REGNUM STUDIES IN MISSION

The Holy Spirit Movement in Korea

Its Historical and Theological Development

Series Preface

Regnum Studies in Mission are born from the lived experience of Christians and Christian communities in mission, especially but not solely in the fast growing churches among the poor of the world. These churches have more to tell than stories of growth. They are making significant impacts on their cultures in the cause of Christ. They are producing 'cultural products' which express the reality of Christian faith, hope and love in their societies.

Regnum Studies in Mission are the fruit often of rigorous research to the highest international standards and always of authentic Christian engagement in the transformation of people and societies. And these are for the world. The formation of Christian theology, missiology and practice in the twenty-first century will depend to a great extent on the active participation of growing churches contributing biblical and culturally appropriate expressions of Christian practice to inform World Christianity.

Series Editors

Julie C. Ma	Oxford Centre for Mission Studies, Oxford, UK
Wonsuk Ma	Oxford Centre for Mission Studies, Oxford, UK
Doug Petersen	Vanguard University, Costa Mesa, CA, USA
Terence Ranger	University of Oxford, Oxford, UK
C.B. Samuel	Emmanuel Hospital Association, Delhi, India
Chris Sugden	Anglican Mainstream, Oxford, UK

A full listing of titles in this series
appears at the end of this book

The Holy Spirit Movement in Korea

Its Historical and Theological Development

Young-hoon Lee

Forewords by David Yonggi Cho and Andrew F. Walls

First published 2009 by Regnum Books International

Regnum is an imprint of the Oxford Centre for Mission Studies
P.O. Box 70, Oxford, OX2 6HB, UK

09 08 07 06 05 04 03   8 7 6 5 4 3 2 1

British Library Cataloguing in Publication Data
A catalogue record for this book is available from the British Library

ISBN 978-1-870345-67-5

Typeset by RBI
Cover by Potion9 Design
Printed and bound in Great Britain
for Regnum Books International
by Nottingham Alpha Graphics

Dedicated to Dr. David Yonggi Cho,
my spiritual mentor and father

Contents

Tables and Figures

Photos

Images in pp. 26, 27, 34, 43 and 49 are the property of www.1907revival.com and used by permission.

Images in pp. 66, 68, and 69 are the property of the Korean Assemblies of God and used by permission.

Images in the cover, pp. 93, 97, 126 and 129 are the property of the Yoido Full Gospel Church and used by permission.

List of Abbreviations

AJPS   *Asian Journal of Pentecostal Studies*
AV   Authorised Version
CNCC   Chosun National Christian Council
ITI   International Theological Institute, Yoido Full Gospel Church
IMF   International Monetary Fund
KCCC   Korean Campus Cruse for Christ
KCRA   Korean Christian Revival Association
KNCC   Korean National Christian Council
PCCNA   Pentecostal/Charismatic Churches of North America
PFNA   Pentecostal Fellowship of North America
WCC   World Council of Churches
YFGC   Yoido Full Gospel Church

Foreword

I have known Dr. Young-hoon Lee since 1964. He has been a faithful member of the Yoido Full Gospel Church, actively serving the Lord as the student representative at Sunday schools, a choir conductor, the Executive Director of International Theological Institute, and in many other important ways. I consider him as a spiritual son of mine.

In response to God's call, he studied Theology and entered into the ministry of God. Now, being elected by the congregation and by the guidance of the Holy Spirit, he is the new Senior Pastor of the Yoido Full Gospel Church.

Dr. Lee has made a great contribution to the academic establishment of the work of the Holy Spirit as shown in the Yoido Full Gospel Church. In this book, he introduces the history of the Holy Spirit movement in the Korean church in connection with the Pentecostal movement.

Readers will learn the characteristics of the Holy Spirit movement of the Korean church, the development and the contribution of the Holy Spirit movement to the Korean church and the World Christianity.

This publication is one of the best academic achievements of Dr. Lee. He was serving the Full Gospel First Church of Washington as the Senior Pastor, while he made researches and preparations for his dissertation. I highly appreciate him for his both academic and vocational achievements.

I congratulate my spiritual son on the publication of his dissertation, and I am very pleased with his great work.

David Yonggi Cho
Emeritus Senior Pastor
Yoido Full Gospel Church

Foreword

Korea holds a unique place in the modern history of Christianity. As an Asian country, never under the colonial domination of any Western power, in which Christianity holds the allegiance of a substantial proportion of the population, it is, to say the least, unusual; and in sending thousands of missionaries, not only where Western missionaries went, but to locations they never reached and hardly considered, Korea is the phenomenon of the modern missionary movement. Further, its expression of Christianity is itself distinctive, combining firm attachment to the formularies and polities, whether Presbyterian, Pentecostal or other, of Western Christianity with an ethos and spirituality that transforms them and which is unmistakably Korean. As this book makes clear, Korean Christianity has grown up in constant engagement with the Shamanistic, Confucian and Buddhist influences that have shaped Korean culture.

In the middle and later twentieth century Korea saw a period of massive church growth, one feature of which was the appearance of Christian congregations of immense size. If Korea did not create the mega-church, the mega-church became more integral to Christian activity in society than was the case elsewhere. And the largest and most celebrated of the world's mega-churches, celebrated not only for its size but for the thoroughness of its structures for pastoral care and fellowship and the scale of its social engagement, is Yoido Full Gospel Church.

One could not wish for a better guide to this whole topic than Dr Lee. With an insider's knowledge he provides a sympathetic picture of Yoido Church and of its remarkable founder, David Yonggi Cho. He sets this in the context of the entire history of Korea, political, cultural and religious, including its wider Christian history. The result is a book that constantly informs and illuminates and sometimes intrigues. There is no way of understanding the most recent phase of Church history without taking account of Korea; and Dr Lee has given his readers an excellent place to start that reckoning.

Andrew F. Walls
University of Edinburgh and Liverpool Hope University

Preface

The life of this research began as I embarked my doctoral study at Temple University in Philadelphia, U.S.A. The dissertation was successfully submitted in 1996. For this reason, the people I want to express my gratitude to were involved in this process in one way or another. They are numerous to name them all, as many people have helped me in various ways to finish this dissertation. I believe it is the work of the Holy Spirit to enable me to finish it, knowing that my ability is limited. With the risk of missing some names, I wish to acknowledge those who made significant contribution to the process.

First, I should like to express my gratitude to my advisors. Professor Leonard Swidler guided me in writing this dissertation as its director. I am greatly indebted to him, for his broad knowledge and understanding helped this work embrace the ideas of various religions and provided it with balance. I am also greatly indebted to Professor Emeritus Gerard Sloyan. With fatherly love for me, he examined the theological aspects of the dissertation thoroughly and guided me with special interest over a long period. On the historical side, Professor Emeritus Franklin Littell assisted me with his breadth of learning. Dr. Littell provided me with useful information and material source in writing the dissertation. Dr. Vinson Synan, former Dean of the Divinity School at Regent University, provided me with a clear picture of the Pentecostal/ Charismatic movement.

I cannot rule out the prayers of my parents and the continuous support of the Rev. Dr. David (Paul) Yonggi Cho, who is my spiritual father. Dr. Cho has encouraged me throughout the years of my postgraduate work. The kind words in his foreword affirm this privileged relationship I have enjoyed for decades. I cannot thank him too much for his spiritual and financial support.

The kind words which Professor Andrew Walls wrote for his foreword bring honour to me and to this book. He has been the most credible voice in the rise of the 'Southern' Christianity in the twentieth century, and the current study of the Holy Spirit movement in Korea is exactly in the same line of his argument.

I give my special thanks to the staff of the International Theological Institute and Hansei University.

I am grateful to Dr. Wonsuk Ma, Executive Director of Oxford Centre for Mission Studies and the editorial team of Regnum Books International, Oxford, U.K. The inclusion of this title in the Regnum's prestigious mission series is a special honour.

Last, but not the least, I give my thanks and love to my wife Inja for her being there for me with dedication and help, for without her I could not have finished this work. Most importantly, I want to express my love to my daughter Grace, who has given me inexpressible joy.

Young-hoon Lee
At the dawn of year 2009
at the Cross Tower of the Yoido Full Gospel Church, Seoul, Korea

Editorial Note

The Romanisation standard of Korean names has gone through several revisions, and the latest one is still in dispute. The convention used in the book is a modification of the latest standard, as some Korean consonants were Romanized normally using stronger consonant values (e.g., 'Kim' for 'Gim" which is closer to the Korean pronunciation). Also there is an uncertainty in the Romanization of some cases. As a result, although most personal and place names are according to the current system, some exceptions have become unavoidable. It is simply because names which were Romanized using different systems have already been used in various publications. To clear the confusion as much as possible, the editors adopted the following rules for this book.

A personal name is presented in the order of the given name followed by the surname, which is opposite of the normal Korean convention. However, there are a few exceptions among archaic names such as ancient kings where the foram Korean sequence is used to follow commonly established identities.

A given name as well as many location names (such as a place, a nation, etc.) often consist of two syllables, but treated as a one word. In some cases, to aid pronunciation, a dash ('-') is added. For this reason the syllable after the dash is in a lower case. This convention is against some common practice which treats the two syllables as if they were two different words.

In footnotes as well as in the bibliography, only the English translations of the original Korean titles are provided, but not their transliterations of the Korean titles. The latter is deemed unnecessary especially for non-Korean readers.

Chapter 1

Introduction

The Scope

This work deals with the historical and doctrinal development of the Holy Spirit movement in Korea. As the Holy Spirit movement consists in and is part of Pentecostalism, the study generally explores the harmony between the Holy Spirit movement and the Pentecostal/Charismatic movement and their relationship within the context of Protestant church history. Specifically, the study researches into the religious, social and historical background of Korean Christians and the life of the Korean churches by discussing the process of the indigenization of Christianity in Korea.

The Procedures

After introducing the background of the Holy Spirit movement in Korea, the study divides the history of the Korean Protestant church into six periods of twenty years each. Then each chapter discusses the historical and doctrinal development of the Holy Spirit movement in the given period paying a particular attention to its socio-cultural and religious context.

The Limitations

It is clear that the task is formidable and ambitious considering the broad span of period it covers. Thus, the study runs into a danger of superficiality and simplification. To avoid such risk and make this study useful, the attention will mainly focus on the historical and doctrinal development of the Holy Spirit movement, especially in connection with the Pentecostal movement, with more than a century of its development in the country. The study will briefly discuss the movement in relation to other Korean religions.

The Research Sources

There are several significant works that deal with similar topics to the present work.[1] A Pentecostal scholar Paul Jaebum Lee produced a Ph.D. dissertation titled 'The Pentecostal Type Distinctives and Korean Pentecostal Church Growth'. A Presbyterian scholar Boo-woong Yoo wrote his doctoral dissertation and later published under the title, *Korean Pentecostalism*. These two remained two major academic references to the subject for a few decades, and they make an interesting contrast primarily because of their perspectives on Pentecostalism. In the new century, another doctoral dissertation was published under the title of *History and Theology of Korean Pentecostalism* by a Korean Pentecostal scholar Ig-jin Kim. This massive study has suffered from its limited availability.

Another group of publications began to appear in the new century in the form of collected essays. First, a dozen studies by insiders as well as outsiders were published: Wonsuk Ma and others (eds) *David Yonggi Cho: A Close Look at His Theology and Ministry*. A similar collection was published by two insiders of the Yoido Full Gospel Church (YFGC): Sung-hoon Myung and Young-gi Hong (eds) *Charis and Charisma*. Also several titled appeared in 2007 to combine various scholarly reflections on Cho and his ministry to mark the fiftieth anniversary of Yoido Full Gospel Church and Cho's ministry. Surprisingly good studies are found in *Asian Journal of Pentecostal Studies*.

The following sources were very helpful in various discussions. For the YFGC, I draw much help from studies of James Sung-hoon Myung. For the matter of the Pentecostal/Charismatic movement, a long list of good sources is available. Among those written with a generally favorable approach to the movement are: *Pentecostals* by John Thomas Nichol, *The Pentecostal Movement* by Nils Bloch-Hoell; and *The Theological Roots of Pentecostals* by Donald W. Dayton, which discusses the theological background of the Pentecostal movement; *Charismatic Renewal and the Church* and *Christian Initiation and the Baptism in the Holy Spirit* by Kilian McDonnell and George T. Montague, Catholic scholars who support the Charismatic movement theologically. Also to be added are: *The Pentecostals* and *Pentecostalism* by Walter A. Hollenweger; *Fire from Heaven* by Harvey Cox; *The New Faces of Christianity* by Philip Jenkins, and *Global Pentecostalism* by Miller and Yamamori. Those written in the Pentecostal circle are: *Restoring the Faith: The Assemblies of God, Pentecostalism and American Culture* by Edith L. Blumhofer; *What Meaneth This?* by Carl Brumback; *The Spirit Himself* by Ralph M. Riggs; *What the Bible Says about the Holy Spirit* by Stanley M.

---

[1] Although there is a long list of academic articles and books on the subject in Korean, my survey discusses only academic publications in English. For a useful bibliography on Cho and related topics, see Chang-soo Kang, 'Resources for Studies of David Yonggi Cho', in Wonsuk Ma, et al. (eds), *David Yonggi Cho: A Close Look at His Theology and Ministry* (Baguio, Philippines: APTS Press, 2004), 273-302.

Horton; *The Holiness-Pentecostal Movement in the United States* and *The Latter Days* by Vinson Synan; Robert Menzies, *Empowered for Witness*; *Spirit and Power* by Menzies and Menzies; and *An Introduction to Pentecostalism* by Allan Anderson. Among those written with a critical view are: *A Theology of the Holy Spirit* by Frederick Dale Bruner; *What about Tongue-Speaking?* by Anthony A. Hoekema.

I find *The Church History of Korea* by Kyung-bae Min quite remarkable in its research on this topic. *The History of Protestant Missions* in Korea by Nak-jun George Baek, a volume written primarily from his Ph.D. dissertation done at Yale University, contains large amounts of the sources that I needed for this research. I have also found great help in the books written by Allen D. and Donald N. Clark and that written by Roy E. Shearer.

In the relationship between Christianity and other religions in Korea, I find *Christian Faith Encounters the Religions of Korea* by Dong-sik Ryu and *Christianity and Korean Thought* by Sung-bum Yun to be useful sources. For the research on the Korean Pentecostal movement, it is useful to study the books published by the International Theological Institute and the books of Yonggi Cho.

Bibliography

The bibliography of this dissertation is divided into three categories. The first consists of biblical, theological and historical references on Pentecostal and Charismatic movements. The second consists of references on the Korean religions, Korean Christianity and Korean Pentecostalism. The third category of the bibliography consists of books of general references.

Definitions

Before going into the main part of the dissertation, I wish to define the following terminologies in relation to the Holy Spirit movement for purpose of a clear understanding.

The Pentecostal Movement

This is a twentieth-century Christian movement emphasizing a post-conversion experience in the Holy Spirit, following the tradition of Wesleyanism. The post-conversion experience is called the baptism of the Holy Spirit and is evidenced by speaking in tongues as recorded in Acts chapter 2. The most distinctive characteristic of the movement is the reemergence of certain patterns reported from the early Christian church. The glossolalia once considered aberrant within Holiness revivalism developed to the Pentecostal movement, which has emerged as perhaps the single most significant development in twentieth-century Christianity.

The Charismatic Movement (Neo-Pentecostal Movement)

This movement succeeded the traditions of the classical Pentecostal movement. While the Pentecostal movement emphasizes Spirit baptism and tongue-speaking, the Charismatic movement emphasizes general gifts of the Holy Spirit. Some advocates of the Pentecostal movement came out of their original denominations and formed new denominations but other advocates of the movement remained in their denominations and spread it, expanding it to all the mainline Protestant churches, the Roman Catholic, and Eastern Orthodox churches.

The Neo-Charismatic Movement

This is the third category of the broad Holy Spirit movement of the twentieth century. The term 'neo-charismatic' has been used by several authors including David Barrett[2] and Stanley Burgess[3] in their well known reference works. In this 'catch-all' category, various groups are included.[4]

The first is an incredible variety of what is called 'indigenous Pentecostals'. Not historically related to the outbreak of the Holy Spirit in the beginning of the twentieth century, many revivals resulted in groups of Christians which manifest some Pentecostal characteristics such as baptism in the Spirit, speaking in tongues, healing, etc. The majority of African Initiated Churches fall into this category. In Korea, the Yongmoon Prayer Mountain established by Woon-mong Nah is an example.[5] They often incorporate indigenous forms and practices of spirituality in their Christian expressions. For this reason, whether they are genuinely Christian is occasionally questioned. Globally speaking, this segment of the movement, however, is the fastest growing and also theologically the most creative.

Another identifiable group in this category is the Third Wave.[6] The designation assumes that it is within the development of the classical Pentecostal movement, referred to as the First Wave, while the Charismatic movement presumably is the Second Wave. They are streams of Evangelical Christians who have embraced Pentecostal beliefs and their ethos, but further developed distinct beliefs in a power encounter, inner healing, territorial spirits,

---

[2] David B. Barrett, George T. Kurian and Todd M. Johnson (eds.), *World Christian Encyclopaedia: A Comparative Survey of Churches and Religions in the Modern World* (2nd ed.; 2 vols.; Oxford: Oxford University Press, 2003).

[3] 'Introduction', *New International Dictionary of Pentecostal and Charismatic Movements* (Grand Rapids: Zondervan, 2003), xvii-xxiii.

[4] Vinson Synan, *In the Latter Days* (rev. ed.; Ann Arbor, MI: Servant, 1991), 138.

[5] Yeol Soo Eim, 'South Korea', *New International Dictionary of Pentecostal and Charismatic Movements* (Grand Rapids: Zondervan, 2003), 241.

[6] Peter Wagner, *The Third Wave of the Holy Spirit: Encountering the Power of Signs and Wonders Today* (Ann Arbor, MI: Servant, 1988).

spiritual mapping and the like.[7] The same group was later known as post-denominational churches, and recently the New Apostolic Movement, claiming that the offices of apostles and prophets have been restored. Like the Charismatics they remain in their churches.

I use the term 'the Holy Spirit movement' to embrace the conceptions of all the above. I will specify which movement I refer to when necessary.

---

[7] Reflections on certain Third Wave practices are available, e.g. Wonsuk Ma, 'A First Wavers Looks at the Third Wave: A Pentecostal Reflection on Charles Kraft's Power Encounter Terminology', *Pneuma* 19 (1997), 189-206.

Chapter 2

Religious Background of the Holy Spirit Movement in Korea

At the beginning of the twentieth century, the Pentecostal movement made its appearance on the world religious scene. [1] This movement was begun in the small city of Topeka in the United States of America by a Methodist minister Charles Fox Parham. He established the Bethel Bible College in Topeka, Kansas in October, 1900, and prayed for the restoration of the apostolic faith. According to the record, on January 1, 1901, there was in his congregation a manifestation of Spirit-baptism and tongue-speaking. The doctrine of Spirit-baptism and tongue-speaking became one of the most important doctrines of the Pentecostal movement. Parham proclaimed the 'full gospel' message that emphasized baptism in the Holy Spirit and healing. Rev. William J. Seymour, of the Apostolic Faith Gospel Mission, the black minister of a Holiness church and one of Parham's students, started a great revival in his Azusa Street Mission of Los Angeles in 1906. The revival continued for three years and contributed greatly to the expansion of the Pentecostal movement all over the world. At the beginning, they did not intend to form a new denomination. As they received severe criticism from the leaders of established denominations, who did not allow the practice of tongue-speaking, they came out of their denominations—mainly Methodist and Holiness churches—and formed a new denomination. At first, no one paid much attention to this movement. But this movement has widely spread all over the world in less than a century. Developed from a movement into several new denominations, it brought about the Charismatic movement (Neo-Pentecostalism) and has become one of the most influential movements in today's Christianity. [2]

---

[1] See for more details John Thomas Nichol, *Pentecostalism* (Plainfield, NJ: Logos International, 1966), 25-39; Synan, In *the Latter Days*, 43-54; Donald W. Dayton, *Theological Roots of Pentecostalism* (Peabody, MA: Hendrickson, 1987), 173–79; Allan Anderson, *An Introduction to Pentecostalism* (Cambridge; New York: Cambridge University Press, 2004).

[2] Walter Hollenweger has been predicting a shift of the centre of Christianity toward the non-Western, non-white, and non-'mainline' world for many years. D.B. Barrett estimates by the middle of the 2000s, Pentecostals in its diverse forms would reach 620 million, outnumbering the category 'Protestants' by almost 200 million. See D.B. Barrett et al., eds., *The World Christian Encyclopedia*, I, 20. See also Henry I. Lederle,

The Pentecostal movement traces its origin[3] back to none other than Wesley's Methodism, which was later linked to the Holiness movement and then to the Pentecostal movement.[4] It advocates the claim that tongue-speaking is the sign of the baptism in the Holy Spirit.[5] Gaining popularity among people all over the world, this movement has spread widely throughout Christian denominations since the 1960s, where it is called the Neo-Pentecostal or the Charismatic movement. This movement was initiated by Father Dennis

---

'The Spirit of Unity: A Discomforting Comforter', *The Ecumenical Review* 42 (1990), 279; W.J. Hollenweger, 'Creator Spiritus: The Challenge of Pentecostal Experience to Pentecostal Theology', *Theology* 81 (1978), 32-40, and 'After Twenty Years' Research on Pentecostalism', *Theology* 87 (1984), 403-12.

[3] According to William Wood, its origin goes back to John Calvin's 'Calvinism'. He wrote, 'Pentecostalism, like other Evangelical systems, varies in certain ways from Calvinism'. See William W. Wood, *Culture and Personality Aspects of the Pentecostal Holiness Religion* (Paris: Mouton, 1965), 5.

[4] John Wesley was the spiritual and intellectual father of the modern Pentecostal movement. He founded Methodism. The Holiness movement was originated by some Methodists. Conflicts between Methodists on the Holiness movement caused the formation of Holiness denominations (1890-1900). The Holiness movement gave rise to the Pentecostal movement and the formation of Pentecostal denominations (1910-1920). See in detail, Vinson Synan, *The Holiness-Pentecostal Movement in the United States* (Grand Rapids, MI: Eerdmans, 1971), 13-22, 43-54; Dayton, *Theological Roots of Pentecostalism*, 35–60. Also Frederick Dale Bruner, *A Theology of Holy Spirit* (Grand Rapids, MI: Eerdmans, 1970), 35-55.

[5] Tongue-speaking prevailed in the Holiness movement. The Pentecostal movement insisted that tongue-speaking was the only initial evidence of the baptism in the Holy Spirit. This, in turn, gave birth to the formulation of another denomination. Synan, *The Holiness-Pentecostal Movement*, 62-65, 98-102, 119. About tongue-speaking, see Carl Brumback, *What Meaneth This?* (Springfield, MO: Gospel Publishing House, 1947); John L. Sherill, *They Speak with Other Tongues* (Old Tappan, NJ: Revill, 1964); Cyril G. Williams, *Tongue of the Spirit: A Study of Pentecostal Glossolalia and Related Phenomena* (Cardiff: University of Wales, 1981); Frank D. Macchia, 'Groans too Deep for Words: Towards a Theology of Tongues as Initial Evidence', *AJPS* 1:2 (2998), 149-173; Mathew S. Clark, 'Initial Evidence: A Southern African Perspective', *AJPS* 1:2 (1998), 203-217; Robert J. Gladstone, 'Sign Language in the Assembly: How Are Tongues a Sign to the Unbeliever in 1 Cor 14:20-25?', *AJPS* 2:2 (1999), 177-94; Simon K.H. Chan, 'Evidential Glossolalia and the Doctrine of Subsequence', *AJPS* 2:2 (1999), 195-211. See also Anthony A. Hoekema, *What about Tongue-Speaking?* (Grand Rapids, MI: Eerdmans, 1966). Hoekema gives theological critiques about tongue-speaking. Studies by non-Pentecostals but open to the validity of tongues are, for example, David Lim, 'A Reflection on the "Initial Evidence" Discussion from a Pentecostal Pastor's Perspective', *AJPS* 2:2 (1999), 223-232; Max Turner, 'Tongues: An Experience for All in the Pauline Churches?', *AJPS* 1:2 (1998), 231-53. Also see James R. Goff, 'Initial Tongues in the Theology of Charles Fox Parham', in Gary B. McGee et al., eds., *Initial Evidence: Historical and Biblical Perspectives on the Pentecostal Doctrine of Spirit Baptism* (Peabody, MA: Hendrickson, 1991), 57–71.

Bennett.[6] On Sunday, April 3, 1960, Father Bennett informed his congregation that he had recently had a new religious experience at St. Mark's Episcopal Church in Van Nuys, California. He said that the Holy Spirit had granted him the 'gift of tongues', the miraculous ability to speak a language he had never learned. An interest in tongue-speaking and other gifts of the Spirit soon gave rise to a new 'Charismatic movement'. This movement spread rapidly to all denominations.[7]

Introduced and influenced by American missionaries, Protestant Christianity in Korea has rapidly developed in a short time—about one hundred and ten years[8]—to claim 25 per cent of the Protestant population, which amounts to twelve million people. Today, Korea has the largest percentage of a Protestant Christian population among all the nations of the Asian mainland. Spencer Palmer describes the situation this way: among the examples of Asian receptiveness to the Christian religion the most remarkable is in Korea, where missionaries have been called 'one of the marvels of modern history'.[9] Judging from such studies and data, Korea deserves to be called one of the most successful Protestant mission fields in the world. Quite differently from the Pentecostal movement in America, however, the Holy Spirit movement in Korea has its own origin and has developed independently.

In the early twentieth century, the Korean Holy Spirit movement began as a repentance movement and developed in a mystical direction while the country was under Japanese occupation. With severe persecutions during the subsequent period, right after the liberation of the nation, the general atmosphere was rather confusing. Out of such confusion, many Korean syncretistic religions developed. The Unification Church and the Olive Tree Church—two representative Korean syncretistic religious sects—were formulated in this period. In opposition to such sects, Korean Christian leaders

---

[6] His autobiographic report is found in Dennis J. Bennett, *Nine O'clock in the Morning* (Plainfield, NJ: Logos International, 1970).
[7] See Robert Mapes Anderson, *Vision of the Disinherited: The Making of American Pentecostalism* (New York: Oxford University Press, 1979), 3-9. The difference between the Pentecostals and the Neo-Pentecostals is the following: 1) while the Pentecostals claim that tongue-speaking is the evidence for the baptism in the Holy Spirit, the Neo-Pentecostals say that each kind of gift of the Holy Spirit is considered evidence of the Holy Spirit at work. Neo-Pentecostal movements are called Charismatic movements; 2) while the Pentecostals came out of their former denominations to keep their faith, the Neo-Pentecostals remain in their denominations, maintaining their theologies.
[8] Rev. Horace G. Underwood, a Presbyterian, and Rev. Henry D. Appenzeller, a Methodist, arrived at Jemulpo Port (now Incheon City) on Easter morning, April 5, 1885, as the first two Protestant missionaries to Korea. Kyung-bae Min, *Church History of Korea*, rev. ed. [in Korean] (Seoul: Christian Literature Society of Korea, 1982), 152.
[9] Spencer J. Palmer, *Korea and Christianity: The Problems of Identification with Tradition* (Seoul: Hollym, 1967), vi.

with traditional denominational backgrounds did not wish to recognize any spiritual experiences and ignored them completely. By repressing the work of the Spirit, they failed to provide spiritual satisfaction for their members. This inevitably resulted in the development of the Holy Spirit movement in Korea. The movement has developed rapidly in Korean Christian history and has had a great influence on all the Christian denominations in Korea.

The rapid growth of the Holy Spirit movement may be attributed to the rich soil of the religious ground of the people. Currently, there are two major religious growths in the country, Buddhism and Christianity. Buddhists constitute 23.1 per cent of the national population and Christianity 26.28 per cent.[10] In addition to these two major growths, there are two strong religious influences,[11] Confucianism and shamanism, which have influenced people's minds almost as powerfully as Buddhism or Christianity. Confucianism is no longer considered a religion in Korea but it still works as an 'ethos' for those in the upper middle classes. Shamanism, on the other hand, has long been a basic conception in the mental outlook of the lower middle classes. The following diagram represents the historical changes and developments of major religions in Korea.

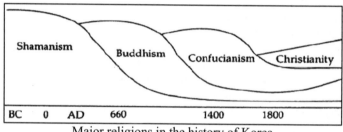

Major religions in the history of Korea

One distinctive characteristic of the history of Korean religions is that the dominating religions dramatically changed as ruling governments or dynasties changed. Shamanism was the dominating religion in pre-historical times;

---

[10] This figure includes 8.76 million Protestants and 2.95 million Catholics, according to the 2005 data published by the Korean National Statistical Office.

[11] These days, Confucianism and shamanism are not considered as religions but as religious functions in Korea. We find the religious function of Confucianism in ancestor worship and that of shamanism in the performance of shamanistic rituals. These two elements still have great influence on the Korean people. Dong-sik Ryu, *The Christian Faith Encounters the Religions of Korea* [in Korean] (Seoul: Christian Literature Society of Korea, 1965), 191–97. For ancestor worship, see Roger L Janelli and Dawnhee Yim Janelli, *Ancestor Worship and Korean Society* (Stanford, CA: Stanford University, 1982) and Wonsuk Ma, 'Three Types of Ancestor Veneration in Asia: An Anthropological Analysis', *Journal of Asian Mission* 4:2 (2002), 201-15.

Buddhism in the Silla and Koryo eras (from the seventh to the fourteenth century); Confucianism in the Chosun Dynasty (from the fourteenth to the nineteenth century); and Christianity from the late Chosun era and following. Nevertheless, none of the religions became completely extinct in any period. All the religions took root in the context of the Korean religious soil, and influenced one another. The background and the influence on Christianity of the other major religions in Korean history will now be briefly discussed.

Shamanism

History

Before Buddhism was introduced into Korea from China in the fourth century, shamanism had been the major traditional religion. It was the common, primitive religion among the tribes of Siberia, Mongolia, Manchuria, Korea, Japan, and the Ural-Altaic region. Although commonly found in various tribes, shamanism had unique features in each of them. In Korea, shamanism formed the basic background of Korean religions, accepted foreign religions, mixed itself with them, and flourished throughout history.[12] Shamanism is the key element in understanding the religious mentality of the Korean people.[13] It is based on animism which is a primitive type of religion believing that everything has *anima* (spirit), and is, therefore, a kind of nature worship. Primitive minds believed that the souls that had left their bodies at the time of death had supernatural power. They also believed that there were spirits in the universe to cause catastrophes like diseases and poverty or to bring blessings upon them. Shamanism, therefore, belongs to a category of polydemonism. There had to be mediators, shamans, between the world of the spirits and the human race.

Shamanism views the universe as consisting of three structures—the upper world, the middle world, and the lower world. The upper world is a bright, heavenly world, the abode of the supreme god and good spirits; the middle world is a world for humans and other living creatures; and the lower world is a world of evil spirits. Humans are supposed to go to one of these three worlds of the dead according to their deeds on earth.

Originally shamanism was a pantheism but it has a notion of the supreme god who controls the whole spiritual world. In Korea the supreme being is called *Haneunim*.[14] The idea of *Haneunim* is related to the foundation of

---

[12] Ryu, *The Christian Faith Encounters*, 13-15.
[13] Bong-bae Park, 'Christianity in the Land of Shamanism, Buddhism, and Confucianism', *Asia Journal of Theology* 1 (1972), 33.
[14] *Haneunim* means 'the highest god of all other gods in nature' as the heavenly king or the heavenly god.

Korean culture and history. We can find the concept of *Haneunim* in the Dangun myth:

> In ancient times, Hwanung, the son of Hwanin desired to descend from Heaven and to live amongst men. His father, realizing his son's intentions, chose among three great mountains to descend upon Taebaek-san and saw mankind would greatly benefit. He gave his son the Three Heavenly Treasures and commanded him to go and rule.... Taking with him three thousand of his followers, Hwanung descended upon the peak of Taebaek-san beneath the Sacred Sandle-wood Tree. That area was called the land of God and he was known as Hwanung Chonwang....[15] At that time, there was a bear and a tiger which lived together in a cave. They prayed incessantly to Hwanung saying, 'Please transform us into humans'. Then Sinung[16] gave them some mugwort and twenty pieces of garlic and said, 'If you eat this and if you do not see light for one hundred days, you will become human'.

> At the end of three times seven days, the bear became a woman. The tiger could not endure and did not become human. As there was no one with whom the woman Ungnyeo could marry, she constantly went to the base of the Sacred Sandle-wood Tree to pray for a child. Hwanung changed his mind and married her. A son was born who was called Dangun Wanggeom. Dangun established a city at Pyongyang and called the nation Chosun.[17]

In the above text, Hwanin is referred to as the 'lord of heaven' who sent his divine son to the human world. This word is related to the present Korean word *Haneunim* meaning 'god'. Dangun was believed to be the representative of heaven and the son of god, performing the functions of priest and ruler while at the same time acting as a healer. Dangun, a grandson of Hwanin, reputedly set up Korea's kingdom in 2333 BC. Dangun became the first human king of Korea and his image became the archetype of the Korean people. Dong-sik Ryu states that the Dangun myth was a product of shamanism, and that Dangun was simply a shaman.[18]

Shamanism has become the folk religion throughout Korean history from pre-historic ages until today. Although Buddhism was the dominating religion in the Silla and Koryo eras and Confucianism during the Chosun Dynasty,

---

[15] The term *chun-wang* means 'heavenly king' and is similar to *chun-gun* ('prince of heaven'). For its Christian implication, see Sung-wook Hong, *Naming God in Korea: The Case of Protestant Christianity* (Oxford: Regnum, 2008).

[16] *Sinung* is another term for *Hwanung*, the son of the lord of heaven.

[17] James Huntley Grayson, *Korea: Religious History* (New York: Oxford University Press, 1989), 282-83.

[18] This idea is supported by many scholars like Nam-sun Choi and Byung-hee Lee. Dong-sik Ryu, *The Christian Faith Encounters*, 19-23. See also Dong-sik Ryu, *The History and the Structure of Korean Shamanism* [in Korean] (Seoul: Yonsei University Press, 1975), 28-35.

shamanism mixed itself with these religions and thus survived in history. Although shamanism, along with Buddhism, was officially prohibited during the Chosun Dynasty, it never became extinct. In the second half of the Chosun era, moreover, shamanism flourished and reached its peak, as Korean society became frustrated by the divisions of its ruling parties.

The influence of shamanism on Korean history is so great that Buddhism and Confucianism were syncretized with shamanism. Even Christianity is partially syncretized in its short history of just over one hundred years.

The Influence of Shamanism on Christianity

Shamanism influenced Christianity significantly, both positively and negatively, having formed the religious background of all Koreans. First, shamanism made it easy for Koreans to accept the Christian God and the spiritual world. Since shamanism professes its belief in a supreme being *Haneunim*, along with many subordinate spirits, the shamanistic background helped people to understand similar concepts of the Christian world of the spirit and the Christian God as supreme. Furthermore, in the Dangun myth Dangun is the incarnation of the heavenly king, a mediator between heaven and earth.

This idea bears certain resemblances to the incarnation of Jesus Christ. The early missionaries attempted to make use of this belief as a way to introduce God and Jesus Christ to the Korean people. The missionaries assumed that the concept of *Haneunim* associated with the Dangun myth bore certain resemblances to Christianity.[19] Although it helped the first Korean Christians to believe in the God of Christians without excessive resistance, there arose the question whether their faith in God is limited by the notion of a supreme being, as in shamanism, rather than the only deity.[20]

Second, its emphasis on the present and material blessings influenced Korean Christianity so as to make it a major concern. Shamanism puts as its primary goal the happiness of individuals and, therefore, performs a ceremony of spirit-worship in order to avoid or overcome personal miseries. As a consequence of these concerns, shamanism does not pay too much attention to social matters. Influenced by such a tendency, Korean Christians, with some exceptions e.g. the Minjung theology influenced clergy and laity, are rather indifferent towards social matters, accepting things as they are. Korean Christians selfishly pray for the solution of their own problems and their own prosperity. Since they are more interested in their personal benefits than in divine providence, their faith is in danger of becoming something akin to sorcery. Being fused with the self-righteousness of individualistic faith and

---

[19] Palmer, *Korea and Christianity*, 90. See also Harry Rhodes, *History of the Korea Mission Presbyterian Church U.S.A. 1884–1934* (Seoul: Chosen Mission Presbyterian Church U.S.A., 1934), 47–48.

[20] Ryu, *The Christian Faith Encounters*, 37.

individual churches, such self-centered Christianity has resulted in the lack of a co-operative spirit.

Third, shamanism implicitly drove Korean Christians to focus on blessings. Throughout the history of Korea, most Koreans have cherished and pursued blessings. This tendency may have resulted from a geo-political cause, as the social atmosphere was unstable due to constant invasions from other countries. This led people to seek individual stability. Another reason may have been the desire of Koreans to overcome uncontrollable natural phenomena by seeking blessings. The concept of blessing in shamanism is the search for secular and material blessings in the present life. In this sense, it resembles the Old Testament concept of blessedness in the Bible but is quite different from the blessing of God that Jesus promised or St. Paul held out to his churches.

Fourth, shamanism influenced the exclusiveness and conservatism of Korean Christianity. Such indifference toward change brought a stagnation of faith and led Christianity into a conservative mode. It caused the Korean Christian faith to be legalistic, lacking an ethical dimension and creative possibilities.

Buddhism

History

Buddhism was transmitted to Korea from the Chinese mainland during the Three Kingdoms period of Korea. The introduction of Buddhism into the country is presumed to have occurred in 372 CE, when King Fu Chien (r. 357–384) of the former Chin dynasty sent a monk-envoy (*sundo*) to the Koguryo court with scriptures and images. The new religion steadily flourished. As many as nine magnificent temples were built in Pyongyang city during the reign of King Gwanggetto (r. 391–412). Twelve years later, Buddhism was introduced into the kingdom of Baekje, where it also flourished. The kings and nobles were converted in no time. It was through Baekje that the Japanese people received the teaching of Buddha.

Koguryo accepted Buddhism from north China, while Baekje, which had no overland access to the Chinese continent, received it from south China by sea.

Buddhism was introduced into the kingdom of Silla, about a half century later than was into Koguryo. In Silla the opposition of conservative court officials prevented its propagation until the martyrdom of Yi Chadon (528) which turned Silla into a Buddhist state.

After the unification of the peninsula under the Silla banner in 668, the fortunes of the new religion expanded on an unprecedented scale. Buddhism flourished mostly in the kingdom of the Unified Silla (668–935).[21]

Many great Buddhist scholars emerged during the kingdom of the Unified Silla. Among them, Wonhyo (617–686) made the greatest contribution. He is considered to be the central figure and crown of Buddhism in the history of Korea. Universalism is one of his unique concepts. He developed the idea of transforming all the people into a single Buddha. A second unique thought of Wonhyo was to eliminate the distinction between the sacred and the secular. To him, religion was secular, it was daily life, and a secular life was religion: the sacred exists and can be found in secular and daily life.

Toward the end of the Silla dynasty, Buddhism seemed to over-ripen, showing signs of decay and decline. At this juncture, Zen was introduced from China, bringing a drastic change in the Buddhism of Silla.

As Koryo replaced the Silla dynasty, its founder King Wang Geon protected Buddhism in a positive way; it accordingly thrived as the guardian religion of the new dynasty. He built almost 4,000 temples and pagodas throughout Korea. Ironically, for this reason Buddhism faced a stagnation period in the Koryo dynasty.

Buddhism, under the protection of the king, was in collusion with political power. When Buddhism became the national religion of Koryo, the monks involved themselves in politics and became interested in power and wealth. Consequently, Buddhism could not help deteriorating. Besides, Buddhism in the Koryo dynasty showed a tendency to syncretism from the beginning. King Wang Geon loved the conventional native religion, worshipped the heavenly gods, great mountains, and great rivers, and restored the Palgwanhoe festival that had been observed in Silla. Thus the native religion, shamanism, flourished along with Buddhism. Although Buddhism prospered rapidly as a result of being syncretized with shamanism, it soon deteriorated into a loss of self-identity and a turned into a merely superstitious religion.

With the revolution in which Yi Sunggye overthrew Koryo to found the Chosun dynasty, Confucianism became the dominant religion. That was because Yi's close followers were Confucianists who strongly rejected Buddhism. Through the five centuries of the Chosun dynasty, Buddhism was suppressed, while Confucianism enjoyed unreserved royal patronage. Buddhism barely maintained its position among ordinary people.

---

[21] Scholars generally agree to view Buddhism in Korea over three periods; the first is the period of advancement, from its first introduction to the Korean peninsula up to the kingdom of Unified Silla; the second is the period of prosperity in the kingdom of Koryo; and the third is the period of decay in the Chosun dynasty. Each period is a span of approximately five hundred years, which when added together, gives us fifteen hundred years of Buddhist history in Korea. Ryu, *The Christian Faith Encounters*, 45.

After the signing of the Korea-Japan Friendship Treaty in 1910, the Japanese took an interest in Korean Buddhism from which they derived their own Buddhist tradition. The Japanese protected and supported Buddhism as a tool to take control of Korea. Thus, Buddhism began to prosper under the Japanese occupation.

The Influence of Buddhism on Christianity

First, Buddhism, along with shamanism, produced a yearning for the material blessings of the present life. Fanaticism in Christian circles of Korea seems to have been influenced by such a tendency. Expectation of blessings in Buddhism belongs to Nirvana. Therefore, the early Buddhists prayed in order to receive blessings and escape disasters. This idea of seeking blessing was influenced by shamanism; again, it influenced Christianity so that Christianity in Korea adopted the idea of blessing as something both tangible and material.

Second, Buddhism brought a focus on the other world into Christianity. Buddhism posits as its ultimate goal denying the self and attaining Nirvana with a philosophy of pessimism and escapism. It may be said that Buddhism does not appreciate the value and meaning of life but inspires faith in the other world. Too much focus on the future world is more like some traditional forms of Buddhism.[22]

It was a coincidence that the futuristic asceticism of Buddhism was in line with the imminent eschatology of Christianity. Christian eschatology includes in itself the danger of denying the present life and over-emphasizing the other world. In so doing, it may lose its sense of responsibility and duty for the present life and end by being apathetic toward society.

Confucianism

History

The introduction of Confucianism from China preceded the era of the Three Kingdoms and it became stronger in Silla than in the other two kingdoms. Alternately with Buddhism, Confucianism has had a long-term influence on Korean religious life.

During one particular period of Korean history, Confucianism had an overwhelming effect on the social and political aspects of the culture. Between 969 and 1036, Confucianism for the first time gained the upper hand in the court, then lost its influence to Buddhism. The Mongol invasion in the twelfth century materially lessened the power of Buddhism. There was some reaction

---

[22] Jang-sik Lee, *The Yesterday and Today of the Korean Church* [in Korean] (Seoul: Korean Christian Literature, 1977), 190.

in favour of Confucianism in the fourteenth century, but it was not until the arrival of the Chosun dynasty in 1392 that Buddhism was totally dethroned from its privileged position.[23]

It was inevitable that the political influence of the Confucianists began to rise with the repression of Buddhism. The fall of Buddhism accompanied the fall of the Koryo kingdom. Buddhism gave evidence of having lost its purity, becoming increasingly more political and contaminated, and its decline seems to have been a natural consequence.

The founders of the Chosun dynasty (1392–1910) sought for a new philosophy of governing by Confucianism that could replace Buddhism. The progenitor of the new dynasty Yi Sunggye (r. 1392–1398) originally professed Buddhism, as did his ancestors. But as a corrupt Buddhism lent no help to his dynastic revolution, but Confucian thought played the major role, he decided to reject Buddhism. He built the Sunggyun-gwan (Confucian Academy) which included a college and a Confucian shrine for the veneration of Confucius and his disciples. He also awarded high positions to Confucian scholars.

As Confucianism became the state religion, all ceremonies for weddings, funerals, and ancestral worship naturally were Confucianized. Confucianism in the Chosun dynasty developed remarkably under the protection of the state. However, due to the governing idea of Confucianism, it was inevitable that it should become connected to politics and involved in the issues and conflicts of the ruling parties. Toward the end of the Chosun dynasty, because of the constant involvement of Confucianism in political conflicts and its constant dependence on protection by the ruling parties, it gradually lost its religious functions. Thus a kind of religious vacuum was created in the Chosun dynasty. At this juncture, shamanism moved in. It not only monopolized the religious life of the masses but also invaded the royal court and upper class.[24] As a result, Confucianism was syncretized with shamanism and the people performed Confucianist ceremonies that became shamanistic.

Toward the end of the Chosun dynasty, Confucianism almost lost its religious function. Ancestor worship was the only actual religious element remaining. It is still common practice for most Korean families to make an annual visit to the grave mounds of their ancestors and there make sacrifices of food.[25]

Confucianism suffered under the Japanese occupation; there was a concerted attempt to bring it under the authority of the Japanese emperor. The Confucian school in Seoul was forced to come under Japanese control. But after the liberation of the country this school was opened again and now has become a

---

[23] Che-kyung Ok, *The Handbook of Korea* (New York: Pageant, 1958), 71-72.

[24] Giyong Lee, 'Religion' [in Korean], in *Korean Studies Today: Development and State of the Field* (Seoul: Institute of Asian Studies, Seoul National University, 1970), 17.

[25] Roy E. Shearer, *Wildfire: Church Growth in Korea* (Grand Rapids, MI: Eerdmans, 1966), 27.

modern university (Sunggyun-gwan University). Nowadays, although the Confucian tradition in Korea hardly has any religious functions, it still affects the mind of the people as an ethos.

The Influence of Confucianism on Christianity

Confucianism has had the following positive effect on Korean Christianity. First, it helped Koreans understand Christianity more quickly. The Confucian concept of heaven (*Tien*) and its concept of the Supreme-Being (*Shang-ti*) helped the Koreans understand the idea of God as Heavenly Father in Christianity. The Koreans had had the concept of God in their old religions even before Confucianism came to Korea but the Confucian conception of heaven and Supreme-Being were closer to those of Christianity than their predecessors and helped Koreans understand Christian conceptions. The ethical viewpoint of Confucianism also helped people grasp the ethical outlook of Christianity. Buddhism can be perceived as negative about life, whereas Confucianism seeks love and righteousness while taking a positive attitude toward life. Under this aspect, the Confucian ethic coincides with the Christian ethic. For this reason, the first Korean Christians were Confucian scholars.

There are, however, many negative effects of Confucianism on Christianity. Confucianism was a religion exclusively for the ruling class. As a result, the common people were compelled to follow Confucian traditions and customs regardless of their preference. This only led people to shamanism and society to stagnate.

When Catholicism was first introduced to Korea in the eighteenth century, it was the ruling class that wanted to learn it as a bridge to the Western culture. Thus, quite naturally, Christianity was influenced by Confucianism and began to stress traditions and forms, eventually turning to legalism. Confucianism was the cause of Korean Christianity's turning into a Pharisee-like observance.

Confucianism deteriorated into a selfishness whereby people pursued nothing but their own good in endless political conflicts. Members of the upper class focused on their own lives, their families, and their political parties, without recognizing others. The Christian idea of being 'people for others' was weakened in Korea. This produced selfish Christians who cared for nothing but their own interest. The exclusivism and conservatism of Confucianism accounted for an exclusive and conservative tendency in Korean Protestant Christianity, thus causing the denominations to be divided into a great number.

Chapter 3

The First Period (1900–1920)

Background

The history of Korea shows that there were several occasions that Christianity reached Korean soil. It was in the late eighteenth century that Christianity started taking root in Korea. However, Kyung-bae Min, a church historian, asserts that the Nestorians, who were actively ministering in China, introduced Christianity to Silla as early as the seventh and eighth centuries. This assertion is supported by scholars like P.Y. Saeki and C.H. Robinson.[1]

The next encounter was possibly in the thirteenth century through Mongolia. Catholics sent many missionaries to Mongolia in an attempt to evangelize it. One of the missionaries, Guillaume de Rubruc was the first one to make the name 'Korea' known to the world.[2] The Catholic missionaries to Mongolia may have contacted some Koreans but there is no sign of success in evangelization.

Catholicism

The next encounter was during the Japanese invasion of Korea in the sixteenth century (1592–1599). The missionaries of the Society of Jesus (Jesuits) were ministering in Japan quite actively. They came to Korea with Japanese soldiers. Gregory de Cespedes stayed in Korea for about six months but had no contact with the Koreans. It was probably Japanese Christian soldiers who baptized some Koreans.[3] Many of the Korean captives to Japan after the invasion were converted to Catholicism. During the severe persecutions in Japan early in the seventeenth century, 21 Koreans were martyred. Nine of them were among the 205 martyrs beatified in 1867.

Later Catholicism was reintroduced to Korea through China. Young Confucian scholars became interested in Western civilization and studied Christian literature. Seung-hoon Yi, a member of the annual delegation to

---

[1] Min, *Church History of Korea*, 31–35.
[2] Rubruc called Korea 'Caulej' in his report. Later it became 'Corée' and then 'Korea'.
[3] C.A. Hervest, 'Korea', *The New Catholic Encyclopedia* (New York: McGraw-Hill, 1967), vol. 8, 254.

China of 1783, went to Beijing and met the Jesuit missionaries there. Yi was converted and baptized by Louis de Grammont in February 1784. He was given the name Pierre (Peter), in the hope that he would be the foundation rock of the Korean church. Upon his return to Seoul, with his friend Pyok Yi, he formed a church and devoted himself to evangelical work. Within five years, there were about 4,000 Catholics in Korea.[4] The Catholic Church was growing rapidly.[5] However, their rejection of ancestor veneration, one of the Confucian traditions, caused socio-political problems and conflicts in society and, consequently, persecutions against the Catholics. Major persecutions went on for about a century and became particularly severe in 1801, 1839, 1846, and from 1866 to 1869, when some 10,000 Catholics were martyred.[6]

It was in 1883, when Korea was opened to foreigners, that religious freedom was finally granted. Then a period of steady growth of the Catholic church followed.

Protestantism

The early Protestant contacts with Korea started in 1832 with Karl Gutzlaff, a German missionary who had served in China. Gutzlaff was the first Protestant missionary to visit Korea. Sent by the Netherlands Missionary Society in 1832, he visited Hwang-hae and Choong-chung provinces. He sent a petition and gifts to the king, requesting an opening for trade. While waiting for a reply, he distributed Bibles and tracts. The petition and gifts were returned with the information that Koreans could not permit them to trade without consulting China. So he had to end his one-month long visit to Korea.[7]

The next Protestant missionary to attempt to enter Korea was Robert J. Thomas, who had come to China as a missionary sent by the London Missionary Society. In 1865, Thomas came to Hwang-hae province and stayed there for two months. In 1866, he embarked on the fully-armed American trade ship General Sherman that entered the mouth of the Daedong River and proceeded up the river to the city of Pyongyang in the northern part of Korea without the permission of the Korean government. The Americans asked for open trade but it was turned down. They reacted violently and even took a few Koreans as hostages. A battle began between the crew and the Koreans. The

---

[4] In the history of world missions, it is quite remarkable that the first church in Korea was established by Koreans, not by missionaries. Min, *Church History of Korea*, 112.

[5] There are 510,000 Catholics in Korea as of 2007.

[6] Min, *Church History of Korea*, 99. Min quotes from the material by S. Neill, J.H. Kane, and Hong-yul Ryu. Like the early Christian church under the rule of the Roman Empire, the Korean Catholic church underwent severe persecutions from the government but survived the 110-year long persecutions.

[7] Allen D. Clark, *History of the Church in Korea* (Seoul: Christian Literature Society of Korea, 1971), 62.

Koreans burned the ship, killing all the crew including Thomas. Thomas gave out copies of the Bible that were on the ship before he died. According to Allen Clark, Thomas offered his slayer a Bible. The man took the Bible home with him and, later, his nephew worked for Korean Christianity.[8]

Subsequent contacts between the Protestant missionaries and Koreans were made in Manchuria, later in Japan and then in America. Starting from 1863, the United Presbyterian Church of Scotland sent missionaries to northern China and Manchuria. John Ross and John McIntyre were among the missionaries. They met Koreans who had travelled to and from Manchuria. They learned the Korean language from them and preached the gospel. Sang-yoon Suh came to Manchuria as an itinerant medicine seller but became sick and was cared for by John McIntyre. Suh was converted and helped Ross and McIntyre with the translation work of the Bible into Korean. He received baptism by Ross in 1882 and continued the translation, publishing the Gospels of Luke and John in 1882 and the Book of Acts in 1883. Suh endeavored to spread this Korean version of the Bible in Korea. In 1883 he built Sorae Church in Jang-yon, Hwang-hae province with his brother.[9] Those who had received the gospel through the Sorae Church were baptized by Horace Underwood in 1887.

The next opening of Korea to the gospel was prepared for from the Japanese side. Soo-jung Yi was one of the Korean students who had gone to Japan for further studies. He made contacts with George W. Knox of the American Presbyterian Mission, Robert S. Maclay of the American Methodist Mission, and Henry Loomis of the American Bible Society. Yi was baptized in 1883. He completed the translation of the Gospel according to Mark into Korean in late 1884 and published 1,000 copies in 1885 in Yokohama, Japan. Underwood stayed in Japan on his way to Korea as a missionary. He learned the Korean language from Soo-jung Yi, while staying in Japan. He took the Korean version of the Gospel of Mark with him and finally arrived at Port Jemulpo.

The next contact took place in America.[10] The treaty between Korea and the United States was signed in May 1882. The Korean government sent representatives to the United States and they came into contact with American Christians and their mission boards. They visited San Francisco, Chicago, New York and Washington, D.C. On their way to Washington, D.C., on a train they met John E. Goucher who was living in Baltimore. During his conversation

---

[8] Clark, *History of the Church in Korea*, 63. Also Stella Price, *Chosen for Choson (Korea)* (Essex, MA: Emmaus Road Ministries, c. 2007).

[9] Sorae Church was the first Korean church built by the Koreans. The church was said to be built in 1883 or 1885. It was at least two years earlier than the Saemunan Church in Seoul that was built with the help of the missionaries in 1887. See Man-yeol Lee, *The Church History of Korea* [in Korean] (Seoul: Evangelical Students Fellowship, 1985), 38.

[10] Clark, *History of the Church in Korea*, 73–75; Min, *Church History of Korea*, 151–52.

with the Koreans, Goucher learned that the gospel had not reached them as actively as in China or Japan. He wrote a letter to the Methodist Mission Board in New York, urging them to start missionary work in Korea and offering $2,000 toward this work. Receiving no encouragement from the Methodist Mission Board, Goucher sent a letter to Robert S. Maclay of the Methodist Mission in Japan, urging him to make a trip to Korea in order to investigate the possibilities of missionary work there. Maclay made a trip to Korea and contacted Ok-gyun Kim, whom he had met in Japan, and sent a letter to the King through Kim. The letter was a petition asking permission to open a school and begin medical work in Korea by the Northern Methodist Churches of America. The petition was granted. Maclay wrote to his mission board urging it to start work as soon as possible. The Methodist Mission Board appointed the first missionaries to Korea toward the end of 1884.[11]

The first medical missionary was, however, a Presbyterian not a Methodist, Horace Allen. The Presbyterian Board was thinking along similar lines. While this was being discussed, Horace Allen arrived in China in 1883 as a medical missionary under the Presbyterian Board. Learning that Korea needed a doctor, Allen wrote a letter to the Presbyterian Board and asked permission to go to Korea. The Board instructed Allen to go to Korea and thus he became the first medical missionary to that country.

The Presbyterian and the Methodist Mission Boards then appointed the first missionaries to Korea. It was on April 5, 1885 that Underwood and Appenzeller came to Korea.[12]

When Korea began to open itself to Protestant churches in the late Chosun Dynasty era, the country was in political, cultural, social, and spiritual chaos. Not only that, Confucianism which had characterized the spirit of Chosun for almost five hundred years had become rather formalistic and legalistic, leaving the people in a period of a religious vacuum. Wars between strong countries such as Japan, China and Russia, in pursuit of expansion of their territories, broke out in the Korean peninsula. At the same time, there erupted internal anti-social movements led by Je-woo Choi and his followers. This movement was called *Dong-hak* ('Eastern Learning').[13]

---

[11] Lak-jun George Baek, *The History of Protestant Missions in Korea 1832–1910* [in Korean] (Seoul: Yonsei University Press, 1973), 81–83.

[12] Min, *Church History of Korea*, 152.

[13] In 1894, the Dong-hak movement began in the south. This was both a religious and a political movement. The founder, Je-woo Choi, was a scholar who had come into contact with the Catholic missionaries. He became ill and had what he considered a revelation from heaven which called upon him to found a new religion. He took the Five Relations from Confucianism, the law of heart-cleansing from Buddhism, the use of charms and magic from animism, monotheism from Christianity, and the use of candles from Catholic worship. He called his deity *Chun ju*, the Catholic term for God, and named the new religion *Dong-hak* ('Eastern Learning') in opposition to *Suh-hak* ('Western Learning'), by which name the Catholic teaching had formerly been called.

In such a confusing situation of conflicts, leaders of society decided to accept Christianity, believing that Christianity could strengthen the already worn-out country. This opened the door to evangelism so that the first Protestant missionaries came to Korea and preached the gospel with the permission of the Emperor Gojong. On April 5, 1885, on the Easter Sunday, a Methodist missionary, Henry Appenzeller, and a Presbyterian missionary, Horace Underwood, took their first steps on Korean soil together. Although not as severe as the persecutions that the Roman Catholic missionaries had suffered, the opposition met by the first Protestant missionaries was considerable. They endured various persecutions from conservative Koreans. Despite the hardships the Protestant church in Korea continued to grow steadily. When the Japanese claimed control over Korea by virtue of the Korea-Japan Friendship Treaty in 1910, the Protestant church of Korea reached a turning-point.

From the signing of the treaty to March 1, 1919, the date of the Declaration of Independence, Korean Christianity grew rapidly. Out of the tragic frustration of losing their country, the people gathered in the churches, for they had no other place in which to concentrate their minds and hopes. The Japanese rulers began to persecute the church for its involvement in the Declaration of Independence and, inevitably, the church stopped growing.

While the Korean Christian leaders were very much interested and involved in issues such as the liberation of the country, the missionaries opposed the involvement of the church in politics. Most of the missionaries in this period were from North America. Their traditions were conservative and evangelical and their background Puritan. [14] They took the separation of the state and religion for granted, not paying too much attention to secular life. The faith style of the missionaries was a crucial influence on the formation of the Korean style of faith and understanding of the gospel. Although there are two major streams of Christianity in the world, the Western and the Eastern churches, Korea did not have a chance to absorb the rich Eastern traditions and inheritance. Moreover, since the Protestant missionaries were in opposition to Roman Catholic traditions to a certain degree, the Protestant church of Korea

---

Choi was executed, but the movement then revived and became primarily a political movement. It was a reform movement rather than purely revolutionary. The leaders professed to be loyal to the king and expressed their opposition to the existing corruption in government. They raised an army in the southern provinces and began to march to Seoul. Chinese troops were called in to suppress the rebellion. The troops were sent, but the notification required by the Sino-Japanese agreement was not observed until several days later. The Japanese were aware of what was going on and sent their troops directly to the capital. With this began the Sino-Japanese War of 1894-1895. At the end of this conflict, Korea was declared free from China, and Japanese influences replaced those of China in the affairs of Korea. Clark, *History of the Church in Korea*, 102-03.

[14] Min, *Church History of Korea*, 134.

could not receive the traditions inherited from its parent church by the continental Protestants. Only the conservative, fundamentalist, and Americanized Christian traditions were planted in the Protestant church of Korea.[15]

As a result, the Korea churches have the following tendencies: passivity in pursuit of theological studies, literal biblicism, uniformity of faith, exclusivism, extreme pietism, and an eschatological faith with an emphasis on the life of the world to come. This tendency was in line with the original Korean mental outlook and formed the tradition of the Korean church. We can see that these tendencies had influenced the Korean church from its early stages by examining the great revival of 1907.

There are a few unique features common to the coming of Catholicism and Protestantism to Korea. First, both were carried out by voluntary requests of Koreans. The Koreans went to China and received Catholicism there, while they went to Manchuria and Japan and accepted Protestantism there. In both cases translation work of the Bible was begun. Second, the Bible and Christian books had been brought in and spread before the missionaries came. In contrast with these common features, the Protestant mission boards took the political situation of Korea into consideration and started medical and educational work first. In this way, they first reduced the prejudice and hostility of the Koreans toward foreigners and then endeavoured to spread the gospel.[16]

The Great Revival of 1907

The revival movement in this period (1900–1920) is of great significance, for through this movement Korean Protestantism experienced the powerful gifts of the Holy Spirit for the first time. The Christians who had entered the church with various motives now came to know what true repentance was and what it meant to be Christain. They also came to feel the excitement of their faith. The Holy Spirit movement in this period not only made the Korean church exuberant but it also energized the already existent Christian traditions and brought about the exceptional growth of the Korean church. The Holy Spirit movement in this period started in 1903 at Wonsan and reached its peak in 1907 at Pyongyang.

---

[15] William Haller, *The Rise of Puritanism* (New York: Harper & Bros., 1957), 339.

[16] Lee, *The Church History of Korea*, 46–47. In the Catholic churches, missionary work has been generally accompanied with educational and medical work, such as the establishment of schools and hospitals. In Korea, however, the Protestant church started this ministry first. The Catholic Church joined the Protestant church in this ministry after the government had opened itself to Christianity.

The Great Revival of 1907 had a most important influence on the life of the Korean church.[17] Many local revivals had characterized the life of the Korean church from the beginning but the Great Revival swept over the country and affected the entire Christian movement.

Its Progress

The origin of the revival may be traced to a prayer meeting of Methodist missionaries at Wonsan in 1903.[18] The outbreak of this movement is attributed to R.A. Hardie. He was a medical doctor and Methodist missionary who was ministering in Gang-won province.[19] Although he had worked very hard, he could achieve little in his missionary work. He felt greatly burdened and began to examine his spiritual state and the motives of his missionary work in retrospect.

While this was going on, he and seven other missionaries gathered for a week-long conference of Bible study and prayer at Wonsan under the leadership of a visiting missionary from China, Miss M.C. White. Hardie was going to report his research on prayer at the 1903 conference. During this, he said that he experienced some unusual feelings as if stirred by the Spirit. When he read Luke 11:13, 'If you then, though you are evil, know how to give good gifts to your children, how much more will your Father in heaven give the Holy Spirit to those who ask him!', he came to realize that his missionary work had failed because he had counted too much on his own effort in his ministry. He said that his heart was stirred by this scripture passage and, in this scripture, he found simple faith in the gift of the Holy Spirit. The feeling he experienced was a deep conviction of sin and captivation by the holiness of God. He knew the power of the Spirit within himself and, inevitably, could not help sharing it with others.

Hardie gave testimony to his fellow missionaries of his experience of the new infusion of power and peace by the Spirit and it touched their hearts.

---

[17] This event was reported by William Blair. He called this event 'The Korean Pentecost'. He was living in Pyongyang (now the capital city of North Korea) as a missionary at that time. See in detail, William Blair and Bruce Hunt, *The Korean Pentecost and the Suffering Which Followed* (Carlisle: Banner of Truth, 1977), 71-74. See also Donald D. Owens, *Revival Fires in Korea* (Kansas City, MO: Nazarene, 1977), 2379.

[18] This is a remarkable coincidence since the contemporary Pentecostal movement was originated by a Methodist minister through a Bible study and prayer meeting in Topeka, Kansas, U.S.A. The Pentecostal movement that had started in the late 1900s moved its centre to Houston in 1903 and then to Los Angeles in 1906. It is around this time that this movement spread from Los Angeles to all over the world, which is about the same period of time as the Great Revival of Korea. Cf. Synan, *In the Latter Days*, 99-102.

[19] R.A. Hardie came to Korea as a medical missionary of the Canadian Mission, but in 1888, joined the Southern Methodist Mission. See Owens, *Revival Fires in Korea*, 26.

Further, he gave the same testimony to the Korean congregation, confessing that his own pride, hardness of heart, and lack of faith had brought shame and confusion upon his ministry.[20] This moved the hearts of the audience and they wanted to follow his example in confessing their sins and in being open to receive such a vital religious experience.[21]

Hardie's public confession of sin must have been painful and humiliating to him. His honest confession, however, made a strong impact on the hearts of the audience. The Korean congregation began to yearn for the same gift of the Spirit that had changed Hardie so dramatically. Such yearning for the gift of the Holy Spirit produced subsequent Bible study classes and prayer meetings. At

these meetings, the Korean congregation confessed their sins, gave testimonies, and experienced and tasted the grace of God in a new way for the first time. These revival meetings were successful from the beginning. The first Holy Spirit movement in Korea thus began to burst into flames at the conference in Wonsan (photo).[22]

The flame of the revival movement was restricted to the Wonsan area in 1903. In 1904, revival movements continued to be held similar to those of the Wonsan conference and the movement became more fervent. The news about the revival at Wonsan spread widely to reach Pyongyang. There the Presbyterian missionaries began to yearn for the spiritual gifts that had been given at Wonsan. They invited Hardie to speak at a united conference in Pyongyang.[23] He spoke on the First Epistle of John and urged them to receive the gift of the Holy Spirit. As they prayed for the spiritual gifts, there was an enormous outpouring of blessings.

Similar conferences and revival meetings were held in Seoul in September, 1906, with great manifestations of the gift of the Holy Spirit. At a missionary conference,[24] Howard Agnew Johnston, a missionary from North America, reported to missionaries and Korean congregations about the Welsh revival and a revival in India[25]

---

[20] Owens, *Revival Fires in Korea*, 26-27.

[21] Owens, *Revival Fires in Korea*, 27.

[22] For an in-depth study of Wonsan revival, see Chang-ki Lee, *The Early Revival Movement in Korea (1903-1907): A Historical and Systematic Study*, Mission 34 (Zoetermeer, the Netherlands: Uitgeverij Boekencentrum, 2003), 74-80.

[23] Min, *Church History of Korea*, 251.

[24] Sung-bum Yun, *Christianity and Korean Thought* [in Korean] (Seoul: Christian Literature Society of Korea, 1964), 185-86.

[25] It is one of the greatest mysteries of the movement of God's Spirit, and the revival that His presence brings, that the years 1905–1910 are often considered the period of the

The air of revivalism which had started from the spiritual experience at the Wonsan conference reached its climax at the great revival meeting at Pyongyang in January, 1907.[26] The meeting was going to continue for ten days, focusing on Bible study and research as they had done in previous conferences. They preached evangelism intensively, however, in the evening meetings. According to the reports of missionaries, it was during the evening meetings that people witnessed the strong manifestations of the Holy Spirit.

On Monday, January 14, 1907, about 1,500 gathered in the evening meeting (photo). As it drew to a conclusion, William Blair reported that they had received the power of the Holy Spirit. Graham Lee was leading the meeting that evening. After a short sermon, Lee took charge of the meeting and called for prayers. So many began praying at the same time that Lee told the whole audience to pray together if they wished to pray aloud. The whole audience began to pray out loudly and in unison. People were feeling an urge to prayer.[27]

The prayer that sounded like the falling of water captivated the whole congregation. They then began to repent of their sins publicly one by one. William Blair, a Presbyterian missionary, who served forty years in the northern part of Korea, gave the following statement of what happened at the

---

great awakening — in Asia, Americas, and Europe. The great Welsh revival is a well-known part of this worldwide movement.

The Revs. Seth Joshua and Evan John Roberts were its leaders. Evan Roberts, especially, had no special technique but he preached with great anointing. As he often said, that there are four main points to revival: 1) the past must be made clear by confession of every known sin to God, and every wrong unto man must be put right; 2) every doubtful thing in the believer's life must be put away; 3) prompt and implicit obedience must be yielded to the Spirit of God; 4) public confession of Christ must be made. During the brief period of the Welsh revival, 100,000 people were converted. In 1910, 60,000 of those who were converted during the six months of revival were still members of the Welsh churches. News of the Welsh revival quickened the Christians in both New Zealand and Australia. The great evangelists J. Wilbur Chapman, Reuben A. Torrey, and the American, Dwight L. Moody, were used mightily in bringing revivals both to America and to these lands 'down under'.

During this same period revivals occurred in India. The pattern of revival there was the same as the sweeping revival that had occurred in Wales. Throughout India prayer meetings, evangelistic campaigns, revivals in boys' and girls' schools, indicated that the Spirit of God was at work in the land. In the main, the awakening of 1905 in India was of an indigenous nature; that is, many of the evangelists were Indian preachers. See Owens, *Revival Fires in Korea*, 23-25.

[26] An analytical study on Pyongyang revival, see Lee, *The Early Revival Movement in Korea*, 100-108.

[27] Blair & Hunt, *The Korean Pentecost*, 73–74.

time of the annual Presbyterian and Methodist Bible Conference in January, 1907:[28]

> The evening meeting connected with the Bible conference began January 6th, in the Central Church (in Pyongyang), with more than 1,500 men present. Women were excluded for lack of room. Different missionaries and Korean leaders had charge of the evening meetings, all seeking to show the need of the Spirit's control in our lives and the necessity for love and righteousness.... After a short sermon...man after man would rise, confess his sin, break down and weep, and then throw himself on the floor and beat the floor with his fists in a perfect agony of conviction.... Sometimes, after a confession, the whole audience would break out into audible prayer, and the effect of that audience of hundreds of men praying together in audible prayer was something indescribable. Again, after another confession, they would break out into uncontrollable weeping and we would all weep together. We couldn't help it. And so the meeting went on until 2 a.m., with confession and weeping and praying.... We had prayed to God for an outpouring of His Holy Spirit upon the People and it had come.

It is reported that the experience of the Spirit at this meeting instantly solved the problem of individual sins and helped people release their grief over the fate of the nation. It was said that this was their first experience of feeling and tasting the dynamic power of the Holy Spirit. The same outpouring of the Holy Spirit continued to take place even more intensely the next evening. Blair gave the following description:[29]

> Then began a meeting the like of which I had never seen before, nor wish to see again unless in God's sight it is absolutely necessary. Every sin a human being can commit was publicly confessed that night. Pale and trembling with emotion, in agony of mind and body, guilty souls, standing in the white light of their judgment, saw themselves as God saw them. Their sins rose up in all their vileness, till shame and grief and self-loathing took complete possession; pride was driven out, the face of man forgotten. Looking up to heaven, to Jesus whom they had betrayed, they smote themselves and cried out with bitter wailing: 'Lord, Lord, cast us not away forever!' Everything else was forgotten, nothing else mattered. The scorn of men, the penalty of the law, even death itself seemed of small consequences if only God forgave. We may have other theories of desirability or undesirability of public confession of sin. I have had mine; but I know now that when the Spirit of God falls upon guilty souls, there will be confession, and no power on earth can stop it.

Three years later, Blair wrote a book about this meeting[30] and in his book he described the Great Revival of 1907 as follows: 'Just as on the day of

---

[28] Clark, *History of the Church in Korea*, 160-62.

[29] Blair & Hunt, *The Korean Pentecost*, 74.

[30] The title of this book is *Pentecost and Other Experiences of the Mission Field*. This little book by William Blair was first printed in 1910 by the Board of Foreign Missions

Pentecost, they were altogether in one place, in one accord praying, and suddenly there came from heaven the sound as of rushing of a mighty wind, and it filled all the house where they were sitting'.[31]

The Great Revival was never restricted to adult congregations but spread to children and high school students, especially to those who went to Christian schools. When Soongsil School, operated by the Methodists and the Presbyterians, reopened in February of 1907, a similar revival movement broke out among its students. It was not restricted to the boys. The Holy Spirit movement in this period was even stronger among girls than boys.[32] In other words, the movement of this period was open to all classes of people in all age groups. The revival continued more broadly as people confessed and repented their sins.

Repentance of sins, however, was not the only phenomenon that was involved in their meetings, for if the Holy Spirit movement had involved the repentance of sins only it would not have had much significance or influence on people. What was more significant was the dramatic change of the lives of those who were involved in the revival meetings. They began to quit their bad habits, forgive each other, and make peace with one another. Korean society in general looked at the tremendous change in the Christians with awe and began to expect something from them for the country,[33] for there was no other help or hope. Despite such expectations of Korean society, however, the missionaries to Korea were leading the Korean church in a more non-political direction as they seized the opportunity of the Holy Spirit movement.

The missionaries who had gathered when the revival broke out in Pyongyang went out to other places all over the country and led revival meetings in order to keep the fire of the Holy Spirit from dying out. The fire of the Spirit thus spread widely and brought about a powerful zeal for evangelism and a resulting explosive growth of the Korean church.[34]

---

of the Presbyterian Church in the U S.A. for use of the board and its missions. The book was later edited and reprinted by Bruce Hunt in 1977 with his instructions.

[31] Acts 2:1-4. Blair & Hunt, *The Korean Pentecost*, 71. However, unlike on the Day of Pentecost recorded in the book of Acts, there is no written record of tongue-speaking in the Great Revival of 1907.

[32] Graham Lee, 'How the Spirit came to Pyongyang', *Korea Mission Field* 3:3 (March, 1907), 36.

[33] We find almost the same record in the community of the apostolic church. See Acts 2:42–47.

[34] The following may be described as the background of the revival: 1) people wanted to find hope from Christianity while Korea was in trouble; 2) the revival came as a result of rapid Westernization; 3) the old religions of Korea had failed the nation and thus Christianity was expected to bring new hope; and 4) there was no great difficulty in the replacement of the old religions by Christianity. Like Confucianism, Christianity taught righteousness and revered learning. Like Buddhism, Christianity sought purity and

We should note that the expansion of the fire of the Holy Spirit that had started in Wonsan can be attributed partly to the effort of Sun-joo Gil. Gil had the experience of the Holy Spirit at the Great Revival and went all around the country leading revival meetings and classes. People often say about this revival that where there were Christians, there was a revival. It certainly was perceived as another fulfilment of the promise of God to Koreans; as in everything human, behind this gracious work of the Spirit there were negative aspects to the revival movement as well. Summarizing the influence of the Holy Spirit movement during this period, however, we find more positive factors than negative ones.

First, it preserved the purity of Korean Christianity. Many Koreans had been converted for various reasons and motives when Protestant Christianity was first introduced. Twenty years after the introduction of this tradition to Korea, large numbers of these believers felt that they experienced the fire of the Holy Spirit and thus began to understand what Christianity meant in their daily lives and could distinguish what was truly Christian from what was not. The revival brought them a great renewal of their thoughts, style of life, and behaviour. It was a new birth of the church by the new birth of changed individuals. W.G. Cram said:

> It was genuine. There was no false fire of lies or deceptions. Missionaries never attempted to force the Christians to confess their sins as a necessary evidence of their purity or as a testimony of the Holy Spirit.[35]

The Great Revival started from a pure, genuine religious motive. It bore the religious fruit of renewal and purified the church. So Albert Outler said that the spiritual movement at this time was very sound and evangelistic, because it was in accord with Wesleyanism, and the people's conviction of faith was shown in their actions. According to him, from 1907 to 1919, the internal and external sanctifications of Korean Christians were well harmonized. For without being intoxicated in their own righteousness, they expressed their conviction of salvation and eternal life in social action and in the independence movement.[36]

Second, the Great Revival raised the ethical standards of Korean Christians to a notable degree. As new-born Christians must act differently than before, so new-born Christians in this revival proved themselves by the changes in their lives. Bishop M.C. Harris, who was in charge of the Korean Methodist churches, filed a positive report about the Holy Spirit movement of this period

---

promised a future life. Like shamanism, Christianity taught that God answered prayer and performed miracles. Owens, *Revival Fires in Korea*, 25.

[35] W.G. Cram, 'A Genuine Change', *Korea Mission Field* 3:5 (May, 1907), 68.

[36] Heung-gi Kim, *World Christian History* [in Korean] (Seoul: Yerusalem, 1992), 228.

to the General Assembly of the Methodist Episcopal Church of the United States in 1908.[37]

> The effects following this movement are wholly good—the church raised to a higher spiritual level, almost entire absence of fanaticism because of previous careful instruction in the Bible; not one case of insanity, but many thousands clothed in their right mind; scores of men called to the holy ministry; greater congregations, searching the Word, as many as two thousand meeting in one place for the study of the Bible; many thousands learning to read, and making inquiries; multitudes of them pressing upon the tired missionary and native pastors, praying, 'Give us to eat'. I beseech you do not listen to any word suggestions of doubt as to the vitality and reality of this. Drunkards, gamblers, thieves, adulterers, murderers, self-righteous Confucianists and dead Buddhists, and thousands of devil-worshippers have been made new men in Christ, the old things gone forever.

Third, the Great Revival brought about an explosive growth in the Korean church.[38] Since one of the major characteristics of the revival was a zeal for evangelism, as stated above, the believers could not keep the gospel to themselves. They gave testimonies of their experience of the Holy Spirit to their families, relatives, and friends, proving themselves and the credibility of their testimonies by their changed lives. This led many people to join the movement. In the year between 1906 and 1907, the number of Christians increased tremendously and the growth continued for a few subsequent years.

Presbyterian churches achieved 34% of growth, increasing from 54,987 members (in 1906) to 73,844 (in 1907).[39] Methodist churches achieved a more rapid growth. The Northern Methodist churches attained an 118% growth, from 18,107 (in 1906) to 39,613 (in 1907).[40] Such growth incited the formation of church organizations. The Presbyterian churches organized an independent Korean district in September, 1907. The Methodist churches did the same one year later and took care of the administration and business aspects of the district independently of the missionary headquarters. While the country was being conquered and spiritually disintegrated by the Japanese, the Korean

---

[37] Joseph B. Hingeley (ed.), *Journal of the Twenty-fifth Delegated General Conference of the Methodist Episcopal Church Held in Baltimore, MD, May 6–June 1, 1908* (New York: Eaton & Mains, 1908), 861-62. At the World Missionary Conference at Edinburgh, England, in June of 1910, the great revival of 1907 was reported to have had the 'pure Pentecostal experience'. *World Missionary Conference, Report of Commission I* (Edinburgh, 1910), 77–80.

[38] For the spread of the revival movement, see Lee, *The Early Revival Movement in Korea*, 108-110 to other parts of Korea, and pp. 112-18 to Manchuria and Japan.

[39] Rhodes, *History of the Korea Mission Presbyterian Church U.S.A. 1884–1934*, 547.

[40] *Annual Report of M.E.C.* (1907), 425. Quoted from Gil-sup Song, *History of the Theological Thought in Korea* [in Korean] (Seoul: Christian Literature Society, 1987, 157.

church was building strong, country-wide structures. The growth of the church during this period led to the global involvement of the church in the Declaration of Independence proclaimed on March 1, 1919.

Fourth, it formed new and unique traditions in the Korean church such as early morning prayer meetings, unison prayer in a loud voice, Bible studies, generous offerings, and zeal for evangelism. The dedication of the Korean Christians for the work of Christ was so genuine that the missionaries envied it.[41]

Fifth, it strengthened the unification of the churches. This Holy Spirit movement was a product of a united spirit. People who were committed went beyond denominational differences in seeking the gift of the Holy Spirit. When the revival broke out in united conferences of Presbyterians and Methodists in Wonsan, Pyongyang, and Seoul, they notified one another of up-coming meetings and shared the grace of God. The united work of Presbyterian and Methodist churches in planning and processing the Declaration of Independence on March 1, 1919 may be cited as a product of this united spirit.[42]

There was also a negative outcome. The missionaries started limiting the interest of the Korean churches to the internal affairs of the churches in an attempt to de-politicize the Korean church.[43] In fact, as early as 1901, the Presbyterian Mission Board had decided to de-politicize the Korean church, as it was then involved in the independence movement. Since the Korean church came to experience the Holy Spirit, through the force of the revival movement, the missionaries decided to turn the interest and activities of the Korean church to matters of faith and away from political and social matters. This led some of the Korean churches in non-political directions. Consequently, many churches laid stress on personal salvation and thus lacked social concern. But some other churches were still involved in political matters and took part in the independence movement as actively as before. Despite the efforts of the missionaries to turn the Korean church towards apathy in political matters, the church planned and processed the Declaration of Independence on March 1 in 1919, independently of the missionaries.[44]

After the Korea-Japan Friendship Treaty in 1910, the Japanese severely oppressed the Koreans, taking away the freedom of religion from them, controlling speech, and taking the land by force from the people. This background and the desire of the people for independence led to the Declaration of Independence. The Korean church served as a channel to spread

---

[41] Song, *History of the Theological Thought in Korea*, 157–58.

[42] Also see Lee, *The Early Revival Movement in Korea*, 155-79.

[43] Kyung-bae Min, *History of Korean Nationalistic Church Formulation* [in Korean] (Seoul: Yonsei University Press), 36–54.

[44] Institute of Korean Church History Studies (IKCHS), *A History of Korean Church* [in Korean] (Seoul: Christian Literature, 1990), 23–41.

the movement all over the country, since churches were almost everywhere in the country and equipped with effective communications, they could carry it on secretly so that the movement would start at the same time throughout the nation. Almost half of the writers of the Declaration of Independence were church leaders — 16 out of 33, to be exact. This again proves that the Korean church was actively involved in the movement. When the Independence of the country was declared all the churches participated in it. The reasons for this involvement of the church can be found in the following: its persistent faith that does not yield to persecutions; the unifying power of the church; the church's strong independent spirit; and its connection to the world church. According to a mission report, 'to be a Christian in Korea is the same as participating in the independence movement'.[45]

The Japanese used all its forces to suppress the movement and persecute the church. According to the data of the Presbyterian churches, the Japanese arrested 3,804 lay Christians and 134 pastors and elders. They imprisoned 202 Christian leaders and killed 41. As of the day of the report, 6 were beaten to death, 1,642 were in prison and 12 churches had been abolished.[46] The ruthless power of the Japanese caused Korea's Declaration of Independence to fail.

The failure of the independence movement and subsequent severe persecution of the Korean church by the Japanese influenced the Koreans to be more concerned about spiritual matters and made them rather apathetic to political and social matters.

However, it is clear that the Holy Spirit movement gave rise to a new style of faith. A new style of escapism in faith focusing on the future life was added to the existing faith style which focused on and participated in matters of the present life. These two styles have continued in Korean Christianity up until now. We find the following problems in each of these two styles: first, people are likely to become apathetic to society and the present life when the future life and hope for the future are exclusively emphasized; and on the other hand, when the present life is overly emphasized, people are likely to focus on personal well-being, and to care more for the material blessings of the present.

Summary

Generally speaking, the characteristics of the Korean churches and their Christian lifestyle have been influenced by this movement. Bible study and prayer, especially characterized by repentance, have become the most important religious traditions of the Korean church.[47]

---

[45] Min, *Church History of Korea*, 304–10.

[46] Min, *Church History of Korea*, 313.

[47] Most church historians in Korea agree with this opinion. For example, see Min, Min, *Church History of Korea*, 252–61; Clark, *History of the Church in Korea*, 165-66.

We may characterize this 1907 revival movement in the first period as a 'repentance movement'. Here we find important similarities among three Holy Spirit movements: the early Christian Holy Spirit movement, the Korean Holy Spirit movement, and the modern Holy Spirit (Pentecostal) movement. Let us first take the early Christian Holy Spirit movement into consideration. One hundred and twenty disciples gathered together to keep the commands of Jesus Christ and devote themselves to prayer.[48] When the Day of Pentecost came the Holy Spirit descended upon them. 'Repentance' was one of the most important topics in the first sermon of Peter.[49]

These three elements are to be found in the other two movements, as in all expressions of biblical faith.[50] In other words, in the two later movements as in New Testament times we find that, 1) they kept God's commandments and studied His Word seriously, 2) they gathered together and devoted themselves to prayer, and 3) 'repentance' was one of the most important messages at the beginning of the movements.

Sun-joo Gil's Holy Spirit Movement: Eschatological Expectation

 Sun-joo Gil (photo) is one of the significant figures to have had a major influence on the formation of Korean Protestant Christianity throughout its hundred and ten years' long history, especially in relation to the Holy Spirit movement. Influenced by his contribution to the revival movement over thirty years, Korean Christianity became rather conservative.[51] Gil led classes and revival meetings all over the country from 1907 to 1935. His emphasis on eschatology gave great hope for the future life to people who had despaired under the Japanese occupation.

Gil's Faith

Sun-joo Gil was born in Pyung-nam province in 1869. He had studied ancient Chinese literature, Taoism, and medicine before he became a Christian at the

---

[48] Acts 1:4-8, 14. The Pentecostal movement started, as stated above, in 1900-01 in Topeka, Kansas, U.S.A. According to the record, about one hundred and ten people had gathered for an all-night prayer meeting on December 31, 1900. On January 1, 1901, they experienced the overpowering of the Holy Spirit, just as on the Day of Pentecost.

[49] Acts 2:1-4; 2:37-38.

[50] See James R. Goff, Jr., *Fields White unto Harvest: Charles F. Parham and the Missionary Origins of Pentecostalism* (Fayetteville, NC: University of Arkansas, 1988). This book explores the beginnings of contemporary Pentecostalism in detail.

[51] For an in-depth study of the pneumatological development around the revival movement, see Lee, *The Early Revival Movement in Korea*, 135-49.

age of twenty-eight in 1897. In 1903 he entered a Presbyterian Seminary in Pyongyang and received the training to become a Christian minister. At his graduation from the seminary in 1907 he was ordained and appointed pastor of Jangdae-hyun Church in Pyongyang. This was the official starting point of his pastoral ministry and also the beginning of the revival. Although he had already played a great part in the 1907 Great Revival as an elder, a new ministry began for him with ordination. From this point until he collapsed during the early morning prayer meeting in November, 1935, after preaching at a class in the Pyung-seo district the night before, he made an immense contribution to evangelism. He had led many classes and revival meetings at churches all over the country.

According to a report, during his 28-year ministry he preached more than 20,000 times. It is estimated that a total of 3.8 million people heard his sermons. He baptized more than 3,000 people and built more than sixty churches.[52] Numberless people became ministers, elders, and social workers under his influence. He wrote a few books, including a theological work entitled *Eschatology*. With the revival meetings and also in his writings, he exercised a great influence on the Korean church.

To demonstrate his influence Gil established the following Christian patterns. First, he encouraged a stubborn faith in the authority of the scriptures. Although he had learned this from the first missionaries to Korea, he was even more conservative than the missionaries regarding fundamental faith in his study of scripture. He held to a conservative faith of fundamentalism[53] that was centered on the inerrancy/infallibility of the Bible's Spirit-inspired word. Consequently, in his classes and revival meetings, Bible study took the first place, with stress on the absolute authority of the scripture. This led the Korean church to admire and venerate the biblical Word with a conservative faith from its early stages.

Gil also stressed the importance of Bible reading. At his classes, he taught that Bible study as well as reading were crucial elements in the Christian life. In his church he organized Sunday school classes for adults so that they could study the Bible before the Sunday worship services.

---

[52] Jin-gyung Gil, *Sun-joo Gil* [in Korean] (Seoul: Jongno, 1980), 326.

[53] It has been taught that fundamentalist theology may be summed up in five basic statements: 1) the inerrancy and infallibility of the Bible; 2) the virgin birth and deity of Jesus; 3) the substitutionary Atonement; 4) the literal, physical resurrection of Jesus; and 5) the literal, physical return of Christ. See David L. Smith, *A Handbook of Contemporary Theology* (Wheaton, IL: Victor, 1992), 22. For further information on fundamentalism, see: James Barr, *Fundamentalism* (Philadelphia, Pa.: Westminster, 1977); Stewart G. Cole, *The History of Fundamentalism* (Hamden, Conn,: Archon, 1963); Reuben A. Torrey, et al, *The Fundamentals* (4 vols.; Grand Rapids, MI: Baker, 1980 [1917]).

He urged his congregation to believe the word literally, especially the book of Revelation that he specialized in. He stressed that Revelation recorded both historical facts and what was going to take place in the future, and insisted that Christians should believe it verbatim. For Gil it would be a great sin to doubt the literal word of the Bible. His fundamentalistic attitude toward the scripture is his greatest legacy to the Korean church.

There is one episode that perfectly illustrates his conservative faith. There arose a debate on a Bible commentary by Irvingdon at the Twenty-fourth Presbyterian Annual Assembly in September, 1935 two years prior to Gil's death. Only a few missionaries talked about the core of this issue. Gil pointed out that most of the editors of the commentary were liberal theologians and urged the Korean Presbyterian church not to allow such liberal interpretations of the Bible.[54] By his efforts the General Assembly of the Korean Presbyterian Church decided to boycott the commentary and levelled some penalties against Presbyterian ministers who participated in the translation of the commentary.[55] This set an example that helped maintain the conservative attitude of the Korean Presbyterian churches. Even today, most Korean Presbyterian churches hold the same attitude.

Second, Gil stressed the importance of prayer. He started the early morning prayer meetings and trained people with special prayers like home prayer, fasting prayer, and all-night prayer.[56] The early morning prayer meeting is a very important Christian tradition in Korea and is reckoned to be a key factor in the rapid development and growth of Korean Christianity.[57]

Third, Gil urged zeal for evangelism. From the time of the 1907 Great Revival he challenged people with zeal for evangelism by stressing the offering of certain days or weeks, which meant that people should give their time to God as an offering as well as monetary offerings.[58] This system was adopted by both the Presbyterians and the Methodists and was practiced actively. They employed the system in the following manner. They set apart a certain number of days per year solely for God's work. In response to the grace of God, people

---

[54] Yang-Sun Kim, *Ten-Year History of the Liberation of Korean Christianity* [in Korean] (Seoul: Education Department of the Presbyterian Council, 1956), 177.

[55] Min, *Church History of Korea*, 414.

[56] Gil, *Sun-joo Gil*, 233.

[57] Most Korean churches hold early morning prayer meeting everyday. One finds some churches, which emphasize early morning prayer meeting, have grown rapidly. For an example, Myung-sung Presbyterian Church, as of February 2008, has an average of 7,000 participants on every early morning prayer meeting. This church offers special sessions of their morning meetings twice a year. During these sessions more than a total of 50,000 church members gather at one of the four morning prayer meetings: 4:30, 5:30, 6:30, or 8:30 in the morning. See Bong-rin Ro, 'The Korean Church: Growing or Declining?', *Evangelical Review of Theology* 19 (Oct. 95), 336.

[58] Gil, *Sun-joo Gil*, 201.

went to villages and preached the gospel for ten days or fifteen days, a month, or longer at their own expense. They would sometimes go in pairs.

This system of 'evangelism by laity' achieved great success. Since many Koreans were involved in agriculture in those days, the scheme was actively practiced in winter. The expansion of the gospel throughout the country was greatly helped by the commitment of lay persons to evangelism.

Gil's Teaching on Eschatology

Among his several publications, *Eschatology* is the only theological work. The core of this book lies in witnessing the signs of the second coming of Christ. He viewed the second coming as the supreme theme and eternal hope of the Christian faith, for without faith in the second coming of Christ, there would be no faith at all. Gil viewed the second coming of Christ as the main eschatological hope.

> Eschatology is one of the doctrines of Christian theology based on the Scriptures. It is a study of the situation of men and the world in the last days. There are different views of eschatology but I would like to explore the mystery of eschatology that is written in the Bible, beyond doctrinal theologies. I wish to contribute to the Christian life and to the eternal hope for the future. Since our Christian faith is based on the cross of the Lord Jesus Christ with the hope for the future of eternal life, the second coming of Christ is the centre and the focus of eschatology.[59]

Although Gil described eschatology as a study of the situation of huans and the world in the last days, the main focus of his eschatology was on the second coming of Christ. He emphasized the imminent second coming by illustrating twenty-nine internal evidences and sixty external evidences. He did not state any theory about the pre-millennium, post-millennium, or non-millennium but forecasted the imminent second coming as he understood it.[60]

He called people's attention to the time of the second coming, commenting on Matthew 24:36, 'No one knows about that day or hour, not even the angels in heaven, nor the Son, but only the Father,' as follows: 'It does not mean that it is forbidden to know the time of the second coming as an absolute mystery. Rather, this verse was given to let people prepare for the imminent second coming by looking at the signs'. [61] According to Gil, we can tell the approximate time of the second coming, although not precisely. As John the Baptist prepared the way of the Lord at the time of the first coming in the incarnation, so the Holy Spirit will come to prepare the second coming of the

---

[59] Sun-joo Gil, *Sun-joo Gil's Works* [in Korean] (Seoul: Korean Christian Literature, 1968), vol. 1, 24.
[60] Song, *History of Theological Thought in Korea*, 276.
[61] Gil, *Sun-joo Gil's Works*, 26.

Lord by making his people aware of its time and be prepared for it. He predicted the year to be 1974 by examining the signs.[62] His calculations were based on Luke 21:24–27: 'Jerusalem will be trampled on by the Gentiles until the times of the Gentiles are fulfilled.... At that time they will see the Son of Man coming in a cloud with power and great glory'.

Gil predicted the year 1974 as early as the 1930s. In some other writings, however, he predicted the year of the second coming to be the year 2002.[63] He added that these estimates could be wrong. Judging from this statement, we should not criticize him as a precise time-predicting eschatologist.[64] His main point in predicting the year of the second coming was to stress its imminence and to stimulate people's faltering faith. He wanted Christians to be aware of the imminent coming of the millennial kingdom and be prepared for it.[65] The effect of his eschatology was to give people the power to overcome persecution and oppression with the spirit of martyrdom, for faith in the second coming would give them real hope and courage. Indeed, the Korean church could overcome the persecutions of Japanese rulers by their faith and hope for the second coming. In predicting the approximate year of the second coming, however, Gil's interpretation of the Scripture seems to have gone to an extreme. He could not have avoided this danger in his theology because he was very much influenced by dispensationalism.

Nonetheless, the Holy Spirit movement inaugurated by Sun-joo Gil contributed greatly to the formation of the patterns and traditions of the early Korean Protestant churches. Gil's puritanical and stubbornly conservative attitude influenced the Presbyterian churches to disallow any liberal interpretation of the scriptures. This conservative exclusivism of Korean Presbyterianism devised by Gil was succeeded and summed up by Hyung-yong Park.[66]

The next grand revival movement following the Great Revival of 1907 was the 'Million Souls movement' of 1909–1910.[67] As the Great Revival started from Bible studies and prayer meetings under the leadership of Methodist missionaries in 1903, the Million Souls movement was also started primarily among the Methodist missionaries. In July of 1909, the Methodist missionaries C.F. Reid, M.B. Stokes, and F.K. Gamble, gathered in Gaeseong City to

---

[62] Gil, *Sun-joo Gil's Works*, 70.

[63] Gil, *Sun-joo Gil's Works*, 72.

[64] International Theological Institute, *When the Holy Spirit Comes upon You* [in Korean] (Seoul: International Theological Institute, 1994), 114. Henceforth International Theological Institute will be referred as ITI.

[65] ITI, *When the Holy Spirit Comes*, 72.

[66] See Song, *History of Theological Thought in Korea*, 319–29.

[67] See Institute of Korean Church History Studies, *A History of Korean Church* [in Korean] (Seoul: Christian Literature, 1989), vol. 1, 276–82.

conduct Bible studies and prayer meetings.[68] After the prayer meeting ten missionaries and fifteen Korean church leaders went to a mountain to have another prayer meeting and there they were filled with the Holy Spirit. After this meeting, M.B. Stokes made an appeal to the congregation to lead 50,000 people in Gaeseong City to the Lord within a year. This challenge made a great impact on people. In September of the same year, at the annual meeting of missionaries of the Southern Methodist Church, they committed themselves to bring 20,000 people to Christ within a year through prayer and with the help of the Holy Spirit.

In October, 1909, the General Council of Evangelical Missions was held in Seoul. C.F. Reid, the chairman of the Council, reported on this declaration and suggested 'A million souls for Christ'. They passed the motion unanimously and thus expanded the movement interdenominationally all over the nation. Millions of tracts and 700,000 copies of Mark's Gospel were distributed during this period.[69] This movement, before the country was annexed to Japan, brought another revival in the Korean church. There were about 200,000 Korean Christians around this time.[70]

Although they did not gain one million Christians in this movement, it gave the Koreans a zeal for evangelism which became one of the traditions of the church. Both positive and negative evaluations can be made of this movement. It helped Korea to maintain peace and order since it drove Christians to be more concerned about religion than politics before the country was annexed to Japan.[71] On the other hand, by depoliticizing Christians, the movement may have weakened the role of Christianity in a political and social sense and lessened its concern for society.

---

[68] Yun, *Christianity and Korean Thought*, 192–93.
[69] Yun, *Christianity and Korean Thought*, 192–94.
[70] Baek, *The History of Protestant Missions*, 444.
[71] Baek, *The History of Protestant Missions*, 405.

Chapter 4

The Second Period (1920–1940)

Background

Early in the 1920s, when the Japanese occupied Korea as a colonial power, there arose hostility among younger Christians against the missionaries, for most of them insisted on the separation of religion from the state. Some Christians, who found favour with the Japanese, also had a haughty attitude toward the Koreans. At the same time, the legalistic attitude of the Korean church leaders with their abusive and authoritative stance provoked discontent among the learned, who began to severely criticize the church. On the other hand, there arose a movement to organize a new church system to involve the church in the nationalist movement.

The Japanese sent Koreans by force to the battlefront after invading Manchuria in 1931 and began to persecute them in various ways in order to achieve their final goal. This Japanese colonialism hoped to destroy the spirit of the nation and make the Koreans a subject of the Japanese emperor. The Japanese built Shinto shrines in all the cities and towns, forced the Koreans to observe Shinto worship and, furthermore, forced them to change their names according to the Japanese style.

Christian churches and schools strongly opposed Japanese policies. This led to terrible persecutions for the Korean church. The Japanese closed more than two hundred churches, put more than two thousand Christians in prison, and martyred more than fifty ministers.[1] In such a depressing situation and under severe persecution, as the Korean church could not find hope in the present life, it began to stress the spiritual side of faith, emphasizing the second coming of Christ and hope for the eternal kingdom of heaven.

The Holy Spirit movement of the suffering Korean church during this period can be classified in three categories. The first was the Holy Spirit movement by Sun-joo Gil (1869–1935) that emphasized eschatological faith and the imminent return of Jesus Christ. The second was the Holy Spirit movement led by Ik-doo Kim (1894–1950) that emphasized the miraculous signs of the

---

[1] Yang-sun Kim, *Abridged Korean Church History* [in Korean] (Seoul: General Assembly of Korean Jesus Presbyterian Churches, 1962), 40.

apostolic church and performed healing. The third was the Holy Spirit movement led by Yong-do Lee (1901–1933) that stressed the suffering Christ and mystical union with Christ. Under the persecution of Japan, these three Holy Spirit movements with different emphases—eschatological faith, faith in divine healing, and faith in mystical union with Christ—had a great influence on the Korean people.

Korea was under Japanese occupation from 1910. At the beginning, there were no major conflicts between the Korean churches and the Japanese rulers. However, there later came a great turning point. The Korean church supported and participated in the Declaration of Independence on March 1, 1919, which caused the Japanese regime to persecute the Korean churches. This, along with other factors to be stated below, brought about the decline of the Korean church in this period after the great revival period which had begun in 1907.

The reasons for the decline of the Korean church may be summarized as follows: 1) severe Japanese persecution of the Korean church,[2] 2) discontent with missionaries owing to their co-operative attitude toward the Japanese rulers, 3) severe economic depression, and 4) the introduction of socialism.[3]

As a result, the Korean church became more interested in the internal world or spiritual world rather than in an external concern for society or participation in society. In other words, Korean congregations in this period appeared to ignore their present life, while they anticipated spiritual blessings and hope for the future. The latter has been called a mystical movement and the term is so used in this study. This mystical movement was inaugurated by Sun-joo Gil.[4] Gil was believed to have read the Book of Revelation 800 times and memorized the whole book while he was in prison for religious activities under Japanese persecution. The mystical movement reached its climax in the work of a Methodist minister, Yong-do Lee, an evangelist well known throughout the country.[5]

Ik-doo Kim's Holy Spirit Movement: Healing Ministry

Ik-doo Kim was a charismatic church leader and famous faith-healer who provided vitality and new strength for the Korean people and the Korean church. Against the streams of new ideas that had begun to emerge in the 1920s including an anti-Christian ideology, he was a man of the power of God who

---

[2] One may compare this with the early church under the persecutions of the Roman Empire.

[3] Min, *Church History of Korea*, 304 ff.

[4] He travelled more than 50,000 miles all over the country to lead revival meetings for 35 years. He always chose scripture verses from the book of Revelation and preached on the future life and the return of Jesus Christ. Min, *Church History of Korea*, 350-56.

[5] We may consider both Gil's Holy Spirit movement and Lee's as mystical movements, but they had different emphases.

maintained the orthodox faith and gave hope through a healing ministry to the lower class of people who had been neglected.

Background

Following the Declaration of Independence in 1919, along with the desire for liberation, new ideas began to infiltrate into Korea. Liberal ideas came in to the country through liberal missionaries, bringing about an era of confusion. An economic crisis also occurred with an annual inflation rate of 400%. The Japanese Governor-General of Korea secretly encouraged smoking, drinking, licensed prostitution, and drugs not only as sources of revenue but also in order to carry out a scheme to destroy the Koreans in body and spirit.

In addition to these, the Japanese kept persecuting Christians for their major involvement in the Declaration of Independence on March 1, 1919, against which the Korean church protested vigorously.

Around this time, new ideas and revolutionary ideologies such as bolshevism and socialism that attracted the younger generation entered the church and shook it to its foundations.

The Life and Healing Ministry of Ik-doo Kim

Kim (photo) was born in November, 1884 as the only son in a farmer's household in Hwang-hae province, North Korea. He was a student of Confucianism in his youth. In February 1900 he listened to a sermon preached by a missionary W.L. Swallon, repented of his sins, and became a Christian. He then led his wife and mother into the church. Kim was active and aggressive enough in his Christian life, reportedly having read the New Testament in Chinese one hundred times from July 1900 to February 1902. It is said that during this time he received the baptism of the Holy Spirit and had mystical experiences.[6]

He began to minister as a church worker at the age of twenty-eight. According to the records, Kim began to heal diseases through prayer, being filled with the Holy Spirit.[7] He entered a Presbyterian seminary in Pyongyang in 1906 and graduated from it in 1910. After graduation, he committed himself as the pastor of Sincheon Presbyterian Church. He began with a small number of members but built a church and gained 700 members in a few years. In 1919

---

[6] In-seo Kim, 'Short Biography of Ik-doo Kim', in *Selective Work of In-Seo Kim* [in Korean] (Seoul: Shinmangae, 1976), vol. 5, 101-102.

[7] Min, *Church History of Korea*, 353–56; Paul Jaebum Lee, *A History of Pentecostal Movement* [in Korean] (Seoul: Voice, 1985), 201–02; Jong-ho Byun, *A History of the Pentecostal Movement in Korea* [in Korean] (Seoul: Shinsaeng-kwan, 1972), 75–76.

he was elected vice-superintendent of the Presbyterian churches in Korea and in 1920 the superintendent. He expanded the revival meetings all over the country to full scale after March 1, 1919.

The centre of Kim's revival was a healing ministry through prayer. In October, 1919, when he was leading a revival meeting in a church in Pyung-nam province, he was inspired by Mark 16:17, 'And these signs will accompany those who believe'. He believed that the same signs and wonders could take place as in the apostolic age when the Lord granted his grace, and he ardently prayed for this manifestation of God's power. After a month he laid his hands on a paralytic man and prayed for his healing. The paralytic was healed within a day. It was from this day forward that he was convinced of the power of divine healing. Many miracles accompanied his ministry. According to the record of the minutes of the Ninth Annual Assembly of Presbyterian Churches, the blind regained their sight, the dumb spoke, paralysis and hemorrhaging were healed.

People began to witness Kim's powerful healing ministry after October 1919. News of it spread among the Koreans who had been dismayed at the failure of the Declaration of Independence. Many sick people gathered around him to be healed of their diseases. Many who received healing donated their possessions to the church. The revival movement that Kim led was marked by unprecedented large-scale public conferences. It is reported that such large-scale meetings were attributed to the power of the Holy Spirit.[8] The revival meeting in Daegu City from April 25 to May 1, 1920 was a huge national meeting marked by miracles, spiritual gifts, and exclamations of praise. According to the record, 808 people were converted. They raised an offering for Sunday schools in the region of 50,000 won (the average monthly wage of pastors was 33 won).[9] Hundreds of people were healed of various diseases.[10] His healing crusade at this time was spread widely as it was reported by daily newspapers such as *Dong-ah* and *Chosun Daily News*. Four to five thousand gathered at the revival meetings of the united Presbyterian churches of Pyongyang from June 30 of the same year. At that time the *Dong-ah Daily News* reported the crusade when thousands of people took leave of their senses and were in an ecstatic state.[11]

They raised more than 60,000 won for the establishment of Sungduk School. In October of the same year, Kim led revival meetings of the united Presbyterian churches in Seoul. It is recorded that ten thousand people gathered in them every day. In Korean church history it was the first time that such a

---

[8] Kyung-bae Min, *History of Korean Christian Faith Movement under Japanese Occupation* [in Korean] (Seoul: Korean Christian Literature, 1991), 299.

[9] Min, *History of Korean Christian Faith Movement*, 300.

[10] Chun-geun Han, *Ik-doo Kim Who Never Perish* [in Korean] (Seoul: Biblical Theology, 1993), 112.

[11] *The Dong-ah Daily Newspaper*, July 3, 1920.

large crowd of people had gathered. [12] The offerings people made at his revivals were used in various ways: some were used to send and support evangelists, and others to build a library for students. Kim's ministry bore fruit through his revival meetings and open-air crusades: about 28,000 people became Christians, and about 10,000 people were healed. Such healing miracles that occurred during his crusades were so well known that five pastors and two elders from Hwang-hae Presbytery formed a panel to investigate and verify the claims of miracles. In July 1921 they proved the miracles to be genuine in the book entitled *The Miracle Verification of Chosun Jesus Church.* [13]

In spite of such publicity and popularity, Kim remained humble ascribing all these works not to human power but to the 'fruit of God's mysterious power'. He claimed that he only followed biblical principles and prayed for the sick. [14]

Kim led revival meetings all over the country in 776 cities and towns. It is estimated that about 10,000 people received divine healing at his meetings. [15] He was killed by a communist soldier on October 14, 1950.

Special Features of Kim's Revival Meetings

Kim's revival meeting had the following special features. First, it was a public crusade. There were no other meetings or conferences that attracted so many people as Kim's in Korea under Japanese occupation. An unprecedented number of people gathered in every town where Kim's revival meeting was held.

Second, his revival meeting had a unique schedule or time-table. The standard time-table of his revival meeting was made up of four meetings a day: an early morning prayer meeting, a two or three-hour long Bible class in the morning, a doctrinal study class in the afternoon, and a revival meeting in the evening.

Third, it had a unique atmosphere. People say that his sermons stirred the hearts of those who gathered there. Although his language was rather direct and harsh, his sermons touched the core of people's hearts. He preached mainly on the love of God, the sacrifice of Jesus on the cross, the power of the precious blood of Christ, and repentance. People would praise, weep, and give thanks to God with enthusiasm and excitement, as a reaction to his sermons.

---

[12] Yong-gyu Park, *Biography of Rev. Ik-doo Kim* [in Korean] (Seoul: Word of Life Press, 1991), 120.

[13] IKCHS, *Korean Church History I* [in Korean] (Seoul: Christian Literature Press, 1980), 188.

[14] Taek-kwon Lim (ed.), *Testimony of Miracles in Chosun Jesus Churches* [in Korean] (Seoul: Chosun Jesus Literature, 1921), 100.

[15] Yong-kyu Park, *Biography of Ik-doo Kim: a Korean Evangelist* [in Korean] (Seoul: Christian News, 1968), 104-105.

Fourth, divine healing was pre-eminent.[16] Being influenced by the healing ministry of Ik-doo Kim, the Presbyterian church council changed an article of their bye-law from 'there are no miracles in the post-apostolic age' to 'there are miracles'.[17] In Ik-doo Kim's ministry mostly people of lower classes were healed. Some were beggars. Kim prayed ardently for divine healing. At the beginning, he laid his hands on each of the sick and prayed for their healing individually but later he put the sick together in one place and prayed over them. After the sick gained the faith to be healed by God's power alone, they were healed during the worship services. Kim encouraged public testimony to divine healing during the worship services and thus gave assurance to the people's faith and helped it grow.

Evaluations

Kim received severe criticism from the socialists and persecution from the Japanese government. They judged his healing ministry a fraud because Kim's revival movement was strongly supported by such a great number of people.

Taek-kwon Lim, a Korean church leader in Kim's day, looked at Kim's healing ministry as 'an unusual, mysterious miracle that is hard to find in the 1900 years of church history'. All this took place in less than forty years of Korea's Protestant history.[18] Lim thought it was worth leaving a record of Kim's healing ministry and so organized a committee of ministers and medical doctors to publish a report entitled, 'Testimony of Miracles in Chosun Jesus Churches'. In this report, Lim made the following statement about the historical meaning and position of Kim's ministry:

---

[16] Divine healing is an important part of the modern Holiness movement and the Pentecostal movement. A.B. Simpson, who had a great theological influence on the Holiness movement, discussed the following four major doctrines found in the Bible: salvation, holiness, healing, and the second coming of Jesus Christ. The Pentecostal movement took such doctrines from the Holiness movement. Although the Holiness churches do not emphasize divine healing as much as formerly, the Pentecostal movement still emphasizes and takes divine healing as an important doctrine. See Dayton, *Theological Roots of Pentecostalism*, 115–41; Nichol, *Pentecostalism*, 2–8, 15–17.

In the doctrine of the Presbyterian Church, divine healing is not emphasized. Although Kim was a Presbyterian pastor and the former superintendent of the Presbyterian Church council, his healing ministry was not very much emphasized. Only a brief comment has been made on his ministry in church history books written by Presbyterian scholars. See Yung-hun Lee, *The History of Korean Church* [in Korean] (Seoul: Concordia, 1992), 122–23.

[17] Byun, *A History of the Pentecostal Movement in Korea*, 76.

[18] Lim, *Testimony of Miracles*, 1-2.

The first was God's comfort and exhortation for the people under persecution; the second was God's providence against anti-Christian criticism and materialistic thoughts, proving the divine intervention, and showing the love of the living God; the third was that the revival movement of Ik-doo Kim urged repentance upon people owing to the signs of the age. This is the age of the last days.[19]

Kim's revival movement contributed greatly to the growth of the Korean church. In 1921, the Korean church achieved a 20% annual growth rate. The Presbyterian church statistics are given in the following table.[20]

Year	1919	1920	1921	1922	1923
Pastors	192	180	208	246	234
Members	133,062	153,915	179,158	187,271	193,850
Churches	3,640	3,659	3,969	4,248	4,503

The Presbyterian Church Statistics

The most impressive feature of Kim's revival movement was that he preached his message to people of the lower social strata who were neglected and were suffering from poverty and disease. His message was focused on the future life, proclaiming the eschatological millennium and criticizing sin and wealth. In consequence he was supported strongly by the lower class on the one hand and, on the other, was severely criticized and opposed by the socialists for his stress on the future life and for his rejection of wealth. He was also persecuted by the Japanese government for his indirect resistance to the Japanese emperor as he emphasized monotheism's demand to serve God alone.

Kim's enthusiastic revival movement with manifestations of miracles and signs was born in a social environment of nihilism and defeatism immediately after the Declaration of Independence of March 1, 1919.[21] The emphasis on eschatological faith in his revival movement provided the vision with a focus on the second coming of Christ in the 1930s, at a time of a critical national ordeal. It also helped a faith in escapism to be engendered among the people.[22] A faith of escapism here means a faith with which people focus on the future life, trying to escape from the present life.

Kim's charismatic revival movement should be evaluated positively, as it challenged and awakened the existing Korean church that was somewhat lethargic and was pre-occupied with ceremonies and forms. By reviving the Holy Spirit movement on the lines of the apostolic church and by encouraging

---

[19] Lim, *Testimony of Miracles*, 3-5.
[20] Kyung-bae Min, 'The Revival Movement of Ik-doo Kim and His Healing Ministry', *Oriental Studies* 54-56 (1987), 298.
[21] Min, *History of Korean Church Faith Movement*, 280.
[22] IKCHS, *The History of Korean Christianity II* [in Korean] (Seoul: Christian Literature, 1970), 41.

those who had been neglected in society to experience the Holy Spirit and receive God's call, he inspired a regeneration of the Korean church.

Christianity without the work of the Holy Spirit cannot be called Christianity in the truest sense. Kim's revival movement broke down the wall of unbelief among churches, gave strength to lethargic churches, ignited zeal for prayer and evangelism, and encouraged a vital and victorious faith.

Kim's revival movement is sometimes criticized as being biblically unbalanced for its emphasis on human feelings and miracles. However, the emotional side of his revival movement may be understood as a natural phenomenon that had to appear in a transitional period of Korea. He certainly was a man of God and forefather of the Pentecostal movement in Korea.

Yong-do Lee's Holy Spirit Movement: Mystical Union with Christ

In the early 1930s, when Korea was going through a most difficult period, the journal of the Presbyterian Theological Seminary carried a foreword that predicted the future of the Korean church. This article spoke of the three turning-points in church history: the first turning-point of Christianity was the conquest of the Roman Empire by Christianity; the second was the Reformation; the third turning-point would be the coming era of the Holy Spirit, when Korea would be the country that would carry it out. The article read:

> When Christianity first arrived at Rome, it resisted heresies there, opposed gentile religions, and endured persecutions, and thus conquered the Roman Empire. It became 'an authoritativeness-centered religion'. This is the first turning-point of Christianity. This 'authoritative Christianity' brought about the dark ages that preceded the Medieval era. It was Luther and Calvin and the other Reformers who protested and changed 'authoritative Christianity' into 'Bible-centered Christianity', standing firmly on the Word of God. This is the second turning-point of Christianity. However, this 'Bible-centered Christianity' also lost its life and it became urgent that the Holy Spirit manifest its great power and work. This is the third turning-point of Christianity that changed from 'Bible-centered Christianity' into 'Spirit-centered Christianity'. Who, then, will carry out the third turning-point of Christianity? Christianity began in the West and will flourish and reach its climax in the East. Who, then, in the East will carry it out? It will be in Chosun that Christianity will reach its third turning-point and become Spirit-centered.[23]

---

[23] In-seo Kim, 'The Third Turning-point of Christianity' [in Korean], *Sinhakjinam* (January, 1931), 23.

This article prophesied the future of the Korean church by examining its characteristics and features. Kyung-bae Min, who wrote the piece, was greatly influenced by the Holy Spirit movement of Yong-do Lee in the 1930s.[24]

Although brief, this stimulated and challenged the Korean church, stirring up a new enthusiasm of faith. Yong-do Lee motivated a revival movement that emphasized 'Jesus-centered enthusiasm' and prayer, thus influencing the development of the characteristics of the Korean church. Many scholars classify these features as revivalism or mysticism.

Background

In 1930 the Korean church was going through a difficult time due to 1) the political frustration that came from the failure of the Declaration of Independence of March 1, 1919; 2) the economic crisis of the Great Panic; 3) the introduction of socialism; and 4) a more severe oppression by the Japanese in line with that country's invasion of Manchuria.[25] The Korean church could not adapt itself to the new and threatening situation but tried to avoid it. Since the missionaries led the church in a non-political direction, the Korean church in this period focused on the future life, denying the present life, and tended to be authoritative and legalistic. This left it in a depressed condition.

Yong-do Lee's ministry made a strong impact on the reformation of the weak church of Korea. The revival movement that he led created an atmosphere favourable to the reform of the Korean church and, as a consequence, he became the target of severe criticism from the existing churches.

Yong-do Lee's Life

Yong-do Lee (photo) was born on April 6, 1901 in Hwang-hae Province. He was a weak child with various diseases, which caused him to be emotional and sensitive. His parents did not expect much of him since they thought he could not live long. His health improved, however, as he began to attend elementary school. His teachers favoured him since he was dexterous and clever, with a great talent for words.

His family background was not very good. The family was poor. His father was an alcoholic who badly abused his wife, a faithful Christian. His mother prayed fervently for her children even under the persecution of her husband and

---

[24] Kyung-bae Min, 'The Influence of Yong-do Lee's Theology on the Holy Spirit Movement' (a paper presented at the Fourth International Theological Seminar, Seoul, 1995), 81-83.

[25] Song, *History of Theological Thought in Korea*, 300.

this impressed little Yong-do, the third son. The boy, being sentimental and faithful, became a prayerful child and practiced the prayer that he had learned from his mother. As early as the age of thirteen he would go to the bell tower of a church and pray there for hours, sometimes overnight. He experienced the grace of regeneration and, later, confessed that he was born again. This was in October 1916. He entered Gaeseong Hanyang School, which later became Songdo Junior High School, in 1915 and there he managed to support himself. While he was a student at this school, being a young man committed to justice, Yong-do Lee participated actively in the Declaration of Independence of March 1, 1919. He was nineteen at the time. He was arrested and put in prison for his involvement in the independence movement. After coming out of prison, he continued to participate in the independence movement. By the time he went to Hyeop-seong Seminary, a Methodist school, in the spring of 1924, he had been imprisoned four times, spending a total of three years in detention.[26]

His primary reason for entering the seminary was that he thought he might lead people into eternal life through the gospel of Christ. It was indeed to save and restore the nation. Lee met two very good colleagues at the seminary, Ho-bin Lee and Hwan-sin Lee. These two men and Yong-do Lee are called 'the three Lees'. They spent much time together, discussing the situation of the Korean church and making their plans for ministry.

Two years later, however, Yong-do Lee was diagnosed to be in the terminal stage of tuberculosis and was told to quit school. This served as a turning-point of his life, although he did not yet have a vivid experience of the Holy Spirit or a strong calling from God. Ho-bin and Hwan-shin decided to send Yong-do to their home town of Kang-dong in Pyung-nam Province in North Korea, to recover from his illness. A church in Gang-dong invited him to lead winter revival meetings. It is said that people experienced the powerful work of the Holy Spirit at the meetings and many souls were touched. A month-long stay at Gang-dong gave Lee an unshakable faith and assurance, the experience of the Holy Spirit, and recognition of the urgent needs of the Korean church. He became deeply concerned about the church and aware of what it needed and what it should discard. Lee pointed out that the Korean church did not have prayer, personal evangelism, hard-work, love, courage, thanksgiving, praise, co-operation, and Bible studies but did have murmuring, laziness, cowardice, complaints, worries, division and greed. He insisted, 'The Korean church must grow'.[27] He likewise kept saying that the Korean church had to change.

---

[26] Jong-ho Byun (ed.), *Biography of Yong-do Lee* [in Korean] (Seoul: Jang-ahn, 1993), 23-26.

[27] Jong-ho Byun (ed.), *Diary of Yong-do Lee* [in Korean] (Seoul: Jang-ahn, 1993), 21 (on February 9, 1927). Byun, as a follower of Yong-do Lee, dedicated his life to research on Lee, defending him in regard to the charge of heresy on him, and editing and publishing Lee's books. Through Byun's effort, ten books on Yong-do Lee were

Lee decided to dedicate his whole life to the work of Christ. He criticized the lethargic church of Korea and emphasized the need for a revival within it. He said:

Today's church yearns for revival. When it revives, it can be a true church; on the other hand, if it fails to revive, it will become the true offspring of the devil. Today's church members are deep in sleep. Not only that, the church is on the brink of deception, division, dispute and murder. It badly needs revival. Why? [It is] because it daily grows weaker and more secular. There is no love or warmth but only coldness in the church. Its excessive jealousy and dispute stuns the people.... The members do not serve God or others but are eager to seek their own profit.[28]

He put a stress on the true Christian life: the life of repentance, prayer, thanksgiving, love, and sacrifice.[29]

Lee graduated from the seminary on January 28, 1928 and, on the following day, set off to Dongcheon Church in Gang-won province to minister there. It was his first church to pastor but since he did not have the experience of the Spirit and conversion, he had a hard time in giving leadership to that church. Until he had the great experience of the Spirit in conversion, he was only a theorist. He always prepared detailed sermon manuscripts. Although he spent a great deal of time in home visitations, his church did not grow. He sensed his own problems, and went to Geumgang Mountain, to pray and fast for ten days. During this time, he received a strong experience of the Holy Spirit and became a totally different person. He returned as a man of prayer and began to preach powerful messages.

On the Christmas Eve of 1928 he was praying through the night and had a mystical experience of fighting with the devil and overcoming him. He had another mystical experience eleven days later, early on the morning of January 4, 1929, at a revival meeting in Yangyang Church, also in Gang-won province. These two consecutive mystical experiences became the source of his revival movement later.[30] When he preached, after these experiences, people began to repent of their sins with loud cries. It is said that people experienced the great work of the Holy Spirit and gained new strength through repentance. There were converts from among those who perverted and persecuted Christianity. From this time to his death in October, 1933,[31] he travelled around the country and made every effort to evangelize it through the repentance movement.

---

published, seven by Byun himself and the other three by Byun's wife after Byun's death.

[28] Byun, *Diary*, 32 on May 2, 1927.

[29] Song, *History of Theological Thought in Korea*, 305–12.

[30] About his conversion, see Gil-sup Song, *The Three Stars of the Methodist Church under Japanese Occupation* [in Korean] (Seoul: Sung-kwang, 1982), 231-34.

[31] Lee died at the age of 33 just like Jesus. Min, *Church History of Korea*, 390.

Yong-do Lee's Ministry

After Yong-do Lee had gained new power through these mystical experiences, he became well-known by 1930 even in the remote islands off the west coast. He led revival meetings in Pyongyang, the Jerusalem of Korea, which were accompanied by great works that shook the entire city of Pyongyang. A widespread repentance took place. 1931 was the peak of Lee's ministry, during which time he led revival meetings even in China and Manchuria. With their success, however, there arose opposition against him, largely because Lee strongly attacked the traditional churches and their ministers. Whenever he had a chance he urged the renewal of Christian thought and uttered messages of reform from the pulpit in order to awaken the lethargic Korean church and make it active. He suggested three keys to this reformation: repentance, prayer, and love, for without these, he thought, no one could expect the true revival of the Korean church.

Yong-do Lee proclaimed the message of repentance wherever he went.

> Korea needs pioneers of the repentance movement more than any pioneers of doctrine or organization. A movement that does not bring regeneration by repentance does not have any significance at all. The pioneers of the church should be truly born-again Christians, dead to sin and born of righteousness, born-again by the Holy Spirit....[32] True repentance is long gone in the church. This is one of the major reasons why the church has not grown.[33]

He urged this repentance mainly for the arrogant church, its ministers, and missionaries. The chief target of his criticism was the Christian congregation of Pyongyang, called the 'Jerusalem of Korea'.

Lee became a voice in the wilderness as he urged church reformation but was attacked for it. His fellow ministers, out of jealousy and slander, made him resign from his church and gave him the position of Secretary for Sunday School Assembly. They promoted him as a way of removing him. The Hwang-hae District of the General Assembly of the Presbyterian Churches ruled to ban invitations for Lee. Subsequently, the Pyongyang District condemned him and the General Assembly of the Presbyterian Churches judged him to be heretical. He was then suspended from the Central District of Methodist Churches. The crucial reason for this judgment was the incident related to an allegedly demon-possessed woman and also the establishment of the 'Jesus Church'.[34]

---

[32] Byun, *Diary*, 59-60 on November 10, 1929.

[33] Byun, *Diary*, 33 on May 2, 1927, 33.

[34] It was not Lee himself but his followers who established the Jesus Church. This church was the first indigenized church in Korea that was founded independently without any connections with western missionaries. Min, *Church History of Korea*, 391–99.

There was a woman named Myung-hwa Yoo at a Methodist church in Wonsan who, around 1927, claimed that Jesus had descended upon her. She went to the revival meeting of a church and pretended to be Jesus by mimicking him. A man named Jeon-myung Han was involved in this act of Yoo. Yong-do Lee became close to them and it led him to be judged and ultimately destroyed.

After hearing the voice of Myung-hwa Yoo in Wonsan he hallucinated as if he had heard the voice of Jesus, bowed down before her, and called her, 'Lord'. He thus came under severe criticism. He defended himself, saying, 'Myung-hwa Yoo was neither Jesus nor goddess. I heard the word of the Lord through her. I prostrated myself before the Word'.

Lee also supported Jeon-myung Han with sympathetic love and indirectly helped him to establish a new sect, the 'Jesus Church'. This also caused criticism from the Korean church. Jeon-myung Han was excommunicated from the traditional church for his involvement with a 'heretical' sect.

Yong-do Lee received both popular acclaim and criticism in his latter days and died of tuberculosis on October 2, 1933 at the age of thirty-three.

Yong-do Lee's Theology

The common evaluation by theologians of Yong-do Lee's theology is that it was a form of mysticism. Theologians evaluate his theology of mysticism in various ways: from the apostolic to the mysticism of medieval Germany; from monastic pietism to the purity of faith on the level of sanctification.

Principles of His Theology

His faith was centered on Christ, emphasizing union with him. Many theologians view Lee's theology as that of a 'mystical union between God and man'. The following diary shows his idea about God:

> The Lord is drawn to me in this way
>   and I to Him:
> We became one.
> I am possessed by the love of the Lord
>   and the Lord by my love;
> I remain in the love of the Lord
>   and the Lord remains in my faith.[35]

He put more value on the integration of love and faith than on the relation between reason and revelation. He called the unity of love and faith the 'principle of unity'. His theology states that the love of the Lord embraces faith and faith embraces love: this mutual inclusion becomes the supreme principle

---

[35] Byun, *Diary*, 118 on January 27, 1931.

of his theological method. In his ministry, Lee expressed this theology of mutual inclusion of the love of Christ and the faith of men. He confessed: 'Only when Jesus-centered love touches us can we cry and be captivated by the sacrifice and love of the Lord'. He urged people to discard loveless faith and to hold on to love-filled faith:

> Love is life. Loveless faith does not have life. Forms such as the recitation of decrees and doctrines or the habit of coming to church should not be all of Christian faith, for such forms deceive people. Can it be called faith? Then, possess you love. Loveless faith is like a lamp without light or eyeglasses for the blind.[36]

His whole emphasis was on love, saying that the goal of Christians was Jesus and that Jesus was the focus of our faith.[37]

Mysticism

Lee's thought was a mysticism that emphasized union with Christ. Mysticism refers to the direct connection or union between God and the human spirit.[38] To be a mystic is simply to participate here and now in the real and eternal life in the fullest, deepest sense which is possible to man.[39] Mysticism, however, is more an active element in all true religions than a religion itself and is seen as a reaction to the lethargic tendency of religions. In the days of Yong-do Lee, the Korean church was becoming formalistic without being concerned about the miserable state of the people. Lee tried to awaken the Korean church and to restore the vitality of the church by 'tears' and 'love'. The mystical movement of Yong-do Lee was a severe warning against the lethargic church and, at the same time, provided a real hope for the people.[40]

Evaluation of Theologians

Professor Kyung-bae Min, a Presbyterian church historian, describes Lee's thought as a 'mysticism of the suffering Christ'.[41] He esteemed Lee to be 'a man of faith who loftily raised his voice for the independence and the indigenization of the Korean church and who then vanished'.[42] Min points out that Lee described Jesus as a suffering God enduring shame, not as the Lord of

---

[36] Jong-ho Byun (ed.), *Letters of Yong-do Lee* [in Korean] (Seoul: Jang-ahn, 1993), 143.

[37] Byun, *Letters*, 118–19.

[38] Everlyn Underhill, *The Essentials of Mystics* (London: Methuen, 1920), 29.

[39] Margaret Smith, *Studies in Early Mysticism in the Near East and Middle East* (Amsterdam: Philo, 1973), 25.

[40] Young-hoon Lee, 'Evangelism and Church Growth in Korea' [in Korean], *Theological Thoughts* 100 (April 1998), 226

[41] Min, *Church History of Korea*, 386.

[42] Min, *Church History of Korea*, 391.

authority and power, not to mention his relation to the triune God.[43] But Min viewed positively Lee's effort to be like Jesus and thus to activate the church, as it was losing vitality by its rigid doctrines.

Many Methodist scholars published research papers about Yong-do Lee. Sun-hwan Byun, the former president of the Methodist Theological Seminary, compared Lee with Meister Johannes Eckhart, a great German mystic. According to Byun, Lee was not much different from Eckhart or his disciple, Tauler. If German mysticism reflected the distress and suffering of human nature that feared the loss of salvation at the end of the medieval era, Lee's theology reflected the pain and suffering of the Korean people in the age of extreme oppression by the Japanese rulers.[44] Byun's claims, however, are criticized for pressing too far in identifying Lee's theology with Eckhart's.[45]

Dong-sik Ryu, a professor at Yonsei University, views Lee as a fanatic and states that through his fanaticism he tried to practice universal love. His attempt at unlimited inclusion, he wrote, has both its merits and demerits.[46] Sung-bum Yun emphasizes that Lee's mysticism was Christ-centered, while Gil-sup Song views Lee as a reformer who tried to reform the Korean church. Jae-yong Park, Sung-hong Han, and Bong-bae Park also published research papers about Lee. He is classified as a mystic by most scholars. This charge calls for more research on the mysticism of the suffering Christ that Lee emphasized.

Influence of Yong-do Lee on the Korean Church

Although he lived only for thirty-three years, Lee influenced the Korean church quite crucially — both positively and negatively.

Positive sides

Lee's revival movement had a great impact on the Korean church in many ways. First, he confronted a formalistic and lethargic faith and provided an opportunity to connect faith and life by an exercise of the emotions in their pure state.[47] He charged self-contented church leaders—missionaries, pastors, and evangelists—with divisions within the church and thus rescued the Korean church from the danger of mere adherence to the repetition of doctrines and forms. Although his time was short, Lee reformed the Korean church in the early 1930s by starting a new way of life. It had been decreasing in numbers

---

[43] Kyung-bae Min, 'The Influence of Yong-do Lee's Theology', 66–78; 89–90.

[44] Sun-hwan Byun, 'Yong-do Lee and Meister Eckhart' [in Korean], *Theology and World* 4 (1978), 83.

[45] Sung-hong Han, 'Research on Yong-do Lee, II' [in Korean], *Ministry and Theology* 12 (June 1990), 211.

[46] Dong-sik Ryu, 'Rev. Yong-do Lee and His Neighbors' [in Korean], *Christian Thoughts* (July 1967), 24.

[47] Min, *History of Korean Christian Faith Movement*, 359.

since 1923 but began to increase from 1929 to 1933 due to the direct and indirect influence of Lee's revival movement.[48]

Second, Lee stressed the prayerful life. He diagnosed that the Korean church had become depressed due to the lack of prayer. Being a man of prayer himself, he showed the example of a prayerful life:

> Alas, the Korean churches, whether Presbyterian or Methodist, have become miserable. Since they do not pray, where could they possibly go to experience spiritual blessing? Oh, Lord, teach them to pray.[49]

He was convinced of the power of prayer, for he himself had experienced spiritual blessing through prayer. People would even describe him as being crazy about prayer.[50]

He prayed with all his effort and might. Through him many people came to understand what prayer was and could taste the beauty of prayer. Some zealots even formed a prayer group in Pyongyang. The revival meeting at a church in Pyongyang led by Yong-do Lee in late February 1930 motivated its formation. They were not large in numbers but by emphasizing a prayerful life they greatly contributed to the igniting of a prayer movement all over the country. There were always fervent prayers where Lee led revival meetings.

Third, he started a new style of revival meeting. His style was mystical and indigenous to the Korean people, quite different from the Great Revival of 1907 that had been led by the missionaries. He did not organize or advertise or make elaborate plans. When he did not feel inspired he did not preach but would lead in prayer for several hours and then dismiss the congregation. His sermons were not skilfully made. He gave himself completely to the congregation. While he was conducting revival meetings, he did not sleep or eat but prayed face down, in awe of God's grace. This set an excellent model. He would stop preaching when he became emotional and sing hymns with the audience while continuing to preach. His revival meetings were always filled with grace. His sermons were sometimes very short, but sometimes went on for hours. This style of revival meeting became popular.

Fourth, Lee's revival meetings caused many young people to dedicate their lives to Christ. Among them were Gyung-woo Cho, Sin-il Cho, Ho-woon Lee, Gwan-jo Myung, Gwan-woo Kim, Jong-ho Byun, and Yong-ryun Kim. They were the main figures who revived the Korean church after the liberation of the country.[51]

---

[48] Song, *History of Theological Thought*, 310-11.

[49] Byun, *Diary*, 105 on January 13, 1931.

[50] Byun, *Biography*, 225.

[51] Song, *History of Theological Thought*, 311.

Problems/Critiques

A few problems of Lee's revival meetings need discussion. First, he put too much stress on the dualism of flesh and spirit. He tended to avoid or neglect the flesh. This was one of the reasons why it is hard to find a *missio Dei* in him.[52] Second, he emphasized mystical union with Christ rather than salvation or grace by Christ. Consequently, his theology lacked a mature faith and a theology of justification or salvation, even of the Trinity.[53] Third, his emphasis on undiscriminating and unconditional love caused many problems in his latter days. We may say that it was because of the character of this love that he was involved with Myung-hwa Yoo and the 'Jesus Church'. His undiscriminating and unconditional love hindered him from discerning the fault of his followers and consequently he inadvertently approved it.[54]

Yong-do Lee was an activist and reformer who constantly and earnestly tried to achieve wholeness in Christ. He tried to plant the message of hope in the minds of the people. As he preached the sermon entitled, 'The Holy Spirit Who Empowers Prayer', 'The Motive of Repentance and Practice of Love' and others, he emphasized the role of the Holy Spirit at a time of national darkness and despair. Also when preaching another sermon entitled, 'Let's Be Humble in This World and the Rich in the World to Come', he stressed the Kingdom of God, and encouraged the people to be eager for spiritual gifts.[55] Despite this he was misunderstood and attacked. He was not fully understood until his death, but his voice in the wilderness and his life of love still awaken today's Korean church.[56]

In this period between 1920 and 1940, as a consequence of his preaching, many Christians who had experienced the power of the Holy Spirit interpreted the Spirit as some kind of spiritual force that would work wonders and perform miraculous healings among people. The Holy Spirit was not yet regarded as the guiding Spirit of the church at that time. This misapprehension of the Spirit has caused immense confusion and disorder in the church. It may be a natural consequence, since the Korean church had not yet conducted enough theological research on pneumatology in its short history.

---

[52] Song, *History of Theological Thought*, 311.
[53] Song, *History of Theological Thought*, 103.
[54] Song, *History of Theological Thought*, 103.
[55] Young-hoon Lee, 'The Influence of the Pentecostal Movement on the Korean Church' [in Korean], *Journal of Pentecostal Theology* (February 1998), 103.
[56] Song, *History of Theological Thought*, 312.

Chapter 5

The Third Period (1940–1960)

Background

The era of confusion and division began in the year 1945, immediately after the liberation of the country from the Japanese occupation.[1] The sudden freedom from colonial oppression caused confusion in both the church and the people. The agreement between the two strong countries, the United States of America and the Soviet Union, divided the Korean Peninsula in two at the thirty-eighth parallel. Communism took root in the North under the influence of the Soviet Union, while democracy assumed its place in the South. The North Korean communists began to persecute Christianity severely, martyring many Christian ministers and, therefore, almost obliterating Christianity in the North. One example of a deliberate attempt was apparent in elections and other important events that were scheduled on Sundays in order to trap Christians who would observe the Lord's day. The churches in North Korea objected to the policy and the communists persecuted the church.[2] Ironically, however, persecution only helped the rapid growth of Christianity in the South.

The church had not yet been equipped with the wisdom and power to face such a challenging situation so conflicts and divisions were inevitable. During the last years of Japanese occupation, on August 1, 1945, the Japanese rulers amalgamated all the Korean Christian denominations and forcibly organized the Chosun Division of the Japanese Christian Church. The leaders of this union were appointed by the Japanese governor and included those from the Presbyterians, the Methodists, the Salvation Army, and a few minor denominations that still existed. Any who did not favour this forced union were either imprisoned, or driven from their pulpits and placed under house-arrest. Prior to this forced union, in 1943, the Holiness, Seventh Day Adventist and East Asia Christian Church (Baptist) were abolished for their emphasis on the second coming of Jesus Christ.[3] This is another reason for the unavoidable

---

[1] This situation is similar to the situation oat the time of the Reformation. After Luther there arose quite a number of divisions in the Protestant churches.

[2] Young-hun Lee, *The History of Korean Church*, 234.

[3] Clark, *History of the Church in Korea*, 231; Min, *Church History of Korea*, 446-47; ITI, *The History of the Assembly of God Churches*, 155-56. In the history of the Korean

division within the Korean church. In fact the Korean churches have been repeatedly divided. A perfect example of church divisions may be found in the Presbyterian churches, the largest denomination in Korea, which comprises two thirds of the whole Korean Protestant population. The reason behind the first division was the subject of Shinto-worship. On September 9, 1938, at the twenty-seventh annual assembly of Korean Presbyterian churches, the delegates declared that Shinto-worship was not an act of idolatry and decided under Japanese coercion to permit Shinto-worship.[4] Despite the decision of the general assembly, a great number of Christian ministers strongly objected to this decision and were imprisoned or martyred for their stand. After the country regained its independence, the conflict between the two groups of ministers, those who permitted Shinto-worship and those who opposed it, began to come to the surface.

In April 1950, two months prior to the outbreak of the Korean War, there was a major conflict between the two groups. During the war, both took refuge in Busan, and finally broke with each other in 1951. The conservative group was separated from the general Assembly and formed another Assembly with the new name 'Koryo-pa' (the branch of Korea). Another reason for the division lies in their different theological interpretations. Jae-jun Kim, one of the Presbyterian leaders, had followed liberal views in biblical interpretation and was criticized by the conservative group. This, too, resulted in the division of the Presbyterian Church.

The General Assembly was again divided into two groups, one liberal and the other conservative. The liberal group formed the Presbyterian Church of the Republic of Korea, while the conservative group formed the Presbyterian Church in Korea, which is also called the Jesus-Presbyterian Church. In 1959, the Jesus-Presbyterian Church was further divided into two groups, one of which was in favour of ecumenical activity and the other strongly opposed it as represented by the World Council of Churches (WCC).[5] The latter opposition group was divided into another two groups in 1974, resulting in five major Presbyterian groups and more than forty minor Presbyterian groups.[6] The five major groups are: 1) the Presbyterian Church in Korea (Tonghap-pa, a moderate group), 2) the reunited anti-ecumenical assembly (Hapdong-pa, a conservative group), 3) the conservative anti-ecumenical Assembly (Hapdong

---

church, this was the first and the only occasion when the Korean churches were unified. It is an irony that the Korean churches have so many denominations and groups, while all the Koreans are from one tribe having the same cultural background and one language.

[4] It was done under compulsion. Min, *Church History of Korea*, 425-32.

[5] Min, *Church History of Korea*, 481-83.

[6] According to the up-to-date statistics, there are 96 Presbyterian groups. Korea Research Institute for Religion and Society, *Annual Report of Korean Religion* [in Korean] (Seoul: Korea Research Institute for Religion and Society, 1995).

Bosu-pa), 4) the Presbyterian Church in the Republic of Korea (Gijang-pa, a liberal group), and 5) the Koryo Presbyterian Church (Koryeo-pa, a fundamentalist group). Divisions have continued to this day. Christianity progressively lost its leadership as a result of such continual divisions. In consequence, certain fanatic, eschatological, and mystical sects made approaches to the people. They focused on the future life more than the present life, propagating eschatological expectations and a faith based on the direct experience of God. While classical churches proclaimed piety, orthodoxy and tradition, their becoming divided at the same time by conflicts and struggles led these sects to spread rapidly after the Korean War.

New Religious Sects: History and Background

In parallel with these divisions in the most traditional churches, a number of heretical Christian sects and new religious movements (*Sinheung Jonggyo*, Korean syncretistic religions) were born during this period. According to Myoung-hwan Tak, there were around 200 new Korean syncretistic religions in the 1960s: 27 were derived from Buddhism, 25 from Christianity, 14 from Eastern learning, 5 from Japanese religion, 19 from Dangun sects, and 51 from Chungsan sects. These new syncretistic religions emerged from the opportunity presented by social chaos.[7] The most well-known groups of these are: the Olive Tree Church and the Unification Church. Their movements may be called a pseudo-Holy Spirit movement.[8]

The Olive Tree Church[9]

The Olive Tree Church founded by Tae-sun Park was the fastest growing and largest of the Korean syncretistic religions during the 1950s and 1960s. The movement is now largely insignificant and may pass away before the end of the century. The Olive Tree Church is a Christian syncretistic movement, a pseudo-Holy Spirit movement, which emphasizes faith-healing.[10]

---

[7] Myung-hwan Tak, *New Syncretistic Religions in Korea*, vol. 1, rev. ed. [in Korean] (Seoul: International Religious Research Institute, 1992), 35.

[8] Some scholars uphold that both the Olive Tree Church and the Unification Church came into existence under the influence of the mystical Holy Spirit movement of Yong-do Lee. Young-kwan Park, *Major Cults* [in Korean] (Seoul: Christian Literature Mission, 1976), I, 30–32, 129–31; *Major Cults* [in Korean] (Seoul: Christian Literature Mission, 1984), II, 35–38.

[9] The original Korean name of the Olive Tree Church was *Hanguk Yesugyo Jundo-gwan Buheung Hyuphoe* (Jesus Church Jundo-gwan Revival Association of Korea). Later it changed its name to the Heavenly Father's Church, the Heavenly Father being the founder Tae-sun Park.

[10] Grayson, *Korea: Religious History*, 245.

History of the Sect

Tae-sun Park was born in North Pyung-an province in North Korea in 1915. His parents died when he was little. Park attended the local Presbyterian church Sunday school from a young age. He finished elementary school in his home town, went to Tokyo, studied at a technical school there, and came back to Korea. He attended the Namdaemun Church in Seoul. According to Myoung-hwan Tak, Park went to a revival meeting led by Rev. Sung-bong Lee, a famous Holiness evangelist, and he was deeply moved by the Spirit at the meeting. He fasted and prayed for three days and he said he had received fire from heaven.

In 1954 Park became an elder of the Changdong Presbyterian Church. In April 1955, he was one of the principal speakers at a massive revival rally held on Namsan mountain in southern Seoul. The church was facing a difficult time after the Korean War and it was trying to reorganize and reconstruct itself. This proved a temporary vacuum when the Olive Tree Church suddenly appeared. Park claimed that a man, who had been a cripple for 30 years, was immediately healed after he had laid his hand on the man's head. This incident served as the starting point of the Olive Tree movement. In 1956 the local presbytery expelled him on charges of heresy after examining his ministry.[11]

He was imprisoned briefly in 1959. The charges were for embezzlement of money, injury or death to believers through faith-healing practices, and promiscuity.[12] However, until the mid- or later 1960s, the Olive Tree Church grew rapidly but by the beginning of the 1970s, various scandals connected with Tae-sun Park and his immediate family created mass defections from the church. Now that Park is dead, it has lost its influence.[13]

The Olive Tree Church is best known for its attempt to establish faith towns, a new Zion in Korea. Two Christian communities were built near Seoul (one at Sosa town in 1957 and the other at Dukso town in 1962 in Gyeonggi Province). He established the third faith town at Gijang town, Gyung-nam province in 1970. These were total communities with all the facilities the members would need. Some of the charges of financial misappropriation of church funds come from claims of abuse of church labour and of mishandling company funds. The revenue office investigated the tax evasion of his company. Due to the constantly arising problems in the community and because of Tae-sun Park's claim of being the 'Heavenly Father' himself, most people left the community. There are now only a few people left.

Doctrines and Beliefs

The followers of Tae-sun Park placed implicit faith in his statements that he was a prophet of God who was to usher in a new society in Korea. Park

---

[11] Tak, *New Syncretistic Religions*, 180; Park, *Major Cults*, vol. 1, 139.

[12] Tak, *New Syncretistic Religions*, 181; Park, *Major Cults*, vol. 1, 140.

[13] He died on February 7, 1990 at the age of 73. Tak, *New Syncretistic Religions*, 212.

identified himself with the mysterious figure mentioned in Isaiah 41:2, the prophet of righteousness who comes from the East. In the 11th chapter of the Revelation of John in the New Testament and in the 4th chapter of the book of Zechariah in the Old Testament, there is a reference to two prophets who are called olive trees.[14] These figures, at first defeated by the forces of this world, will be proven victorious and assumed into heaven. Park claimed to be one of these trees and it is for this reason that his movement has been known popularly in English as the Olive Tree Movement. He claimed that he would judge the sinners, as a prophet of God, in the last days and gather the 144,000 righteous men. Then the chosen people will live in the millennial kingdom.

The power that Park was given was the power of healing, called by believers *anchal*, a kind of massage.[15] Park's followers believed that his power was transmitted to the body through Park's *anchal* and that they would be healed. Some of the faithful believed that even drinking the water in which Tae-sun Park had washed himself would cure any disease.[16] Park denied the authority of the scripture and deity of Christ publicly in January, 1980. Since then he called himself the 'Heavenly Father'. Ironically, once a famous faith healer Park died of many diseases—tuberculosis, diabetes, nephritis, high blood pressure and schizophrenia.

The Unification Church

'The Holy Spirit Association for the Unification of World Christianity,' also known as the Unification Church or *Tongil-gyo* in Korean, is the best known of Korea's syncretistic religions and the most controversial. It was formally founded in Seoul by Sun-myoung Moon (1920–) in 1954, although its roots date back to the early 1940s. The movement claimed to be he fulfilment of God's plan for the universe, and it centered its belief on the anticipated second coming of the Lord.[17]

History of the Sect

Sun-myoung Moon, born in Cheongju in North Korea in 1920, was brought up in a Presbyterian home. In 1945, following the liberation from Japanese rule, Moon set up a movement in the Pyongyang area to reform Christianity. He based this movement on a claim that he had been given the authority to reform the churches when he had heard the voice of God at the age of sixteen. His claims caused dissension among the local Christians in Pyongyang. Moon was imprisoned by the Communist authorities in 1948 for demoralizing society.[18]

---

[14] Park, *New Syncretistic Religions*, vol. 1, 150–52.

[15] Grayson, *Korea: Religious History*, 247.

[16] Grayson, *Korea: Religious History*, 165.

[17] Grayson, *Korea: Religious History*, 247.

[18] Tak, *New Syncretistic Religions*, 52–53.

He was liberated by the United Nations troops in 1950 and made his way down to Busan. There Moon met Hyo-won Yoo, who became his most important assistant in the formation of the Unification Church. In May 1954, Moon and Yoo started a new religious body, the Holy Spirit Association for the Unification of World Christianity in Seoul.

In July 1955 Moon was imprisoned for demoralization but he was released three months later.[19] In the following year his church was registered with the government as a religious body. From that point the Unification Church was involved in evangelism, expanding its mission base within Korea and spreading its beliefs into foreign countries. In 1959 the first Unification missionary was sent out to the United States. In succeeding years, missionaries were sent to the USA, Japan, Europe, Great Britain, the Near East, and Latin America. In the early 1970s, Moon moved the centre of his operations from Korea to the United States, at which time he combined his evangelistic efforts with a campaign against Communism. The Unification Church seminary was organized during the mid-1970s in Tarrytown, New York. In 1983 Moon was tried on charges of tax evasion by the Internal Revenue Service and was sent to jail.

His ministry in Korea was not successful. The significant growth of the Unification Church was outside of Korea. But it aroused considerable criticism from orthodox Christian churches as well as from various human rights groups. The criticism of the church was along these lines: 1) criticism of its heretical doctrine; 2) criticism of its methods of attracting members and of the education of these members, called by some persons 'brainwashing'; 3) criticism of the affluent style of living of the church's leadership; and 4) criticism of the extensive business holdings of the church. The Unification Church had been successful as a business conglomerate.

The church received most criticism, for its methods of recruiting members, and its 'heretical' doctrines. Though not numerically strong in Korea, the church found support through its appeal to young Western intellectuals.

Doctrines and Beliefs[20]

According to Young-gwan Park, Moon was a disciple of Baek-moon Kim, a mystic. Moon learned Kim's teaching of the 'fundamental truth of Christianity' for six months.[21] *Wolli Gangnon* (Exposition of the Divine Principle, or simply, The Divine Principle), the principal textbook of the Unification Church, is a copy of Kim's 'fundamental truth of Christianity'.[22]

Wolli Gangnon consists of seven principal chapters and an extensive section of appended material. The chapters discuss in turn creation, the fall, the

---

[19] Tak, *New Syncretistic Religions*, 53–54; Park, *Major Cults*, I, 37–38; Grayson, *Korea: Religious History*, 247.
[20] For the critique on the Unification church's doctrine, see Park, *Major Cults*, I, 50–74.
[21] Park, *Major Cults*, 52.
[22] Park, *Major Cults*, I, 50–51.

eschaton, the advent of the Messiah, resurrection, predestination, and Christology. The appended material consists of additional six chapters. These chapters develop themes in the main text, especially the role of the predecessors and patriarchs of Israel, Adam, Noah, Abraham, and Moses. The sixth chapter is perhaps the most important as it is there that the second coming of its lord is discussed.

The Unification Church belief is that God, the eternal creator of the universe, is attempting to restore the state of perfection in the world which existed at the time of the Garden of Eden. Sin, it is said, came into the world through the violation of God's commands. Eve is believed to have had sexual relations with Satan in the form of a serpent, and sin has been transmitted physically through Satan's blood to succeeding generations. Jesus, son of God but not God himself, failed in his mission to save mankind because he did not marry and produce sinless children. Physical sin continued to be transmitted to later generations. Jesus' death on the cross only brought spiritual salvation, not physical salvation. For there to be a complete restoration of the world, its physical salvation is necessary. In the Unification Church schema, Jesus is the 'True Father' and the Holy Spirit is the 'True Mother' of spiritual salvation. Jesus having failed in His task, it was necessary that Another should come to fulfil God's mission, Someone who would marry a perfect woman and so restore mankind physically as well as spiritually. This person who is to come is called the 'Lord of the Second Coming'. His marriage, which will restore humanity, is called the 'Feast of the Lamb'. Sun-myoung Moon was identified as the 'Lord of the Second Coming' and his wife, Hak-ja Hahn, as the 'Mother of the Universe'.[23] They received special courtesies such as bows from the believers, as did their children who were believed to be sinless.

One of the most important functions of the Lord of the Second Coming is the physical restoration of humankind. Moon selected suitable marital partners for the faithful and conducted sacred ceremonies of marriage in large groups. It should be noted with regard to the purging of physical sin that Moon was accused of acts of gross immorality that were denied by the church authorities. This doctrine was criticized by many Christian scholars for being sexually motivated.[24]

Besides the two major sects, the Olive Tree Church and the Unification Church, there have been many new religious sects, which were popular in the country at one time or another.[25] The reasons for the flourishing of the heretical sects may be summarized as follows: 1) social disorders due to the Korean War, student demonstrations,[26] and military overthrow,[27] and 2) the lack of

---

[23] Grayson, *Korea: Religious History*, 249–50.

[24] Grayson, *Korea: Religious History*, 59–64.

[25] Tak, *New Syncretistic Religions*, 33–35.

[26] April 19, 1960.

[27] May 16, 1961.

spiritual leadership of Korean churches due to their frequent divisions over trifling matters.

The Beginnings of the Korean Pentecostal Movement

Its Background and History

It is remarkable that the Holy Spirit movement kept going even amidst this chaos. Evangelists like Sung-bong Lee from the Holiness Church and Jae-bong Park from the Methodist Church, during this period of confusion, led a great number of revival meetings all over the country. Many incidents of miraculous healing were witnessed during their meetings. In this period the Assemblies of God, the largest Pentecostal body in the world, was organized in Korea. It provided a direct connection between the Holy Spirit movement in Korea and the worldwide Pentecostal movement, since the former had developed quite independently.

The Pentecostal faith was first brought to Korea by Mary C. Rumsey (photo) in March, 1928. Rumsey was the first missionary to Korea who had a Pentecostal background. Originally, she was a Methodist. She participated in the Azusa Street revival meeting in 1906, received the baptism in the Holy Spirit, experienced speaking in tongues, received God's call as a missionary to Korea, and came to Korea twenty years later.[28]

The history of the Azusa Street revival is as follows:[29] William J. Seymour, a black Holiness preacher, was a student of Parham's Bible school in Houston, Texas. He was convinced that an experience in the Spirit was necessary. In 1906, he was invited to be the associate pastor of a church in Los Angeles. Upon his arrival in Los Angeles, he began to preach at nightly meetings. In addition to the familiar themes of conversion and sanctification, he stressed divine healing, the imminent second coming of Christ, and speaking in tongues as a sign accompanying the baptism in the Holy Spirit. Most of his audience had until then considered sanctification and the baptism in the Holy Spirit to be synonymous. Seymour now made a distinction between them. As a text for his first sermon before the California congregation, he selected Acts 2:4 and preached about the new Pentecostal experience: 'Anyone who does not speak in tongues is not baptized with the Spirit.' While some members of the church

---

[28] Korean Assemblies of God, *The 30 Year History of Korea Assemblies of God* (in Korea; Seoul: Jong-ryo, 1983), 28–29.
[29] For an extensive study of the Azusa Street revival, see Cecil M. Robeck, Jr., *The Azusa Street Mission and Revival: The Birth of the Global Pentecostal Movement* (Nashville, TN: Thomas Nelson, 2006).

responded favourably to his sermon, others doubted or rejected it. Because of the unacceptable sermon he was expelled from the church.

One of the church families invited the ousted preacher to conduct worship services in their home. There in April 1906, seven seekers received the Holy Spirit baptism and began to speak in tongues. For three days and nights they shouted and praised God. People who sought spiritual experiences began to come from everywhere. Later Seymour and his followers obtained an old frame building (once a Methodist church) on Azusa Street in the industrial section of Los Angeles. People came at ten o'clock in the morning (and often remained until three o'clock on the following morning), seeking salvation, sanctification, the Holy Spirit baptism, or healing. They practised prayers, sermons, and testimonies in their meetings but no subjects or sermons were announced ahead of time, and no special speakers for such an hour; so that no one neither knew what might be coming, nor what God would do but all was spontaneous, ordered by the Spirit. Black, white and every race worshipped together without segregation. It was very unusual in the United States at that time. Their meetings lasted for three years.

This Azusa Street Mission is regarded by Pentecostals as the place of origin of the worldwide Pentecostal movement. For three years without interruption prayer meetings took place there with speaking in tongues, singing in tongues, healing and prophecy. The Azusa Mission newspaper, *The Apostolic Faith*, founded in 1906 increased from 5,000 to 50,000 copies by 1908.

In the subsequent years, the Pentecostal movement grew rapidly and expanded to Chicago, Winnipeg and New York. The 'Full Gospel' has flourished throughout America since 1906.[30]

Many went into the world as missionaries from the Azusa Street Mission. This Pentecostal faith spread to Canada, to Europe and Asia, to Africa, and to Central and South America. Rumsey also was a missionary of the Azusa Mission.

Upon arriving in Korea, Rumsey stopped off for some rest in the Jungdong hospital where R.A. Hardie had been staying.[31] It is an important detail that the first Pentecostal missionary became connected with Hardie who had initiated the Holy Spirit movement in Korea.

---

[30] See Iain MacRobert, 'The Birth of a Movement: William J. Seymour and the Azusa Mission,' in *The Black Roots and White Racism of Early Pentecostal Church in the USA* (London: Macmillan, 1988), 48–59; Stanley M. Burgess and Gary B. McGee (eds.), *Dictionary of Pentecostal and Charismatic Movement* (Grand Rapids, MI: Zondervan, 1988), 31–36, 778–81. See also Frank Bartleman, *Azusa Street* (Plainfield, NJ: Logos International, 1980).

[31] This hospital was founded by William B. Scranton and Jack F. Heron. It was the first Methodist hospital. ITI, *The History of the Assemblies of God*, 149–50.

Rumsey paid her visit to the headquarters of the Salvation Army of Korea in 1931. There she met Hong Huh (photo), who was working at the headquarters,

and asked him for help in her missionary work. Huh took Bible lessons from her and received the baptism of the Holy Spirit.[32]

Rumsey emphasized two characteristics of the Pentecostal faith—speaking in tongues and divine healing. [33] In March 1933, Rumsey and Huh together established Seobinggo Church (photo) in Seoul, the first Pentecostal church. It was in the fifth year of Rumsey's stay in Korea. Seong-san Park was appointed as the first pastor of this church.[34] Park had studied the Bible in Japan and experienced the Pentecostal faith.[35]

Park preached Pentecostal messages that speaking in tongues was the sign of the baptism in the Holy Spirit and that the Christian faith should be expressed by participation in social activities. He further claimed that the Pentecostal faith was a fundamental faith with its foundation on the Book of Acts and that the three gifts—speaking in tongues, divine healing, and power—could be manifested only after Spirit-baptism. In 1930, two years after Rumsey had begun her ministry, T.M. Parsons, an American Pentecostal missionary, came to Korea and, upon his request, the British Pentecostal missionaries E.H. Meredith and Vessey joined him.[36]

The Pentecostal church in Korea continued its ministry even under the Japanese persecution. At this time, there were two Pentecostal missionary teams: Seong-san Park and Hong Huh with Rumsey formed one, while Bu-geun Bae, who had gone to the same Bible seminary as Park, formed another with Parson, Vessey and Meredith. Huh, Park, and Bae were ordained as the first Pentecostal pastors of Korea on October 5, 1938 (photo). Members of the ordination committee were Bishop Katha of the British Pentecostal Church and five American and British missionaries, including Meredith. It was held in

---

[32] For Rumsey's earlier spiritual experience, call and others, see Ig-jin Kim, *History and Theology of Korean Pentecostalism: Sunbogeum (Pure Gospel) Pentecostalism* (Zoetermeer: Uitgeverij Boekencentrum, 2003), 57-60.

[33] Byun, *The History of the Pentecostal Movement*, 90.

[34] Rumsey stayed in Japan for a short period of time on her way to Korea and met a Bible seminary student Sung-san Park there. A few years later, Rumsey invited Park to Korea in order to establish a church. ITI, *The History of the Assemblies of God*, 151-52.

[35] ITI, *The History of the Assemblies of God*, 293.

[36] Kim, *History and Theology of Korean Pentecostalism*, 60-62 under the heading of 'Other Women Missionaries (1930-1939)'.

 Jeongdong Hospital which housed the mission headquarters of the Chosun Pentecostal Church.

The Pentecostal churches grew rapidly up until 1938 but began to decrease as a result of continuous persecution by the Japanese. The following is a table of the statistics of the Chosun Pentecostal Church during these years according to data by the Japanese Government-General of Korea.[37]

year	churches	ministers	Members
1934	2	7	99
1935	3	8	113
1936	3	9	130
1937	6	10	173
1938	6	11	129
1939	6	11	99
1940	5	4	80
1941	4	4	80

The Statistics of the Chosun Pentecostal Church (1934–1941)

The Chosun Pentecostal churches were also to be persecuted for their opposition to Shinto-worship. The first Pentecostal missionary, Rumsey, was deported in February of 1937 and British missionaries Vessey and Meredith in December 1940. The churches were shut down and the church members scattered.[38]

When the country was liberated from the Japanese occupation on August 15, 1945, the Pentecostal church leaders came back to Korea after years of exile and the scattered Pentecostals gathered together and formed a Pentecostal denomination. Among the Pentecostal church leaders, Bong-jo Gwak[39] had the greatest influence on the organization of the Pentecostal denomination. Gwak established a Korean Pentecostal church in Osaka, Chosun Christian Pentecostal Church, in 1933.[40] This church grew rapidly to have 200 members within a year. Gwak also raised many Pentecostal leaders such as Sung-duk

---

[37] ITI, *The History of the Assemblies of God*, 153-54.
[38] For an elaborated report of persecution, see Kim, *History and Theology of Korean Pentecostalism*, 74-75.
[39] Bong-jo Gwak was 87 years old at the time of this research and living in Los Angeles, U.S.A. I received a lot of valuable information about Gwak's ministry from an extensive interview with his son, Mr. Eun-sik Gwak. Also see I. Kim, *History and Theology of Korean Pentecostalism*, 69-70, 78-79, 103-107.
[40] Kim, *History and Theology of Korean Pentecostalism*, 63, 69-70.

Yun, Sung-hwan Kim, Gil-yun Kim and Mrs. Ja-sin Park,[41] who later became leaders of the Korean Pentecostal Church.

Gwak returned to Korea in order to establish a Pentecostal church but, because of Japanese persecution, had to go to Manchuria, where he established a congregation. After the liberation of the country, Gwak returned to Korea, went to the south coast, served a church and worked as the principal of an elementary school. The Pentecostal churches in Jolla province achieved rapid growth during these years. Hun-geun Park came from Japan and pastored the Sooncheon Pentecostal Church, which grew to have more than 300 members within a year. After the outbreak of the Korean War, however, the communists from North Korea took control over this area. They tortured and killed Park. Park became the first martyr of the Korean Pentecostal Church. This took place in September of 1950, twenty years after the Pentecostal faith had entered Korea.[42] In 1948, Sung-hwan Kim came back to Korea from Japan and established a church in Mokpo, Jolla province. Sung-duk Yun established a church in Gwang-san, Jolla province in 1945 and built and dedicated a church in 1948. The Pentecostal churches were being established around the whole country.[43] Boo-geun Bae, Hong Huh, and Sung-san Park ministered and preached the Pentecostal faith in Seoul; Mrs. Gwi-im Park in Sooncheon and Gwangju;[44] Sung-hwan Kim in Mokpo and Mu-an; and Sung-duk Yun in Gwang-san.[45]

At last, the Korean Pentecostal Church held the first Korean Pentecostal Conference on April 9, 1950. It was of great significance that the Korean Pentecostals could have held such a conference in the Sooncheon Pentecostal Church since there were only a few scattered Pentecostal churches at the time and their activities were insignificant. The participants in the first conference were Sung-san Park, Hong Huh, and a few other Pentecostal ministers, along with about 200 laity.[46] The conference was more a revival gathering than an organizational meeting, since they did not discuss the organization of a denomination. The Assemblies of God (AG) in the United States sent the

---

[41] Ja-sin Park expanded the Pentecostal faith in Jolla province in the southwestern section of Korea. The expansion of the Pentecostal faith in this region is due to the dedication of many women Christian leaders who were influenced by Park. ITI, *The History of the Assemblies of God*, 158–59; Kim, *History and Theology of Korean Pentecostalism*, 70, 81.

[42] ITI, *The History of the Assemblies of God*, 159.

[43] Kim, *History and Theology of Korean Pentecostalism*, 69-70, 79.

[44] Kim, *History and Theology of Korean Pentecostalism*, 76-77, 80-84; Ig-jin Kim, 'A Prominent Woman in Early Korean Pentecostal Movement: Gui-Im Park (1912-1994)', *AJPS* 9:2 (2006), 199-218.

[45] Kim, *History and Theology of Korean Pentecostalism*, 69-70, 79.

[46] Kim, *History and Theology of Korean Pentecostalism*, 84.

missionary A.B. Chestnut to the third Korean Pentecostal Conference on May 4, 1952.[47] His confession is revealing:

> One time when I was alone before God in my room, I began asking him to help the Christians in Korea. Suddenly He seemed to place a certain pressure on my back, as I was kneeling. Then He asked me, 'Why don't you go?' There was no long discussion or promise given.[48]

After the third conference the AG in Korea (KAG) was organized. Chestnut joined in the third Korean Pentecostal conference and led the fourth conference, officially organizing the Assemblies of God in Korea on April 8, 1953.

The AG developed rapidly in the period of confusion after the Korean War as the leading faction of the Korean Pentecostal movement. It gave people hope and a strong faith based on personal spiritual experiences, while most other traditional churches were not paying attention to spiritual experiences.

There were fourteen AG congregations in October of 1953, 28 in August, 1954, and 44 at the end of 1955. They established the Full Gospel Bible College in May of 1953 in Seoul and raised many Pentecostal Christian leaders.[49]

A Pentecostal evangelist, Harold Herman, visited Korea and led great crusades for 24 days in the fall of 1957.[50] In 1958, an evangelist Ralph Byrd came to lead revival crusades in many major cities.[51] In May of 1958, Yonggi Cho started a church which became the Yoido Full Gospel Church, later to be the centre of the Korean Pentecostal movement. The Pentecostal movement played the major role in the Holy Spirit movement of Korea.

Distinctiveness of the Pentecostal Theology:
Doctrine of the Baptism in the Holy Spirit

Like most churches in the Protestant tradition, the Pentecostals follow the Reformation principles that salvation is a free gift of divine grace apart from

---

[47] KAG, *The 30 Year History*, 65.

[48] Arthur B. Chestnut, *Put...Shoes on His Feet* (Tulsa, Okla.: Christian Publishing Services, 1989), 77.

[49] Full Gospel Bible College later became Hansei University, a Christian university fully accredited by the Korean government. Its undergraduate school consists of the Departments of Theological Studies, Journalism, Computer and Information Management, Business and Management, History, Industrial Design, and Music. Its graduate school confers Master and Ph.D. degrees in Theology and Music. Hansei University, *2003 Hansei University Catalog* [in Korean] (Gunpo, Korea: Hansei University, 2003).

[50] Kim, *History and Theology of Korean Pentecostalism*, 101, 107.

[51] Kim, *History and Theology of Korean Pentecostalism*, 96, 113.

deeds and effort, and that the word of God must be the norm for faith and practice. Beyond this, the emphases of the Pentecostals place them in the radical (or left) wing of the Reformation. Like the Anabaptists, the Pentecostals declare 1) that individuals as well as the corporate body of believers should seek and submit to the leading of the Spirit; 2) that there should be a return to apostolic simplicity in worship; 3) that believers ought to separate themselves from the world; 4) that believers' baptism replaces infant baptism; and 5) that believers should look for the imminent, visible return of Christ who will set up his millennial reign.

In matters of doctrine, Pentecostals can be described as Evangelicals whose theology is akin to Fundamentalism.[52]

In 1948, fifteen of the major Pentecostal bodies in North America organized the Pentecostal Fellowship of North America and adopted the Statement of Faith[53] in eight articles.

1) We believe the Bible to be the inspired, the only infallible authoritative Word of God;

2) We believe that there is one God, eternally existent in three persons: Father, Son and the Holy Spirit;

3) We believe in the deity of our Lord Jesus Christ, in His virgin birth, in His sinless life, in His miracles, in His vicarious and atoning sacrifice through His shed blood, in His bodily resurrection, in His Ascension to the right hand of the Father, and His personal return in power and glory;

4) We believe that for the salvation of the lost and sinful men regeneration by the Holy Spirit is absolutely essential;

5) We believe that the full gospel includes holiness of heart and life, healing for the body and the baptism in the Holy Spirit with the initial evidence of speaking in other tongues as the Spirit gives utterance;

6) We believe in the present ministry of the Holy Spirit by whose indwelling the Christian is enabled to live a godly life;

---

[52] Useful studies are available to present Pentecostal beliefs in the context of Evangelicalism. See for example, William W. Menzies and Robert P. Menzies, *Spirit And Power: Foundation of Pentecostal Experience: A Call to Evangelical Dialogue* (Grand Rapids, Mich.: Zondervan, 2000); Nichol, *Pentecostalism*, 2–3.

[53] The Statement of Faith in Nichol, *Pentecostalism*, 4. This Statement of Faith is quoted from a brochure published by the Pentecostal Fellowship of North America (PFNA). PFNA was disbanded in 1994 in what was later called the "Memphis Miracle" to join the more racially inclusive Pentecostal/Charismatic Churches of North America (PCCNA). Its 8-point statement of faith is similar to that of PFNA. See PCCNA, 'Constitution and By-law' (http://www.pccna.org/constitution_bylaws200510.pdf, Oct 2005), accessed on 3 Feb 2008.

7) We believe in the resurrection of both the saved and the lost; they that are saved unto the resurrection of life and they that are lost unto the resurrection of damnation;

8) We believe in the spiritual unity of believers in our Lord Jesus Christ.

Seven out of the eight (except Article 5 that is about Spirit baptism) were taken from the Statement of Faith of the National Association of Evangelicals (NAE) of 1943.[54]

Pentecostalism evolved from the Holiness movement and was greatly influenced by it. Holiness came from the post-Civil War revivals of America among Methodists with an attempt to revive John Wesley's doctrine of sanctification (Christian perfection), for they felt that this emphasis had been neglected. They used the revival meeting, the camp meeting, and holiness literature, all of which were disappearing. Their theme was that 'the Christian can attain full holiness (sanctification) only when he abandons all efforts and allows the Holy Spirit to live within him the life of Christ'. Pentecostals call this experience the second blessing, the baptism in the Holy Spirit. In 1894, Methodist bishops issued a pastoral letter in opposition to this movement. So the Holiness group withdrew themselves from Methodism and formed independent bodies such as: Church of the Nazarene, Pilgrim Holiness Church, and Church of God (Anderson, Indiana). Some of these Holiness people felt that the experience of sanctification (the baptism with the Holy Spirit, or the second blessing) would be certified by some supernatural signs such as visions, dreams, and speaking in tongues. They became the Pentecostals.

Among the Pentecostal doctrines,[55] the doctrine of the baptism in the Holy Spirit is the most distinctive and the most important. Pentecostalism finds its theological centre in the event of the descent of the Holy Spirit on the day of Pentecost as written in Acts (2:1–4). They believe in the presence of the same religious experience today as in that day of Pentecost. They claim that every believer should have this experience. For Pentecostals this experience, baptism in the Holy Spirit, is authentically biblical: it is an experience subsequent to conversion; and the initial evidence of being filled with the Holy Spirit is

---

[54] Pentecostals, Conservative Baptists, Reformed Presbyterians, Wesleyan Methodists, Conservative Congregationalists, and Mennonites belong to NAE.

[55] They preach the 'full gospel': 1) the biblical emphasis on salvation and justification by faith which the Reformers had revived; 2) the doctrine of the pre-millennial return of Christ which John Nelson Darby and the Plymouth Brethren had preached so vigorously in the nineteenth century; 3) the stress on divine healing which had resulted from the teaching and evangelistic efforts of A.J. Gordon, a Baptist, A.B. Simpson, a Presbyterian, and John Alexander Dowie of Zion, Illinois, and 4) the doctrine of the Holy Spirit whose baptism empowers a Christian to live victoriously and to witness effectively, and whose gifts enables a Christian believer to perform the supernatural; providing him, as one Pentecostal expressed it, with ' a spiritual capacity far mightier than the finest natural abilities could ever supply'. Nichol, *Pentecostalism*, 7–8.

speaking in other tongues.[56] They also claim that the events on Pentecost in Acts 2 are in no way connected with conversion. This fact has led some to locate the baptism in the Holy Spirit in a second moment or second blessing separated in time from conversion.[57]

It is the view of Pentecostals that they have a strong basis in the Bible for seeking a post-conversion blessing. They believe that the experience of the baptism in the Holy Spirit was foretold by the Old Testament prophet Joel.

According to the Pentecostal doctrine, there are two kinds of Spirit-baptism in the Bible. At the time of conversion the convert is taken by the Spirit and placed into the body of Christ. This is called the 'baptism by the Spirit' (1 Corinthians 12:13) in the sense that the Spirit is the personal agent who does the baptizing.[58] On the other hand, Christ is the agent who baptizes us with the

---

[56] The following is a brief statement on the baptism in the Holy Spirit by P.C. Nelson, who is one of the leading scholars among the Pentecostals: 'All believers are entitled to and should ardently expect and earnestly seek the promise of the Father, the baptism in the Holy Ghost and fire, according to the command of our Lord Jesus Christ. This was the normal experience of all in the early Christian Church. With it comes the enduement of power for life and service, the bestowment of the gifts and their uses in the work of the ministry (Luke 14:49; Acts 1:4-8; I Corinthians 12:1-31). This experience is distinct from and subsequent to the experience of the new birth (Acts 8:12-17; 10:44-46; 11:14-16; 15:7-9). With the baptism in the Holy Ghost come such experiences as an overflowing fullness of the Spirit (John 7:37-39; Acts 4:8), a deepened reverence, intensified consecration to God and dedication to His work (Acts 2:42), and a more active love for Christ, for His Word and for the lost (Mark 16:20)'. P.C. Nelson, *Bible Doctrine* (Springfield, Mo.: Gospel Publishing House, 1948), 71.

The most important characteristics of the Pentecostal understanding of the baptism in the Holy Spirit are: 1) that the event is usually 'distinct from and subsequent to the new birth'; 2) that it is evidenced initially by the sign of speaking in other tongues. See in detail: Brumback, *What Meaneth This?*, 191-201; Donald Gee, *Concerning Spiritual Gifts* (Springfield, Mo.: Gospel Publishing House, 1949), 73-82; P.C. Nelson, *Bible Doctrine*, 71-83; Ernest S. Williams, *Systematic Theology* (Springfield, Mo.: Gospel Publishing House, 1953), vol. 3, 39-52. From New Testament scholarship, see for example, Robert P. Menzies, *Empowered for Witness: The Spirit in Luke-Acts* (London: T. & T. Clark, 2004).

[57] As early as 1915 the AG rejected the identification of the reverse in order, and the baptism in the Holy Spirit, as false doctrine. R.M. Riggs, *The Spirit Himself* (Springfield, Mo.: Gospel Publishing House, 1949), 47-48.

[58] In six cases of the New Testament that compare John's baptism in water with Jesus' baptism in the Holy Spirit, the word 'baptize' is used with the Greek word *en*, which here means 'in'. But the Pentecostals believe the context in 1 Corinthians 12:13 justifies the translation of *en* as 'by', so that the baptism here is 'by one Spirit.' They make a distinction between the baptism by the Spirit, which incorporates believers into the body of Christ, and baptism in the Holy Spirit, in which Christ is the baptizer and where the purpose is to empower the believer through the filling of the Spirit (Luke 24:49; Acts 1:8, 2:4).

Holy Spirit.[59] This experience is called the 'baptism in the Holy Spirit' or the 'baptism with the Holy Spirit.' This experience normally takes place after conversion.[60] To explain this doctrine, the Pentecostals take some instances from the book of Acts:[61] 1) on the day of Pentecost (Acts 2:1-4) all the disciples were already converted;[62] 2) Peter's sermon at Pentecost is evidence of a concept of two separate events: 'Repent and be baptized...', and 'you will receive the gifts of the Holy Spirit' (Acts 2:38); 3) the converts at Samaria believed and were baptized but received the baptism in the Holy Spirit later (Acts 8:12-17); and 4) the same was true of the converts at Ephesus (Acts 19:1-7).[63] Furthermore, the Pentecostals point out that many statements in the New Testament reported Jesus and John the Baptist were closely related with 'baptism in the Holy Spirit.' For example, John the Baptist said, 'I will baptize you with water. But one more powerful than I will come.... He will baptize you with the Holy Spirit and with fire'.[64] The Pentecostals make every effort to prove the validity of baptism in the Holy Spirit by carefully examining the scripture. The table below shows a clear picture of this doctrine.[65]

---

[59] Matthew 3:11; John 1:13; Acts 2:33; Luke 24:49. See G. Raymond Carlson, *Our Faith and Fellowship* (Springfield, Mo.: Gospel Publishing House, 1977), 47-48. L. Thomas Holdcroft, *The Holy Spirit: A Pentecostal Interpretation* (Springfield, Mo.: Gospel Publishing House, 1962), 129-33. Also Young-hoon Lee, 'The Understanding of Pneumatology in the Pentecostal Church' [in Korean] (unpublished Master's Thesis, Yonsei University, Seoul, 1983), 28-33.

[60] One exception can be found in Acts 10:1-48.

[61] 'The major source of the Pentecostal doctrine of "the subsequent baptism in the Holy Spirit" is the Book of Acts'. See Frederick Dale Bruner, *A Theology of the Holy Spirit: The Pentecostal Experience and the New Testament Witness* (Grand Rapids, Mich.: Eerdmans, 1970), 61. Criticism of this interpretation has been also arisen from within Pentecostal scholarship.

[62] Jesus declared that disciples' name were written in heaven (Luke 10:20). cf. Matthew 16:16; John 15:3.

[63] Carlson, *Our Faith and Fellowhsip*, 48. Normally Pentecostal theologians add one more example: the baptism of Saul of Tarsus (Acts 9:17, 18). See also Brumback, *What Meaneth This?*, 215-17; Holdcroft, *The Holy Spirit*, 111. Someone might raise a question: Who are these 'disciples'? The case for their being Christian lies in two points of the text: 1) 'Disciples' elsewhere in Luke always means 'Christians' and a number of authorities would see no exception here; and 2) The verb 'believe' (*pisteuein*) used here ordinarily means the act of Christian faith. See Ernst Hanchen, *The Acts of the Apostles* (Philadelphia, Pa.: Westminster, 1971), 308.

[64] Luke 3:16; cf. Luke 11:13; 24:49; John 7:37-39; 14:16; 15:26; Mark 16:17.

[65] Holdcroft, *The Holy Spirit*, 131.

Designation	Time	Subject	Agent	Element	Scripture
Baptism by the Spirit	At conversion	Penitent sinner	Holy Spirit	Body of Christ	1 Cor 12:13
Water Baptism	After conversion	convert	pastor	water	Mt 28:19
Baptism in the Spirit	After conversion	believers	Christ	Holy Spirit	Acts 2:4

Elements of Baptism

According to the AG Statement of Fundamental Truth, sections 7 and 10:[66]

With the baptism in the Holy Spirit come such experiences as an overflowing fullness of the Spirit (John 7:37–39; Acts 4:8), a deepened reverence for God (Acts 2:43; Heb. 12:28), an intensified consecration to God and dedication to His work (Acts 2:42), and a more active love for Christ, for His word and for the lost (Mk. 16:20).... This experience:

a) Enables them to evangelize in the power of the Spirit with accompanying supernatural signs (Mk. 16:15–20; Acts 4:29–31; Heb. 2:3–4);

b) Adds a necessary dimension to a worshipful relationship with God (1 Cor. 2:10–16; chaps. 12–14);

c) Enables them to respond to the full working of the Holy Spirit in expression of the fruit and gift and ministries as in New Testament times for the edifying of the body of Christ (Gal. 5:22–26; 1 Cor. 14:12; Eph 4:1–11; 1 Cor. 12:28; Col. 1:29).

They believe that the baptism in the Holy Spirit is not a climactic experience. The day of Pentecost itself signified only the beginning of the harvest. It brought believers into a fellowship of worship, teaching, and service. The baptism in the Holy Spirit is thus only a door into a growing relationship with the Spirit as a divine person and with fellow members of the body of Christ. It leads to a life of service marked by gifts of the Spirit that bring power and wisdom for the spread of the dospel and the growth of the church.

The baptism in the Holy Spirit is the central doctrine of the Pentecostal churches. The experience of the baptism in the Holy Spirit assumes a very important position in the Christian life, especially in connection with sanctification.[67]

---

[66] Stanley M. Horton, 'Pentecostal Perspective', in *Five Views on Sanctification* (Grand Rapids, MI: Zondervan, 1987), 131.
[67] Horton, 'Pentecostal Perspective', 105–35. Holdcroft, *The Holy Spirit*, 133–35.

Chapter 6

The Fourth Period (1960 1980)

The socio-political situation in the late 1960s and in the early 1970s called for two types of the Holy Spirit movement in Korea. One was the Minjung theology [1] movement that was advocated by people a liberal group who recognized the third era of the Holy Spirit. [2] The other was the Holy Spirit movement by a conservative group of people: the evangelical movement with large-scale crusades and the Pentecostal/Charismatic movement.

The socio-political and religious situation during this period had the following characteristics. First, the country was under a dictatorship. President Jung-hee Park amended the constitution and extended his political power. He declared the renovation of the constitution, issued an emergency measure, curtailed free speech, put anti-government leaders in detention, and laid off anti-government professors. The consequence was the emergence of an anti-government elite group.

Second, the economy made rapid progress. Korea achieved a ten billion dollar export trade and a one thousand dollar gross national product per capita. This changed the industrial structure, decreasing the rural and agricultural population and increasing the urban population. This in turn caused problems and brought about harmful effects: the difference between the rich and the poor became more noticeable; social anarchy ensued. An alienated group of people was formed who were socially and financially oppressed.

---

[1] For an explanation of Minjung theology, see: The Commission on Theological Concerns of the Christian Conference of Asia (ed.), *Minjung Theology: People as the Subjects of History* (Maryknoll, NY: Orbis, 1983); Cyris H.S. Moon, *A Korean Minjung Theology—An Old Testament Perspective* (Maryknoll, NY: Orbis, 1985); David Kwang-sun Suh, *Theology, Ideology and Culture* (Hong Kong: World Christian Student Federation, 1983).

[2] This idea is similar to that of the monastic prophet of Southern Europe, Joachim of Fiore, in the Middle Ages. He divided the history into three ages. The Old Testament age has its time of beginning and bloom. So has that of the New Testament. But a third age is to follow. The first of the three ages was the age of the Father, the second the age of the Son, of the Gospel, and the sacraments, the third, the age of the Holy Spirit, was yet to come. David Schaff, *History of Christian Church*, vol. 5, *The Middle Ages* (Grand Rapids, MI: Eerdmans, 1957), 373-78. Cf. Paul Tillich, *A History of Christian Thought* (New York: Simon & Schuster, 1967), 175-80.

Third, the religious congregations increased rapidly. The Buddhist population jumped from one million to over ten million, the Christian population increased to 2.24 million in 1970, 4 million in 1975, and 7.18 million in 1980. Christianity was outstanding in its religious activities. There were several phenomenal crusades with more than one million participants in attendance. Then the struggle between Christianity and the government ensued.

During this period, Korea achieved rapid economic growth under the dictatorship and at the same time witnessed the eruption of social anarchy and an alienated segment of the populace. Against this social background there arose two types of the Holy Spirit movement: the Minjung theology of the elite and the revival movement by and for the people.

Minjung Theology and the Holy Spirit Movement

Its Background and Progress

Since the 1960s, many theologians in Korea had been discussing numerous issues such as the question of an indigenized, contextual, secular, and political theology. Especially among the liberal wing, the centre of the discussion was 'Minjung'[3] theology. Although the economy grew rapidly, the difference between the rich and the poor became more noticeable as the dictatorship of Jeong-Hui Park continued. College students kept protesting. Many liberal theologians were dismissed from their posts for defending the oppressed and the imprisoned students. The dismissed theologians and others who were still able to teach under government supervision began to experience the suffering of the *minjung* (people). They were willing to learn and reflect theologically upon the *minjung* and life in Korea. They began to write, sometimes while in prison, on the theme of the liberation of these *minjung*. They were highly educated scholars who wrote articles in English or German and published them in journals. They also made contracts with foreign publishers and published books about Minjung theology. Thus Minjung theology became internationally recognized.[4] On the other hand, the mainstream Christians maintained an

---

[3] *Minjung* is a Korean word composed of two Chinese characters: *min* ('people') and *jung* ('the mass'). Literally, this would be translated as 'the mass of people'. However, this simple translation does not fully reflect what is meant by the term. Minjung expresses a living reality which is dynamic, changing and complex. Suh defines the term: 'The *minjung* are those who are oppressed politically, exploited economically, alienated socially, and kept uneducated in cultural and intellectual matters'. David Kwang-sun Suh, 'Korean Theological Developments in the 1970s', in *Minjung Theology: People as the Subjects of History* (Maryknoll, N.Y.: Orbis, 1983), 42.

[4] In Minjung theology special attention is being given to studies on theodicy, apocalyptic, the suffering servant, and the messianic Spirit (Holy Spirit). Suh, 'Korean Theological Developments in the 1970s', 42.

apolitical ideology and were more interested in personal salvation than in political issues, thus taking an opposite position from the Minjung theologians. Minjung theology received worldwide attention but it did not receive any official recognition in Korea.

This theology, which is a kind of re-casting of the liberation theology of Latin América, asserts the uniqueness of Korea. It stresses that the history of Korea is one of an oppressed, frustrated, and neglected people. Minjung theology is deeply related to the Koreans' unique mind-set *han*.[5] The *minjung* are *han*-ridden people. Andrew S. Park explains, '*Han* is an Asian, particularly Korean, term used to describe the depths of human sufferings'.[6] *Han* is a repressed anger mixed with depression over a situation that cannot be changed.

Minjung theology was first initiated by theologians who belonged to a liberal group, the Presbyterian Church in the Republic of Korea, whose leader was Nam-dong Suh. Suh was influenced by the historical perspectives of Joachim of Fiore (ca. 1132–1202) and began to talk about the era of the Holy Spirit. According to Joachim, the development of world history is related to God's redemptive work and the era of God the Father was the Old Testament period. People had to observe the law with fear and, as a punishment for not keeping the law, lived like slaves in this era. When Jesus Christ came, the era of God the Son began. This is the era of the New Testament and of the church. Christians, with their faith, could now live in freedom. However, Christians were still dominated by the structured institutional church of the Pope and the authorities, and by literalism. The era of the church, the era of a Christian kingdom that began in the days of the empire at Constantinople, came to an end. The era of the Holy Spirit began. In the era of the Holy Spirit, people now can have fellowship with God, receive revelations from God, and live in the kingdom of freedom, love, and joy. People were oppressed and neglected in the previous eras but can enjoy the glorious sonship of God. It is the new era of eschatology, the era of the millennial kingdom. From the standpoint of these interconnections, Minjung theology may be viewed as an apocalyptic-oriented movement. It believes that the Christian mission is to participate in the third era of the Holy Spirit and God's mission (*missio Dei*).

---

[5] *Han* is a Korean word, which may be translated as 'grudge' or 'resentment'. *Han* is an underlying feeling of the Korean people. Han is the anger and resentment of the *minjung* which has been turned inward and intensified as they become the objects of injustice upon injustice. It is the result of being repressed for an extended period of time by external forces: political oppression, economic exploitation, social alienation, and restrictions against becoming educated in cultural and intellectual matters. Cyris H.S. Moon, *A Korean Minjung Theology*, 1-2. See also Chimo Hong, 'Han is Minjung Theology' [in Korean], *Theological Studies* (Spring 1990), 136–51.

[6] Andrew S. Park. *The Wounded Heart of God: The Asian Concept of Han and the Christian Doctrine of Sin* (Nashville, TN: Abingdon, 1993), 15.

Minjung theologians not only gave theological interpretations about historical and social reality but also participated in the realities of society. They felt a duty to challenge the status quo for the sake of ordinary people and protested against injustice and oppression no matter how powerful. It is a romantic ideology, an interesting mixture of pessimism and optimism. Minjung theology is a movement by which Christians try to participate in the mission of the triune God who controls human affairs. Dong-sik Ryu said that Minjung theology is in line with Sun-joo Gil's Holy Spirit movement in the sense that it has an affinity with apocalyptic literature.[7] However, this movement was not fully recognized by many Christians. The reason was that this movement was initiated primarily by a liberal group who become overly radical, while the Korean church has always had conservative tendencies.

Evaluations

The first question that we raise regarding Minjung theology is whether the movement can really be considered a Holy Spirit movement. Ryu and other scholars on the liberal wing consider Minjung theology to be such. Since all the movements of the church and Christians may be viewed as Holy Spirit movements, in a broad sense, Minjung theology might be included in this category. Boo-woong Yoo, in his paper, referred to Minjung theology as one of the Pentecostal movements.[8] However, by the definition of the Pentecostal movement given by its advocates, this interpretation cannot be acceptable.[9]

A major task that Minjung theology faces is how to handle *minjung*'s *han*. Minjung Christian leaders stand by the protests of the activists but this Minjung activism has caused many problems. For example, they organized an Urban Industrial Mission engaged in activism among factory workers and encouraged them to protest against unfair treatment and injustice. The result, however, was that the factories were bankrupted and the workers lost their jobs. College students also protested against the government so strongly that the stores near the campuses were severely damaged. Thus the students' activism did not receive support from the people, the *minjung*.

On the other hand, since Minjung theology was initiated by a group of intellectuals and scholars, there developed an unbridgeable gap between the leaders and the poor and the uneducated in their thinking and actions. The

---

[7] Dong-sik Ryu, 'Korean Church and the Holy Spirit Movement' [in Korean], in *A Study on the Pentecostal movement in Korea* (Seoul: Christian Academy, 1983), 17.

[8] Boo-woong Yoo, *Korean Pentecostalism: Its History and Theology* (Frankfurt-am-Main: Peter Lang, 1987), 191–215. This volume is his Ph..D. dissertation submitted to the University of Birmingham under the guidance of Walter J. Hollenweger.

[9] Yoo includes both the evangelical movement and the Minjung theological movement in the category of the Pentecostal movement. However, it is ambiguous when differentiating these two movements from the classical Pentecostal movement.

leaders claim that they serve and work for the *minjung* but what the *minjung* gained from the extreme activism and protest was a deteriorating situation.

One thing noticeable is that the demonstrations of the students sometimes feature quasi-religious folk dancing and ceremonies from Korea's shamanistic tradition. These are meant to underscore the *han*, or suffering, of the common people under oppressive regimes and, are of a piece, therefore, with Minjung theology. For example, one expression is found at the seventh General Assembly of the WCC in Canberra in 1991. Hyun-kyung Jung, a Korean female theologian, invoked the spirits of the women, children and men killed by oppression. Next she set fire to long strips of rice paper on which she had written the names of the spirits she had summoned. The audience was divided in their reaction. Some received it well—perhaps seeing in it something similar to the early Christian practice of celebrating the Eucharist over the relics of the martyrs and reading out loud a martyrology. However, some others rejected it as a shamanistic ceremony. It may be viewed as a practice of Minjung theology and hence was not acceptable to many conservative Korean Christians. The early missionaries to Korea strictly banned such practices.[10] Even on Christian college campuses one sees mock ceremonies and sacrifices that are based on shamanistic practices. Minjung theology accepts those practices as means of removing the abuse of oppression that has been rooted in Korean history. It is interesting that the most intellectual group adopts the most unintellectual and shamanistic practices.[11] Despite everything, this theology did not solve the problem of the *han* of the common people. It only confirmed that there is *han* in the heart of Koreans. Conservative scholars criticize the Minjung theology, saying it cannot be considered a theological movement but it can be considered a social one.[12]

In line with the perspective of considering Minjung theology a social movement, Young-han Kim, a professor at Soong-sil University, criticizes Minjung theology for not representing the *minjung* of the Bible, since it is understood only in a social context.[13] According to Kim, the image of Jesus that Byung-moo Ahn, a Minjung theologian, claims is different from the image of the suffering servant in redemptive work that C.H. Dodd, John Bright, Oscar

---

[10] Harvey Cox, *Fire from Heaven: The Rise of Pentecostal Spirituality and the Reshaping of Religion in the Twenty-first Century* (Reading, MA: Addison-Wesley, 1995), 213–18.

[11] Donald N. Clark, *Christianity in Modern Korea* (Lanham, MD: University Press of America, 1986), 45.

[12] See Myung-hyuk Kim, 'It Is Not a Theological Movement but a Social Movement', in *Minjung and Church* [in Korean] (Seoul: Inter-Varsity Christian Fellowship, 1983), 47-53. See also Bong-ho Sohn, 'Can We Call Minjung Theology as a Theology, and Korean Theology?', in *Minjung and Church*, 54-61; Young-han Kim, 'Confusion in Own Characteristics of the Church—A Response to Byung-moo Ahn's "Nation, Minjung and Church"', *Minjung and Church*, 39-46.

[13] Kim, 'Confusion in Own Characteristics', 40-41.

Cullman and others hold. The image is closer to a messiah who stood on the side of the *minjung* who fought and was executed for them.

Ahn claims that the kingdom of God that Jesus proclaimed is a new world for the *minjung* and an 'expression of the *han* of the oppressed people'. The biography of Jesus in Mark is not a biography of a person but of a group of *minjung* and should be understood as a social biography. The image of Jesus according to Ahn makes a contribution by calling attention to the socio-political and economic *Sitz im Leben* ('life setting') of Jesus who bore the cross. In his theory, however, the socio-political and economic situation of Jesus has become less an aspect and more the very core of Jesus' life. Thus, the Christology of the New Testament would present Jesus sociologically, overshadowing the Christology of the divinity of Jesus, the recognition of him as Messiah, and his redemptive work as the Saviour of the world. Ahn also describes the cross from a sociological perspective, as the heroic symbol of a martyr for the liberation of the people. This departs from the context of a theology of redemption.[14] Ahn's interpretation totally ignores the work of redemption by the Trinity that was manifested in Jesus.

A conservative theologian, Myung-hyuk Kim, takes the same position as Young-han Kim and criticizes the Minjung theology of Nam-dong Suh. Suh asserts that the framework of theology should not be supernatural revelation or the personal realization of human nature but 'the social conditions of human nature'. In comparison with the framework of liberation theology in Central and South America under dictatorship, Suh points out that the framework of Minjung theology of Korea is the grievance and *han* of Koreans as people of a weak country. Theirs is the *han* of a people who have suffered and groaned under the oppression of their rulers, the *han* of women who have been discriminated under the dominance of men. Suh does not try to find the existence and the activity of God in the context of the Bible, Kim charges, but in the grievance harboured by Koreans in connection with various struggles in the country's history.[15] According to Kim, Suh does not understand salvation spiritually but socio-philosophically, interpreting it as the liberation from or the satisfaction of a grudge, in a word, merely as the realization of the people's humanity. If the charge is true, Suh's theology is a contextual theology that ignores the text. It denies that revelation is an absolute standard of theology.[16]

Bong-ho Sohn, a professor at Seoul National University, supports the claims of Young-han Kim and Myoung-hyuk Kim and points out that Minjung theology is completely different from traditional Christianity. Sohn thinks that being influenced by the liberation theology of Latin America and the structure of Marxism is sufficient to disqualify it as Christian.[17]

---

[14] Kim, 'Confusion in Own Characteristics', 43.
[15] Kim, 'It Is Not a Theological Movement', 47-48.
[16] Kim, 'It Is Not a Theological Movement', 50.
[17] Sohn, 'Can We Call Minjung Theology', 60.

Since Minjung theology seems to place more stress on social concerns than theological concerns with their conventional religious traditions, it cannot escape being called a social rather than a theological movement.

One of the contributions of Minjung theology lies in its calling for attention to society, especially to the plight of the oppressed. The evangelical group had been focusing on personal salvation and the growth of the churches, and was not very much interested in the oppressed if at all. Therefore, the evangelical group obviously needs to be more concerned about the socio-political and economic situation and must elaborate on how to lift the burden of *han* from the people. Identifying the failures of Minjung theology must be a prelude to overcoming them.

Another contribution of Minjung theology lies in giving Messianic hope to the *minjung*. Armed with this hope they can overcome the despair of the present life and look forward to the coming of the Messiah. Minjung theology awaits and proclaims the year of jubilee:

> We believe that God protects the oppressed, the weak, and the poor by his righteousness and that God judges the evil power in history. We believe that Jesus the Messiah will destroy the power of unrighteousness and bring the kingdom of the Messiah. The kingdom will be a resting place for the poor, the oppressed, and the despised. We also believe that the Holy Spirit works for the new creation of history and the universe.[18]

As discussed earlier, Minjung theology may have recognized the problems of *minjung* but fails to provide the *minjung* with the solutions to their problems beyond the important one of instilling hope.

Evangelistic Crusade and the Holy Spirit Movement

The Korean church began to enjoy a revival in the 1960s as Korean society became more stable in an economic sense, although it was far from stable in a political and social sense. There were demonstrations and protests almost every day. In such an unstable situation, a great number of people wanted to find peace of mind through religion and they came to the churches.[19]

Since the 1960s revival meetings have become popular in the Korean churches. Almost every church has held at least one revival meeting each year.

---

[18] 'Declaration of the Korean Christians' that was drafted and announced by the Minjung theologians in 1973.

[19] Jun-sik Choi says that Christianity emerged as an influential religion in Korea in the 1970s with its explosive growth, denying the church historians' claim that Christianity has been an influential religion from the early years of Korean Christianity. Jun-sik Choi, 'Intercultural Theology from Perspective of Korean Religions', *Theological Thought* 82 (1993), 103.

This has helped the qualitative and quantitative growth of the Korean church.[20] The leading evangelists are Hyun-gyoon Sin from a Presbyterian church and Man-shin Lee from a Holiness church. Most evangelists in the 1960s emphatically spoke of eschatology. They even claimed that Korea was the spiritual Israel, espousing the responsibility of Korea as a country of prophets and priests with a strong nationalist outlook. The following are some of the results of the revival movement in the 1960s: zeal for evangelism; active involvement in foreign missions; active work in publishing and distributing Bibles; and active participation in special missions in urban and industrial areas.[21]

In the 1970s large-scale inter-denominational crusades made a great contribution of the growth of Christian churches. Among the large-scale crusades were: the Billy Graham Crusade in 1973, the Explo Crusade in 1974; the National Crusade in 1977; and the Mission Centenary Crusade in 1984. The Korean church has been revived dramatically through these crusades. One amazing fact about this is that all the Protestant churches, which used to be divided, co-operated with one another as much as they could beyond their denominational differences, in the preparation for those crusades. The unity and harmony that the churches showed were received quite positively by Korean society. According to the research data, 350,000 people were known to have experienced conversion at the Billy Graham and Explo Crusades combined. These crusades proved that the Holy Spirit movement is crucial to church growth and that the unification of churches may be established only through the power of the Holy Spirit.[22]

The growth of the Korean church in the 1970s is worth noting: the Christian population in 1974 was 3 million; in 1978, four years later, it had grown to seven million. This indicates that Christians were added to the Korean church at an average rate of 1 million per year.[23] According to the 1978 statistics, six new churches were born every day in South Korea.

Some church growth statistics were reported in the November 7, 1978 issue of *Christian Weekly*. According to the report, the Hapdong, conservative Presbyterian denomination established 1,200 new churches in the two years following January 1976. It means that almost two churches were established each day on average. Hapdong had 1,484 churches in January of 1976 and in 1978, they had increased to 2,684. Their membership almost doubled over this

---

[20] Jin-hwan Kim, *The History of the Revival of the Korean Church*, rev. ed. [in Korean] (Seoul: Seoul Books, 1993), 238–39.

[21] Kim, *The History of the Revival*, 242–43.

[22] Young-hoon Lee, *The Holy Spirit Movement and Korean Church* [in Korean] (Seoul: Young-san, 1982), 193-94.

[23] Joon-gon Kim, 'Six New Churches Everyday Korean Church Growth' (A report for the Asian Leaders' Conference on Evangelism [ALCOE], Singapore, November, 1978), 5.

period of time, from 680,000 to 1,100,000. This gigantic growth started with the launching of a 10,000 new churches planning project. This idea and strategy came from the Korean Campus Crusade for Christ (KCCC).[24]

Even in such a socio-politically dark age, the Korean church grew remarkably, especially in the evangelical wings. The Pentecostal church became noteworthy in this period. For example, Yonggi Cho of the YFGC hosted the Pentecostal World Conference in 1973, at which more than 3,000 Pentecostal leaders from all over the globe gathered. This served to make known the Korean Pentecostal Church throughout the world. Another Pentecostal World Conference took place in the same church in 1998.

One more factor to remember in this period was the formation of the Korean Christian Revival Association (the KCRA), with the participation of leading evangelists and ministers. The KCRA was organized inter-denominationally and has led the revival movement of the Korean church. The formation of the KCRA was the first achievement of the evangelical movement in Korea through the Holy Spirit movement.

---

[24] Kim, 'Six New Churches Everyday', 2-3. Kim was appointed to take charge of the KCCC in November 1958. Since then the KCCC has greatly contributed to campus ministry and evangelism. They use the tract called 'Four Spiritual Principles' in preaching the gospel to non-believers and focus on personal evangelism. They have gained a great number of new converts.

Chapter 7

The Fifth Period (1980–2000)

The Ecumenical Movement and the Holy Spirit Movement

The ecumenical movement was not very successful in the Korean church until the 1980s. There are two key reasons behind this. First, the conservative and the liberal groups of the Korean churches confronted each other. Since it was the liberal group that supported this movement, the conservative group opposed the ecumenical movement. In addition to this, the liberal group was in favor of the World Council of Churches, while the conservative group thought that the WCC was in favour of communism although it proclaimed anti-communism.

History of the Ecumenical Movement of the Korean Churches

The ecumenical movement of Korea started from the translating of the scriptures.[1] The Bible Society was organized in 1885 and worked inter-denominationally to publish the Bible in the Korean language.[2] In 1918, the Presbyterian and Methodist churches formed the Chosun Christian Church Presbyterian and Methodist Association. It was disbanded in 1923. In 1924, the Presbyterian and Methodist churches, mission groups, the England Bible Society, and the YMCA organized the Chosun National Christian Council (CNCC). This association was disbanded by the Japanese during the last years of the Japanese occupation. It was reborn as the Chosun Christian Church Association in 1946 and renamed the Korean National Christian Council (KNCC) in 1948, and further renamed the National Council of Churches in Korea (NCCK) in 2002.[3] Since the NCCK has had a close relationship with the World Council of Churches, it had a liberal tendency, with emphases on the social participation of churches and the prophetic role of the churches. For this reason, currently, eight Christian denominations participate in the NCCK[4] and

---

[1] Gi-moon Lee (ed.), *Christian Encyclopedia* [in Korean] (Seoul: Christian Literature, 1980), II, 1094-98.

[2] So-young Kim, 'Yesterday and Today of the United Movement of the Korean Churches' [in Korea], *Christian Thought* (April 1994), 45.

[3] Kim, 'Yesterday and Today', 48.

[4] The eight denominations are: the Presbyterian Church of Korea, the Korean Methodist Church, the Presbyterian Church in the Republic of Korea, Korea Evangelical Church,

it is not generally supported by the Korean churches.[5] Currently, there is another organization of the Korean ecumenical movement, namely the Christian Council of Korea (CCK), with most evangelical, conservative and some liberal denominations participating. Its membership is around 11 million which means 92% of Korean Protestant Christians (of whom there are 12 million).

The NCCK and the CCK work quite independently on their own projects but have worked together on special occasions. The first is the united Easter Sunday worship services. The NCCK and the CCK work quite independently on their own projects but have worked together on special occasions. The first is the united Easter Sunday worship services. On April 6, 1947, Christian Council of Chosun (later the NCCK) and US army in Korea held the first United Easter Sunday worship service. However, in 1962 they were divided into progressive and conservative and stopped having the United Easter Sunday worship service till 1973 when they were reunited. In 1977 they were split up again but reunited in 1978 and have continued to have the United Easter worship service until now. In 1993, as they were united, they even received a congratulatory message for the United Easter worship service from the Korean Christian (Protestants) Federation of North Korea (*Chosun Grisdokyo Ryunmaeng*). The second is the project of the Bible Society. What is remarkable about the ecumenical work is that the Protestant and the Catholic churches formed a translation committee in 1968 and published a new version of the Holy Bible in 1977.[6]

The Holy Spirit Movement and the Ecumenical Movement

Since the Great Revival of 1907, the Holy Spirit movement has become an agent of the ecumenical movement because revival meetings and large crusades naturally led to the co-operation and unity of the various denominations. This had positive effects on the ecumenical movement. As stated earlier, the large-scale crusades in the 1970s and the 1980s made a great contribution to the unification of the Korean churches which previously had kept dividing. This

---

the Anglican Church of Korea, the Assemblies of God of Korea and the Orthodox Metropolis of Korea.

[5] In opposition to the liberal tendencies of NCCK and its close relationship with WCC, the evangelicals and the conservative groups organized the Association of Conservative Christian Denominations in Korea.

[6] Korean churches do not use various Bible versions but widely use the Authorized Korean Version that was published in 1954. The new version of the Bible that the Protestant and Catholic churches translated together is written in contemporary Korean language. Until now, however, most Korean churches use the Authorized Version.

shows that the ecumenical movement can be carried out under the aegis of the Holy Spirit movement.[7]

There are two movements that call for attention in the 1980s: the activities of the World Holy Spirit Club and the theological dialogue centered on the YFGC. Young ministers of the Pentecostal churches and other denominations first formed the World Holy Spirit Club. It soon became an interdenominational organization with church leaders in almost all denominations working for the expansion of the Holy Spirit movement in the Korean churches and the churches of the world. The World Holy Spirit Club organizes large annual interdenominational crusades. The most outstanding crusade the World Holy Spirit Club hosted was the 1992 World Holy Spirit Crusade in Yoido Plaza, Seoul, in which a total of one million people gathered. It ignited the spirit of new revivalism in the Korean church, which was undergoing a temporary stagnation.[8] The World Holy Spirit Club operates a training school for evangelists and tries not to go in the direction of extreme emotionalism as in the Holy Spirit movement.

On the other hand, the International Theological Institute (ITI), a branch institute of the YFGC, hosts the annual International Theological Seminar on the Holy Spirit and the annual interdenominational ministers' conference. The institute invites scholars of all denominations to the International Theological Seminars and holds dialogues to assist in the understanding of pneumatology. World renowned theologians have been invited to speak at the seminars.[9] It also engages in dialogue with scholars throughout the world.[10]

Leading ministers of various denominations participate in the Annual Ministers' Seminars that is hosted by the ITI, exchanging ideas and information on their ministry and co-operating with one another for church growth.

The Holy Spirit movement has also been active among the Catholics. From the beginning of the charismatic movement in Korea, the Korean Catholics have had an ecumenical spirit. The person who first brought the charismatic movement to the Korean Catholic Church was Miriam Knutas, a Swedish Lutheran. Knutas, a charismatic, received a calling from God to go to Korea and to introduce and expand the charismatic movement in the Korean church.

---

[7] Young-hoon Lee, 'Korean Churches and the Holy Spirit Movement' [in Korean], *World of Faith* (Oct. 1995), 136. See also William G. Rusch, 'The Thought of the Holy Spirit and the Pentecostal Churches in Ecumenical Movement', *Pneuma* 9:1 (1987), 17–30.

[8] The World Holy Spirit Club belongs to the Third Wave movement according to the classification by C. Peter Wagner, a professor at Fuller Theological Seminary.

[9] Some non-Korean speakers include Mac B. Stokes (Methodist), Rodman Williams (Presbyterian), Vinson Synan (Holiness Pentecostal), and Harvey Cox from Harvard University (for the 1996 seminar).

[10] The YFGC and Soonshin University (now renamed as Hansei University) hosted seminars by inviting Jürgen Moltmann (Tübingen University, Germany) and Ralph Martin (Sheffield University, England).

She came to Korea and met Tim Clark, a Catholic and American soldier stationed in Korea. Knutas studied the Bible with Clark, during which time he received the baptism in the Holy Spirit. Afterwards Clark introduced Knutas to Sister Erna Schmid, the founder and chairperson of the Board of Trustees of the John Bosco Technical Training Center. Knutas prayed for Schmid's baptism in the Holy Spirit. On 2 January 1971, Schmid was baptized by the Holy Spirit and began to hold regular prayer meetings every Saturday at her training center. In May of 1971 she gathered 13 foreign priests and friars and invited Reuben A. Torrey, an Episcopal priest, to speak at the Seminar on the Life in the Holy Spirit—the first Catholic charismatic renewal seminar in Korea. De Porres Stilp (whose Korean name is Young-ho Cho)—a member of the Maryknoll community—was one of the participants in the seminar. He experienced the new life in the Holy Spirit at the seminar. For more than fifteen years since this experience, he has been working on the charismatic renewal of the Korean Catholic church.

After Schmid had gone back to Germany, Young-ho Cho (De Porres Stilp) took up his residence in the training center and took charge of the Saturday prayer meetings. He led the Saturday prayer meetings for Koreans. In January 1974, twelve people finished the 8-week-long training program of the Seminar on Life in the Holy Spirit. They received Spirit-baptism and spoke in tongues. In May 1974, at a charismatic renewal retreat at Wae-gwan in Gyoung-nam province, a Korean priest, Bong-do Choi, received Spirit baptism. Father Choi was the first Korean Catholic priest to receive baptism in this fashion.

The Catholic charismatic renewal movement has witnessed continuous growth. Twelve Korean Episcopal priests likewise participated in the Seminar on Life in the Holy Spirit from 30 November through 2 December of 1980. On 3 January 1981, the Catholic charismatic renewal leaders and Protestant missionaries had a special ceremony at the John Bosco Technical Training Center in celebration of the tenth anniversary of 2 January 1971, when the Catholic charismatic renewal of Korea was born.[11]

The Catholic Charismatic Renewal movement, unlike the Protestant Charismatic movement, had an ecumenical spirit from the very beginning. One cannot deny that the Catholic Charismatic Renewal has a great influence on the Catholic churches.[12]

---

[11] The Catholic Charismatic Renewal Committee, *Handbook of Charismatic Renewal in Korea* [in Korean] (Seoul: Catholic Charismatic Renewal Committee, 1986), 7–24. There were 350,000 Catholic Charismatics in Korea around 1990, and the number was estimated to have reached 675,000 in 2007.

[12] Gwang-sup Song, 'Catholic Charismatic Renewal' [in Korean], *Prospects of Theology* 67 (Winter 1984), 29.

Future Prospect and Task

The Korean church has witnessed continuous struggles between the conservative group with an emphasis on personal salvation and the liberal group with an emphasis on social salvation. To overcome such struggles, the Holy Spirit movement should make every effort to have dialogues among its component members and to continue the ecumenical movement through co-operation in world missions. Since evangelism includes both personal, spiritual salvation and social concerns,[13] the co-operation of the two groups in the world mission projects can provide a good example in the ecumenical movement. In fact the Third Wave movement pursues such an emphasis.[14]

True ecumenism should be carried out by the Holy Spirit movement and must have a sound doctrine as a characteristic of the movement. Since the indigenization theology, Minjung theology, and global theological trends that came to Korea have deepened the divisions between the conservative and liberal groups, sound standards of doctrine that are acceptable to both groups are needed. Such standards must be taken from the major teachings of the scriptures as the Reformers proclaimed them. The Reformers thought it necessary to establish objective standards to deal with the issues of Christian faith and practice, and tried to fulfil this need from the Old and the New Testaments.[15] Therefore, it is desirable to establish a sound doctrine for the Protestant ecumenical movement in the dialogue between the conservative and the liberal groups, as well as their co-operation through the continual calling upon the Holy Spirit to expand the work of the gospel.

Church Growth and the Holy Spirit Movement

The 1980s saw an exponential growth of Korean Christianity. The popular statistics indicate that there were six churches added every week.[16] Even the conservative government annual reports attested to this claim. The growth momentum, which began in the 1970s, reached its peak in the 1980s. Korean Christianity which struggled to survive under the harsh rule of the Japanese achieved 508,000 membership by the time of liberation in 1945. The decadal

---

[13] J. Herbert Kane, *The Christian World Mission: Today and Tomorrow* (Grand Rapids, MI: Baker, 1981), 144.

[14] The scripture advocates both personal spiritual salvation and charity work for the poor. The church that is led by the Holy Spirit must show their social concerns to the society as well as the salvation of individuals. Christian Press, 'The Community with Society' [in Korean], in *The Truth and the False of Korean Churches I* (Seoul: Cumran, 1993), 69.

[15] John Wimber and Kevin Springer, *Power Healing* (San Francisco, CA: Harper & Row, 1987), 236.

[16] Bon-rin Ro, 'The Korean Church: Growing or Declining?', *Evangelical Review of Theology* 19 (1995), 336-53.

growth since then shows steady growth with 3,193,000 in 1970, 7,181,000 in 1980 and 8,760,000 in 1990.[17]

This period of growth also coincides with the time of economic growth and social changes, particularly from a military dictatorship to a full democratic political system. Unlike the previous period where Minjung theology represents the socially conscious approach and Pentecostals represent the spiritual approach, this period gradually removed the theological and social agenda for Minjung theology.[18] This changed situation has left the Pentecostal approach as the only visible player in the theological field, perhaps until the inter-Korean situation and economic disparity toward the end of this period provide a new theological impetus.

At the core of the growth in this period are two notable phenomena. The first is the general and popular acceptance of a Pentecostal-type of worship and preaching, popularized by David Yonggi Cho of the Yoido Full Gospel Church.[19] Although suspicions toward Pentecostalism persisted in some theological sectors, pastors observed the explosive growth of Pentecostal-type churches throughout the world. This link between church growth and Spirit-empowered Christian life was further advocated by church growth authorities at Fuller Theological Seminary in California.[20] The fact that Cho was the first speaker for the newly established Annual Church Growth Lecture of the seminary epitomizes the Korean church growth phenomenon. The second is the appearance of mega-churches. According to Hong, a mega-church is defined as a single congregation whose adult Sunday attendance is 10,000 and more.[21] By the end of this period, it was popularly known that Korea had ten of the world's twenty largest churches! Denominationally, the world's largest Pentecostal, Presbyterian, Methodist, and Baptist churches were all found in Korea. What is more striking is that most of the mega-churches (12 out of 15 Protestant mega-churches) in Korea were Pentecostal-charismatic in their orientation in worship and preaching.[22] It is unanimously agreed that the main growth engine of the Korean church has been the YFGC and its network. In this period, the YFGC

---

[17] Young-gi Hong, 'The Backgrounds and Characteristics of the Charismatic Mega-Churches in Korea', *Asian Journal of Pentecostal Studies* 3:1 (Jan 2000), 99.

[18] Some authors interestingly connect Pentecostalism and Minjung theology. See for example W.J. Hollenweger, Pentecostalism: Origins and Developments Worldwide (Peabody, MA: Hendrickson, 1997), 102-105, heavily relying on Boo-woong Yoo, *Korean Pentecostalism: Its History and Theology* (Frankfurt-am-Main: Peter Lang, 1988), esp. 223ff.

[19] For a more detailed treatment, see the next section.

[20] E.g., C. Peter Wagner, *Look out! The Pentecostals Are Coming* (London: Coverdale House, 1974).

[21] Hong, 'The Backgrounds and Characteristics of the Charismatic Mega-Churches', 100, no. 4.

[22] Hong, 'The Backgrounds and Characteristics of the Charismatic Mega-Churches', 101.

grew to an unprecedented size and influence with about a dozen daughter churches of the YFGC becoming either mega- or large churches.

In spite of growing criticism toward the church growth movement particularly in North America, it is important to place the concept in a proper context. Theologically the presence of a local church in a given society, be it a Christian or non-Christian one, is a visible sign of God's kingship over the universe. Especially in a non-Christian society, the growth of the church is critical, as it would serve as the proof of God's reality. A Korean Pentecostal's study of church growth and its influence on society is noteworthy: 1) a change in attitudes towards positive life and hope; 2) social integration; 3) redemption and uplift; 4) cultural reform; and 5) leadership and social change.[23]

Yoido Full Gospel Church and the Pentecostal Movement

As the Korean church grew explosively in the 1970s, one congregation has attracted the attention of the churches of the world. That church is the Yoido Full Gospel Church founded by David Yonggi Cho. This church has the largest single congregation in the world with a membership of 755,000 by the end of 2007. Cho founded the YFGC in 1958 and has pastored the church since then. Many view the YFGC as the base of the Pentecostal movement in Korea. This section will discuss the history, development, characteristics and influence of this church in relation to the ministry of Cho.

The Life and Ministry of Yonggi Cho[24] and the Yoido Full Gospel Church

It is impossible to understand the YFGC and its ministry without considering the man behind it—David Yonggi Cho (photo). He was born on 14 February 1936, in a small town in Ulju County, Gyung-nam Province in the southern part of Korea, while the country was under Japanese occupation. From the time that Japan invaded Manchuria and started a war with China (1931), the Japanese exploited most crops and requisitioned Koreans to harvest them. It was in this devastating situation that Cho spent his

---

[23] Young-gi Hong, 'The Influence of Rev. Cho's Church Growth on Korean Society', in Sung-hoon Myung and Young-gi Hong (eds.), *Charis and Charisma: David Yonggi Cho and the Growth of Yoido Full Gospel Church* (Oxford: Regnum, 2003), 203-208.

[24] His story was published by an American reporter. Nell L. Kennedy, *Dream Your Way to Success: The Story of Dr. Yonggi Cho and Korea* (Plainfield, NJ: Logos International, 1980). See also Woonhak Yeo, *Thy Will Be Done: World Mission and Yonggi Cho* [in Korean] (Seoul: Gyujang, 1982). For a brief biographical study, see Young-hoon Lee, 'The Life and Ministry of David Yonggi Cho and the Yoido Full Gospel Church', *AJPS* 7:1 (2004), 3-20.

childhood. The country was liberated in 1945 but divided in two—South and North—by American and Soviet forces: the North became a communist country and the South a democratic one. But South Korea was still going through major crises both politically and socially.

Cho's Father, Doo-cheon Cho, ran for election to Congress on 30 May 1950 but failed. The Cho family was suffering financially. Less than a month later the Korean War broke out. Young Cho witnessed the destruction and suffering caused by the war.

In the spring of 1953, when he was a sophomore in high school, he was injured in the chest while exercising. He gradually became weakened. Since it was during the war and his family was poor, he could not get proper medical treatment. Later he was diagnosed as having a terminal case of tuberculosis. Without proper treatment he became severely weakened and close to death. On what was thought to be his deathbed he was visited by a Christian girl who was a friend of his sister. His Buddhist parents had forbidden her to visit their home but she persisted and gave Cho a Bible, preaching the gospel to him. Soon Cho became a Christian and his health began to improve dramatically.

He happened to meet Kenneth Tice, an AG missionary, and began to interpret his sermons for him and another missionary, Lou Richards. Richards taught the Bible to Cho. While Cho was reading about divine healing in the Bible, he was touched by it and repented for not having fully believed it. He prayed and fasted for three days. On the third day he had a vision of Jesus in which he was called to dedicate his life to preaching the gospel.[25]

After this experience, in 1956, he moved from Busan to Seoul and enrolled in the Full Gospel Bible College, which belonged to the Assemblies of God denomination. Although he was not in very good health, he managed to continue his studies. As his Christian faith grew deeper, his health also gradually improved. During these years of study, Cho met Jasil Choi, his classmate and a former registered nurse, who took care of him. She later became his associate pastor and mother-in-law.

Cho started a tent church in 1958. Its 50-year history, although it assumed different names as the church moved from one location to another, may be divided into three periods. The first is the pioneering period (1958–1961)[26] in which the YFGC was the instrument of the Pentecostal faith's taking root in Korea by its strong full gospel message and divine healing. The second is the developing period (1961–1973) when the church took the leadership in the Pentecostal movement of Korea and spread the Pentecostal faith in the Korean church. The third is the current period of expansion (1973–).[27] The church has

---

[25] Kennedy, *Dream Your Way*, 118–21.

[26] ITI, *Yoido Full Gospel Church: Its Faith and Theology* [in Korean] (Seoul: Seoul Books, 1993), vol. 2, 96.

[27] This three-stage division is also the interpretation of the YFGC: 'History: The Tent Church' (http://english.fgtv.com/yoido/history.htm, 2007); 'History: The Church at

taken the lead in the Holy Spirit movement of the entire Korean church, has become mature enough to show its concern for Korean society, and has greatly expanded the Holy Spirit movement.

History of the Yoido Full Gospel Church

The Pioneering Period (1958–1961)

Cho, a new seminary graduate, put up a tent in a slum area of Daejo-dong, Sudaemun-gu, Seoul on 18 May 1958 with Mrs. Jasil Choi and her three children. The tent church that had started with only five members grew rapidly as Cho's powerful message and healing ministry, with his ardent prayer and street evangelism, made a great combination. Many who had various diseases came and were healed. The news of the work of the Holy Spirit at this tent church spread among the people and, by 1961, the church had a membership of 600.

The primary characteristic of this pioneering period was its ministry among city slum-dwellers. This was a post-war time of devastation and most people despaired in emptiness and frustration.[28] To these city slum-dwellers in Daejo-dong, Cho preached the good news of hope. He proclaimed that they could gain not only spiritual blessings but also material and situational blessings from God if they came to Jesus Christ and lived by the word of God. Cho's message of salvation in body and spirit gave enormous comfort and hope to people who were poor and suffering.

The second important characteristic of the YFGC was the experience of Spirit-baptism and divine healing. Cho preached a Pentecostal faith, which emphasized Spirit-baptism and the subsequent signs such as speaking in tongues, based on the prophecy of Joel that God would pour out his Spirit in the last days. The most outstanding manifestation of God's power in Cho's tent church was divine healing. Many were healed from various diseases. Cho's sermons penetrated the lives of city slum-dwellers. Divine healing and Spirit-baptism were the driving forces behind the growth of the church. The explosive growth of the YFGC was not only because of divine healing, but also because the members who were changed by God's power went out and preached the Word of God to others.[29]

The third was powerful prayer. Just as the early apostolic church was born by the descent of the Holy Spirit upon the disciples, as they devoted themselves

---

SeoDaeMun' (http://english.fgtv.com/yoido/History2.htm, 2007); and 'History: The Church at Yoido' (http://english.fgtv.com/yoido/History3.htm, 2007), all accessed on 2 Feb 2008.

[28] Min, Church History of Korea, 470.

[29] Yonggi Cho, More than Numbers (Waco, TX: Word, 1984), 87.

to prayer in the upper room,[30] Cho focused on prayer and devoted himself to it. He prayed at dawn, fasted and prayed, and prayed through the night.[31] Prayer became one of the most important elements of his ministry.

The Developing Period (1961–1973)

Cho interpreted the sermons of Sam Todd, an American evangelist, during revival meetings held for one month in September 1961, at Sudaemun Rotary. A great number of people came to these meetings and experienced God's grace. Many received Jesus and many were healed. After the meeting, Cho decided to establish a second church and held an opening worship service on 15 October 1961. The Full Gospel Revival Center was the name of his second church. He started construction and finished it on 18 February 1962. Cho was ordained as a minister on 26 April 1962. On 13 May of the same year, he changed the name of the church to the Full Gospel Central Church. The membership reached 3,000 in 1964.

Cho over-worked to the point of fainting and suffered quite some time from bad health. One Sunday, while he was administering baptism[32] to hundreds of people, Cho collapsed and spent a week in a hospital. A week later, he returned to the pulpit to preach but collapsed again. He was hospitalized. While reading the Bible in the hospital, he received a revelation from Exodus 18 and used it to organize a cell-unit system,[33] which has become a trademark of the YFGC.

Cho appointed women as cell-unit leaders, a revolutionary attempt in the tradition of the Korean church or any Korean society with a strong Confucian background. Until then, the position of women in Korean society was not well recognized, if at all. The cell-group system brought liberation to the status of women in Korea. These women leaders devoted themselves to the growth of the cell groups by effective home visitations and street preaching. Cell units conceived as sub-churches grew rapidly practising worship, prayer, and fellowship. The growth of cell units thus made a significant contribution to the growth of the church. Meanwhile various departments of the church were organized, including men's and women's mission and service groups. The church started publishing a Christian monthly magazine *Sinanggye* [The World

---

[30] Acts 1:14; 2:1–4, 42–47.

[31] Dawn prayer was initiated at Jangdae-hyun Church in Pyongyang, during the 1907 revival meeting and expanded by Sun-joo Gil. Fasting prayer and all night prayer were expanded by Yonggi Cho and Jasil Choi.

[32] The Assemblies of God approve of nothing but baptism by immersion, following the traditions of the apostolic church in the New Testament and also the traditions of the Anabaptists.

[33] ITI, *Yoido Full Gospel Church*, 185–86,

of Faith] in 1967 in order to expand the Holy Spirit movement based on the word of God. This has been renamed as *The Plus Life* from January 2008.[34]

The primary characteristic of this period was the work of the Holy Spirit experienced in the community. If the work of the Holy Spirit in the pioneering period was individual experience, the work of the Holy Spirit in this period was the revival and renewal of the church as a community. The outpouring of the Spirit restored the Christian lives of the discouraged people of God. By this experience, the church could follow the model of the church as presented in the book of Acts. When the church acknowledged and worked with the Holy Spirit it became Spirit-filled and this partnership brought with it the rapid growth of the church.[35]

The second characteristic of the period was the cell-group structure. Other churches had neglected cell-group structures but as employed in the YFGC cells proved to be a great turning-point. All members joined the cell system. Cho educated and trained the cell-group leaders so that they could take care of their groups. The structure of the cell-unit system contributed greatly to the effective training and pastoral care of the new members. With the help of this system, Cho can minister to the 755,000 members of his church. This subject will be discussed further.

The Expanding Period (1973-present)

Since the church could not accommodate the rapidly growing numbers, it decided to build a new church and started construction in Yoido, an island of nothing but sand. Despite economic depression, opposition and hardships, Cho finished construction and dedicated the new church on 23 September 1973. Church growth accelerated after moving to Yoido. Its membership reached 100,000 in 1979; 200,000 in November 1980; 500,000 in 1985; 700,000 in 1992, and 755,000 in 2007.[36] During this time, the church built a prayer mountain (1973), opened a publishing company (1976), and

---

[34] The impact of this publication, especially through many published testimonies, was studied by Myung-soo Park, 'Korean Pentecostal Spirituality as manifested in the Testimonies of Believers of the Yoido Full Gospel Church', *AJPS* 7:1 (2004), 35-56.

[35] Yonggi Cho, *The Practical Church Growth That I Experience,* Church Growth 2 [in Korean] (Seoul: Seoul Books, 1985), 147-49.

[36] Church Growth International, *Church Growth Manual 7* (Seoul: Church Growth International, 1995), 145.

started a weekly newspaper, the *Full Gospel News* (1978). To propagate the
Pentecostal faith and for the effective training and education of its members,
the YFGC established the Institute for Full Gospel Education, which became
the International Theological Institute in 1993.

The YFGC also fully supports the Full Gospel Bible College to educate
Christian leaders. The college later became Hansei University with full
accreditation from the government.

The primary characteristic of this period was the explosive growth of the
church. Some try to explain such growth in relation to the sociological,
economic, and political background in the 1970s.[37] The following factors
contributed to the growth: the message and the leadership of Cho, divine
healing, the baptism in the Holy Spirit, and the proper training of the church lay
leaders by the Holy Spirit movement leadership.[38]

Second, the church began to take the primary role in the Holy Spirit
movement of the Korean churches. In this period of expansion, the YFGC has
dispersed the Holy Spirit movement all over the country and contributed
greatly to the spiritual movement of the Korean church.[39]

Third, the Pentecostal movement of the YFGC expanded into the world.
Since the 1970s, the YFGC has facilitated women workers and stirred a revival
movement through the cell-unit system. They have brought the Pentecostal
movement to thousands by concerted prayer, person to person evangelism,
publications and broadcasting.[40] Pentecostal mission theology puts stress on
eschatological expectation and the realization of the kingdom of God.[41] The
YFGC has made every effort to further the Holy Spirit movement with its
eschatological expectation, thereby to fulfil the vision of the Lord Jesus: to
evangelize the world before the end comes by reviving the church.

Fourth, it emphasized the renewal of the church and its participation in
society, realizing that the church must go into modern society in order to
continue its growth. The YFGC has concentrated on church renewal since
1993.[42] It practised Christian love by extensive charity work for the lower class
and the underprivileged. The charity work of the YFGC includes: providing
cardiac operations to children with heart disease; donating blood; 'bread of

---

[37] Choi, 'Intercultural Theology', 126–28.

[38] ITI, *Yoido Full Gospel Church*, 111.

[39] ITI, *Yoido Full Gospel Church*, 125-26.

[40] Young-hoon Lee, 'Korean Churches and the Holy Spirit Movement', *Shinanggye*
(October 1995), 137.

[41] L. Grant McClung, Jr., 'Truth on Fire: Pentecostals and Urgent Missiology', in L.
Grant McClung Jr. (ed.), *Azusa Street and Beyond* (South Plainfield, NJ: Bridge, 1986),
52.

[42] ITI, *Yoido Full Gospel Church*, 139-40.

love' (distributing food to the needy); giving relief to foreign refugees; a sharing movement; the establishment of a training institute, and so on.[43]

The operation of the YFGC is as follows.[44] Worship services are the core of YFGC spirituality. There are seven worship services each Sunday, three each Wednesday, and two each Saturday. The seven Sunday services have different focuses. Cho used to preach in three services until his successor was elected in 2006. Then Cho preached in two services, while the pastor-elect preached in one for about a year. From May 2008, Young-hoon Lee, the Senior Pastor, preaches in two services, Cho preaches in one service, and executive assistant pastors preach in the other worship services. Among the seven gatherings, one is with an emphasis on praise and worship while another is on healing.

There are also daily early morning prayer meetings and all-night prayer meetings. Sunday schools and various mission groups have their own worship services on Sundays.

Organizationally the operation of the YFGC is centered on the leadership of its senior pastor. As of January 2009, under the leadership of its senior pastor, the church has 14 departments and subordinate branch departments. There are 4 regional chapels, 17 branch churches, 13 districts, 313 sub-districts, 14,888 cell units and 755,000 members.

For the educational ministry, the Department of Pastoral and Theological Studies of the ITI takes care of the continuing education and training of pastors and lay workers. A lay education institute ministers to the needs of lay people. Sunday schools and various mission groups have their own education programmes.

For evangelism and world missions, various mission groups and committees participate in evangelical programmes. The Mission Department supports Cho's overseas evangelistic campaigns, sends missionaries, and establishes and supports overseas Bible schools. As of 2008, the YFGC has sent 648 missionaries, established seven Bible seminaries[45] and one university, and expands its missionary work in the two-thirds world.

---

[43] For detail, see ITI, *Yoido Full Gospel Church*, II, 141-44.

[44] Statistics are as of January 2009.

[45] As an effective missionary strategy, the YFGC builds up Bible seminaries in the mission fields and raises native pastors and Christian leaders to evangelize their own countries. There are seminaries and Bible colleges in Malang (Indonesia), Nairobi (Kenya), Chimkent (Uzbekistan), Hong Kong (China), Tel Este (Bolivia), Osaka and Tokyo (Japan).

Unique Features of the Holy Spirit Movement of Cho and the YFGC[46]

Cho claims that the Holy Spirit movement can bear fruit when it is accompanied by the fullness of the word, prayer, and the Holy Spirit. If one is neglected or overly emphasized, the dynamic work of the Spirit will be impossible. [47] Since the Holy Spirit movement of the YFGC has been established and developed through the ministry of Cho, a discussion of Cho's message, prayer, Spirit-baptism and speaking in other tongues, divine healing, and cell unit system is in order.

Message

The distinguishing elements of the Holy Spirit movement of the YFGC are: salvation of the spirit; faith centered on the word of God; experience of the Holy Spirit; and world evangelization. [48] They are made concrete by Cho's messages. [49]

Jin-hwan Kim has described Cho's message: 'It is positive and hopeful with stress on Bible-centered genuine faith and on the work of the Holy Spirit'. [50] Karen Hurston has said: 'Cho does not prepare his sermons exclusively by his own planning but by calling on the Holy Spirit'. [51] E.J. Peterson wrote: 'A preacher who is called by God and possessed by the Spirit becomes a powerful tool of God'. [52] Cho's Bible-based and positive sermons have contributed not only to the growth of the YFGC but also to the expansion of the Holy Spirit movement.

The framework of Cho's sermons is the fivefold gospel and threefold blessing. During the 1950s and 1960s when Cho started the ministry and even until the 1970s, Korea was suffering from poverty, starvation, and violent political change. Therefore, Cho felt that it was impossible to preach the gospel without solving existing problems. As he was trying to find the biblical

---

[46] Daniel J. Adams, a professor of systematic theology at Hanil Theological Seminary in Korea, published a brief theological research report on the YFGC. Daniel J. Adams, 'Reflections on an Indigenous Movement: Yoido Full Gospel Church', *Japan Christian Quarterly* (Winter 1991), 36–45.

[47] Yonggi Cho, *A Key to Successful Church Growth* [in Korean] (Seoul: Seoul Books, 1976), 40-44.

[48] Young-hoon Lee, 'Suggestions for the Holy Spirit Movement of Korean Churches' [in Korean], *World of the Spirit* 1 (1992), 27.

[49] For a study on Cho's sermons, see Wonsuk Ma, 'The Effect of Rev. Cho's Sermon Style for Church Growth on the Development of Theology', in Sung-hoon Myung and Young-gi Hong (eds.), *Charis and Charisma: David Yonggi Cho and the Growth of Yoido Full Gospel Church* (Oxford: Regnum Books, 2003), 159-71.

[50] Kim, *The History of the Revival* (1993).

[51] Karen Hurston, *Growing the World's Largest Church* (Springfield, MO: Gospel Publishing House, 1994), 153.

[52] Eugene James Peterson, *A Theology of Church Growth* (Grand Rapids, MI: Zondervan, 1981), 47.

solution for many practical and concrete problems in Korea, he found such a solution at 3 John 2.[53] In 1977 Cho presented the threefold blessing by publishing *Threefold Salvation,* and in 1983 he theorized it by means of publishing *The Fivefold Gospel and Threefold Blessing.* Here is his graphic exposition:[54]

> The major premise of fivefold gospel and threefold blessing is faith in the good God.[55] Then, what is threefold blessing? Before giving you an answer, I will take you to the front door of blessing house named 'threefold salvation'. Such a front door is the good God. We need to humbly see "the good God" before reaching threefold salvation. Firm belief of God should sink deep into our hearts. Nowadays many people are not positive as to the truth of God being the good God. We just vaguely think God as fearful and threatening and God of taking away good ones. Or we misunderstand Him as God who has nothing to do with us right now.

To him, the threefold blessing is practical faith (real and applicable) and the fivefold gospel is the principle of the full gospel.[56]

The fivefold gospel consists of the gospel of salvation; the gospel of the fullness of the Holy Spirit; the gospel of divine healing; the gospel of blessing; and the gospel of the second coming of Jesus Christ.[57] The threefold blessing is based on 3 John 2 and describes the blessing that Christians receive by the work of the cross of Jesus Christ. It consists of: spiritual blessing; physical blessing; and the blessing of circumstances.[58] Cho places great emphasis on the importance of the threefold blessing as follows:

> If we comprehend the deep meaning of the threefold blessing, we get to understand all the Scriptures from Genesis to Revelation based on the threefold

---

[53] In the Christian academic world, it was dominant to view 3 John 2, "Dear friend, I pray that you may enjoy good health and that all may go well with you, even as your soul is getting along well," as a typical compliment used in the correspondence of ancient Greece. However, the special point of 3 John 2 was that the soul going well is the basis of being prosperous in everything. Cho saw this verse as God's blessing to all Christians. See Young-hoon Lee, 'Influence of Dr. Cho's "God Is So Good" Faith in the Korean Churches' [in Korean], *Journal of Youngsan Theology* 7 (2006), 89.

[54] Yonggi Cho, *The Threefold Salvation* [in Korean] (Seoul: Seoul Logos, 1989), 19-20.

[55] According to Cho, the good God is on the basis of the love of God and God loves us so much that He wants to bless us. Because of the good God, the threefold blessing is possible. Y. Lee, 'Influence of Dr. Cho's "God Is So Good" Faith', 92-93.

[56] Y. Cho, *Fivefold Gospel and Threefold Blessing,* 'preface'.

[57] The structure of the fivefold gospel is similar to that of the fourfold gospel of the Holiness Church. The Holiness Church stresses regeneration, sanctification, divine healing and the second coming of Christ.

[58] See Yonggi Cho, *The Fivefold Gospel and Threefold Blessing* [in Korean] (Seoul: Seoul Logos, 1983) and ITI, *Yoido Full Gospel Church,* 13–141.

salvation. Then, all the truth of the Bible is vividly brought to life and lightens our lives.[59]

Cho emphasizes that only with the help of the Spirit can such a message effectively reach people[60] and change them to trust in Jesus completely.[61] Hence, Cho's Holy Spirit movement is based on the word of God and is a movement to proclaim Jesus. Since the Spirit testifies to Jesus (John 15:26), it is a 'Jesus-witnessing movement', because Christians testify to Jesus when they are filled with the Spirit.

Prayer

Cho is a man of prayer, saying that he learned in the early days of his ministry that he himself should pray before telling people to pray.[62] Cho has stressed that Christians must learn how to pray, discipline themselves to pray, and devote themselves to prayer, for prayer is a hard and long process.[63] He regularly attributes the growth of the YFGC to prayer.

An emphasis on prayer is epitomized in two particular areas. Firstly, various prayer gatherings are part of the YFGC's weekly programme. As part of the Korean spiritual tradition, the YFGC has daily dawn prayer meetings. To accommodate varying individual circumstances, the church conducts three daily dawn prayer meetings. Sometimes special dawn prayer meetings are planned. For example, in July 2008 right after the installation of the new senior pastor, the church held a special swan prayer meeting for a week. It is reported that each morning, an average of 50,000 everyday participated in this special prayer programme. Another prayer tradition which the YFGC began is an overnight prayer meeting, normally beginning in the evening and ending early next morning. The church now has a daily overnight prayer from 11 in the evening until 4 in the morning. However, the Friday overnight prayer between 9:30 and 4 in the morning attracts the biggest crowd. In fact, just like the dawn prayer meeting, the Friday overnight prayer is now a common feature of most Korean churches. Equally regular are special prayer programmes, for example, called the Daniel Prayer (for 21 days) and the Jericho Prayer (for 7 days). These are special prayer programmes to cater for the common needs of the members such as an economic crisis or a university exam season.

Secondly, the renowned Choi Jashil International Fasting Prayer Mountain is another important expression of this emphasis. Founded in 1973 in the north of Seoul close to the De-militarised Zone, the prayer mountain was initially an addition to numerous prayer mountains throughout the country. As in

---

[59] Yonggi Cho, *The Threefold Salvation*, 19.
[60] Yonggi Cho, *I Preach This Way* [in Korean] (Seoul: Seoul Books, 1989), 173.
[61] Cho, *I Preach This Way*, 174.
[62] Paul Yonggi Cho, *Prayer: Key to Revival* (Waco, TX: Word, 1992), 62.
[63] ITI, *Yoido Full Gospel Church*, 119-20.

Pentecostal spirituality from the West, the Korean revival tradition has placed a strong emphasis on prayer. For example, the dawn prayer meeting of the Korean Christian tradition was the fruit of the Pyongyang Great Revival. After liberation from the Japanese colonial rule in 1945, prayer mountains began to emerge in many parts of the country, to the point that most large churches now have their own prayer mountains. However, the unique contribution of the YFGC to Korean Pentecostal spirituality is found in its prayer mountains and Rev. Jashil Choi, co-founder of the prayer mountain (as well as the FGYC itself), Cho's mother-in-law. In its early years, Choi strongly emphasized fasting as a distinct practice of Pentecostal prayer, as she regularly prayed with fasting. [64] Fasting prayer is often considered as an extreme form of one's resolute prayer. The spirituality aligns with the western Pentecostal practice of 'praying through'. The number of fasting days varies, but it ranges from three to forty days. Soon testimonies of miraculous healing, family reconciliations, the spiritual renewal of individuals and churches, miracles, and the resolution of problems such as interpersonal relations and business difficulties began to attract more visitors. Soon the prayer mountain was crowded by many from outside of the YFGC. The news of miracles through fasting prayer also attracted many international visitors, from Japan and Taiwan in the early years and then from countless countries. The prayer mountain had to construct more prayer chambers, now numbering more than three hundred. It is customary for the staff, cell leaders and members of the YFGC to spend the first few days of a new year at the prayer mountain for prayer and fasting. This has become an important practice of Korean Pentecostal spirituality.

Underlying these prayer programmes is a firm conviction of Cho and the church leaders that prayer creates a mindset of faith and anticipation of God's miracles. Testimonies of God's supernatural intervention, be it healing or miracles, are generously shared in the pulpit, through the church's weekly newspaper and its monthly magazine. Weekly cell group meetings are an exceptionally effective venue in spreading such 'good news'.

Baptism in the Holy Spirit

The 120 disciples of Jesus devoted themselves to prayer before the descent of the Holy Spirit on the day of Pentecost (Acts 1:14). They then received the baptism of the Spirit and became bold witnesses to the gospel. Therefore, any prayer movement is directly connected to the Holy Spirit. Many churches and Christians of other countries have learned the prayer patterns of the YFGC and effective methods for running and managing houses of prayer. When they apply them correctly, they experience the power of the Holy Spirit. The Holy Spirit movement of the YFGC has thus expanded swiftly.

---

[64] Julie C. Ma, 'Korean Pentecostal Spirituality: A Case Study of Jashil Choi', *AJPS* 5:2 (2002), 235-254.

According to traditional Pentecostal faith, baptism in the Holy Spirit is an experience distinct from conversion.[65] The disciples of Jesus confessed 'Jesus is Lord' by the Holy Spirit (1 Cor. 12:3) and Jesus confirmed that they were all clean—that they were already saved except Judas Iscariot, since Jesus had called them (John 13:10). Nonetheless, Jesus said that they should be baptized with the Holy Spirit (Acts 1:4–5). Since Cho emphasized this type of baptism as the second blessing after conversion, churches and denominations with different doctrines have long attacked him.[66] John Wesley's second blessing, which is described as sanctification or as the wholeness of Christ, points to Spirit-baptism.[67] Charles G. Finney, Dwight L. Moody, Reuben A. Torrey, and J.W. Chapman have supported this truth.[68] The doctrine of Spirit-baptism is an integral part of the Holy Spirit movement.

There has been a long-running debate on the signs of Spirit-baptism. Cho says that it has various signs, but speaking in tongues is the most common and unique external sign. He also proposes testifying to Jesus Christ as evidence of Spirit-baptism.[69] Cho divides speaking in tongues into two categories, 'sign' and 'gift'.[70]

The YFGC encourages people to receive Spirit-baptism, edify the church, and be witnesses to Christ, armed with the power of the Spirit.

Divine healing

Healing is an integral part of the development of the YFGC and the expansion of the Holy Spirit movement. Cho preached the power of the Holy Spirit in the Book of Acts to the despairing. This brought miracles, signs and the healing of people with various diseases, all contributing to the rapid growth of Cho's tent church. The sick came and Cho provided them with the opportunity to listen to the gospel.

We may ascribe the continuous manifestation of divine healing in the tent church to Cho's own experience of healing from the terminal stage of tuberculosis and his faith in the gospel of divine healing. Cho claims that divine healing is the will of God, the prime ministry of Jesus, and the task and command that He gave to us, for God himself has said: 'I am the Lord, who heals you' (Exodus 15:26).[71] Moreover, Jesus devoted two-thirds of his ministry to healing.

---

[65] Yonggi Cho, *Pneumatology* [in Korean] (Seoul, Youngsan, 1980), 141. See also footnote 185.

[66] See ITI, *When the Holy Spirit Comes upon You* [in Korean] (Seoul: ITI, 1994).

[67] Nichol, *Pentecostalism*, 5-6.

[68] Dayton, *Theological Roots*, 101.

[69] Cho, *The Fivefold Gospel*, 117.

[70] Yonggi Cho, *The Full Gospel Truth* [in Korean] (Seoul: Seoul Books, 1979), vol. 1, 246-47.

[71] Cho, *Divine Healing*, 22-23.

Some advocates of divine healing misused the healing ministry but Cho presented salvation as whole and entire: salvation through the healing of the spirit, the body, and the person's circumstances. He retained a balanced theology in his healing teaching. Problems that arise among advocates of healing are due to a lack of the correct understanding of the gospel.

The cell system

One of the primary grounds of the explosive growth of the Pentecostal movement lies in the house church movement. This movement has its root in the Christian community of the early church. Meeting in houses was one of the foundations of the growth of the early church (Acts 2:42-47). Christians in the first century, through their small-group house meetings, had fellowship, Bible study, and communion service. They may also have shared an *agape* meal, although the evidence on this is not clear.

John Wesley, the founder of the Methodist church, developed the house church movement.[72] Before John Wesley, the sacraments were at the centre of the faith of the church but he wanted to practice the faith patterns of the early church of the New Testament. Wesley emphasized discipleship, small group meetings (classes), and circuit quarterly meetings. It is worth taking note of the circuit quarterly meetings. They were begun in 1748 to promote the unity and fellowship of Methodists. Wesley, or another leading preacher, was the chairman/leader of the meetings, which were attended by the class teachers and the stewards of societies. Leaders discussed the spiritual activities of preachers and financial support, while the stewards managed financial matters. Wesley wrote 'circuit plans' and posted them at the head office. According to the plans, the preachers would become circuit riders and go to the churches and class meetings in their assigned district for a certain period.

Wesley efficiently utilized the system of bands, classes, and societies and believed this type of system was taken from the early church. In their band and class meetings, they disciplined, edified, and helped one another. The class meeting was the first step to becoming a Methodist and served to form well-disciplined and sincere members, leaving out less committed ones.

Such small group meetings made a great contribution to the development of the Methodist church. The circuit rider system was successfully practised in the pioneering period of America. Asbury developed it and thus added to the growth of the American Methodist church.

---

[72] For the research on the House Church Movement, see Arthur L. Foster (ed.), *The House Church Evolving* (Chicago: Exploration, 1976); Tony Higton and Gilbert Kirby, *The Challenge of the House Churches* (Oxford: Latimer, 1988); Joyce V. Thurman, *New Wineskins: A Study of House Church Movement* (Frankfurt-am-Main: Peter Lang, 1982); and C. Kirk Hadaway, et al., *Home Cell Groups and House Churches* (Nashville, TN: Broadman, 1987).

Small group meetings also had a significant influence on the holiness revival. In the nineteenth century, they were established weekly meetings and considered important for the promotion of holiness. Phoebe Palmer began regular meetings on Tuesdays. Hence it became 'Tuesday meeting'.

Also influential were the revival meetings of Charles G. Finney, D.L. Moody, as well as the twentieth century Pentecostal movement.

Cho reorganized the structure of the small community of the early church into a cell system and made it a 'permanent revival center',[73] so members may experience fellowship, renewal and revival of faith, and engage in evangelical work. In the early stages of the cell system, there were some difficulties because of the lack of places for gathering, the position of women in society (since the majority of the cell leaders were women), and the fact that lay leaders did not have confidence in the cell system. As the problems were resolved, the cell system is considered an internationally registered mark of the YFGC. Cho recently called this 'the smallest churches in the largest church'.[74]

People learn the word of God, pray together, and practice a fruitful Christian life through cells. The nature of the cell unit system is described as follows:[75]

Five to seven families in the same neighbourhood form a cell group, where the strongest spiritual members are the leader and the assistant leader. Metropolitan Seoul is divided into 13 districts, 4 regional chapels, 17 branch churches, and 172 prayer houses. In each district or chapel, a pastor is assigned as the senior district pastor. Each district is divided into several sub-districts with sub-district pastors. Currently there are 313 sub-districts. Each sub-district has several sections with section leaders, and each section has several cell groups and leaders. As of January 2009, there are 14,888 cell units in total. Both the section leader and the cell leader are in charge of a cell group, and the section leader takes charge of one section.

About 5 cell groups form a section, 10 to 15 sections form a sub-district, and 12 to 23 sub-districts form a district. Currently the YFGC has 634 full-time pastors, who are in charge of districts and other parts of church education and administration.

With their cell group leaders, members pray together and are receptive to spiritual experience. When a cell group grows to ten families, it is divided into two units, five families for each. The assistant leader of the original cell unit becomes the leader of the new one, and each leader appoints its own assistant leader. This procedure is repeated as the size of the cell grows. The focal point of each cell is its members and his or her needs. In reality it includes not only

---

[73] Yonggi Cho, *A Secret of Church Growth* [in Korean] (Seoul: Seoul Logos, 1995), 221-42. Cho recently describe this as 'the smallest churches within the largest church'. See

[74] Yonggi Cho, *Small Group Miracle* [in Korean] (Seoul: Institute for Church Growth, 2004).

[75] Lee, 'Yoido Full Gospel Church: Its History and Structure', 3-4, 12-17.

those already registered in the church, but also those who stand on the fringe of making a decision. See Figures below.

The Schematic Representation of the Home Cell Unity System

The YFGC consists of 14,888 home cell units as of January 2009, each of which has one sectional leader or one cell group leader as its own leader. The YFGC has 755,000 members. Home cell group meetings are held once a week at each member's home by turns. They study the Bible in seven steps by themes and each step is a year-long course.[76] This study as a whole is repeated every seven years. At cell meetings, they also pray together for new members, Spirit-baptism, for healing, concerning their personal problems, etc.

This system is the driving force of the unity and fellowship of the church and its growth, following the example of the early church. The target of the YFGC's cell unit system is its members. Each level of leadership represents not the hierarchy of authority but the scope of pastoral responsibility and accountability. The main calling of a position is that of service. Each level of pastoral leadership is organically connected with other levels of pastoral work.

Seoul City has been divided into 13 districts, 4 regional chapels and 17 branch churches by the YFGC. Each district is further divided into 12 to 23 sub-districts, and each sub-district contains about 10 to 15 sections. Each section contains 5 to 15 home cell units, and each home cell unit is composed of members from 5 to 10 households.

---

[76] David Yonggi Cho, *Home Cell Group Study Guide* (vols. 1-2; in Korean; Seoul: Seoul Logos, 1990); Yonggi Cho, *Home Cell Group Study Guide* (vols. 1-7; in Korean; Seoul: Seoul Logos, 1980-1986).

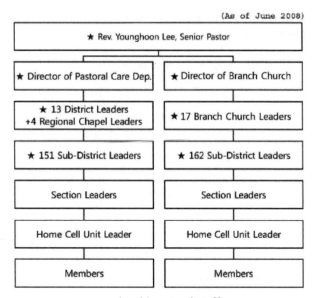

(As of June 2008)

* paid pastoral staff
The Home Cell Unit System

The Contribution of the Holy Spirit Movement of the Yoido Full Gospel Church

Leading Korean theologians and religionists published a research report on the YFGC in 1982. In the foreword of the report, Won-yong Gang pointed out, 'The Holy Spirit movement of the YFGC attracts the interest of the churches around the world, as well as the Korean churches, both positively and negatively'.[77]

I will discuss some negative and positive effects of the Holy Spirit movement of the YFGC and Yonggi Cho and their influence on the Korean church.

First, it promoted people's recognition of the personhood of the Holy Spirit. Cho's emphasis on the personhood of the Holy Spirit presents a clear guideline as to the aim of the Holy Spirit movement, lest it might run in a wrong direction. Although the Korean church recognized the Holy Spirit as the third person of the Trinity, it was almost ignorant of and uninterested in the ministry of and fellowship with the Holy Spirit. For ignoring the personhood of the Holy Spirit but acknowledging the Holy Spirit only as the power of God and mysterious power, Tae-sun Park's Olive Tree Church became the typical Korean heresy. Cho frequently declares, 'Holy Spirit, we acknowledge,

---

[77] Won-yong Kang (ed.), *A Study on the Pentecostal Movement in Korea* [in Korean] (Seoul: Korean Christian Academy, 1981), 3-4.

welcome, and trust you'.[78] This statement is one of the expressions that stresses the Holy Spirit as an existence with personhood. In his book, *Pneumatology*, Cho emphasizes that we should recognize the Holy Spirit as existence with personhood and always associate with Him in our lives.[79] Cho's Holy Spirit movement taught Christians how to minister and work with the Holy Spirit. Consequently, many of the Korean churches recognize the Holy Spirit as a distinct person of the Godhead and experience the Spirit's dynamic work.[80]

Second, it increased people's understanding of the Holy Spirit movement. The YFGC had to go through many difficulties due to the lack of understanding of the Korean church of the work of the Holy Spirit. One Presbyterian denomination in its annual general assembly of 1983 said that Cho had heretical tendencies in his theology, and ruled that its members should not have fellowship with Cho. Theological debates on this issue continued for about a decade, which caused increased, widespread knowledge of Pentecostal theology and the faith of the YFGC. The publications ITI and international seminars on the Holy Spirit, also organized by the ITI, have changed the prejudices of the Korean church about the Holy Spirit movement of the YFGC and of Cho. This has provided the ground for other denominations to understand and accept the Pentecostal theology.[81]

Third, it brought church growth. Church growth means spiritual revival rather than just an increase in numbers[82] and is crucial. It gives glory to Jesus Christ, the head of the church.[83] The YFGC is a model church with a rapid growth rate. When the YFGC was in Seodaemun (1961-1973), the membership of the church increased from 3,000 to 18,000 in 5 years. Also a tremendous revival arose after the church moved to Yoido, and it grew phenomenally, becoming the largest church in the world with a registered membership of 700,000 by 1990.[84] Cho confessed that he accomplished such church growth as he started to commune and associate with the Holy Spirit.[85] Cho has introduced the key factors of church growth in and out of Korea and has

---

[78] See Benny Hinn, *Good Morning, Holy Spirit* (Nashville, TN : Thomas Nelson, 1990) and *Welcome, Holy Spirit* (Nashville, TN : Thomas Nelson, 1995). Hinn adopts Cho's conception of the Holy Spirit.

[79] Yonggi Cho, *Pneumatology* [in Korean] (Seoul: Seoul Logos, 1998), 7, 17.

[80] Young-hoon Lee, 'Dr. Yonggi Cho's Influence on the Korean Church in Relation to His Pneumatology' [in Korean], *Journal of Youngsan Theology* 7 (August 2004), 138-39.

[81] See ITI, *Yoido Full Gospel Church*, 142–205.

[82] Donald A. McGavran, *How Churches Grow* (New York: Friendship Press, 1959), 99.

[83] R.B. Kuyper, *Evangelical Theology* (trans. Su-joon Park; in Korean; Seoul: Hope, 1980), 113.

[84] Y. Lee, 'Dr. Yonggi Cho's Influence on the Korean Church', 140.

[85] Yonggi Cho, Do You Really Want Your Church to Grow? [in Korean] (Seoul: Seoul Logos, 1995), 250-56.

challenged churches by publishing books and lecturing at meetings and seminars.

Fourth, it renewed the thoughts of the people. Cho's sermons are positive and active. Robert Schuller has said that positive thought is just another expression of the faith that Jesus spoke of.[86] Cho presents a positive, active faith to his people and encourages them to practice it daily. This reformed thought has brought changes in many lives.[87] Christians with renewed minds have contributed to the development of society as the country was going through rapid changes in its political and economic aspects.

Fifth, it contributed to the indigenization of the Christian gospel in Korea. Indigenization is a process whereby Christianity adapts itself to the culture of a people for greater acceptance. Each country or nation has its own cultural background and traditions.[88] Indigenization combines the harmonious growth of a native culture in the light of the gospel and Christian principles, into a new Christian unity.[89] Cho, with his belief in a good and sovereign God, presented fresh hope to despairing people. He proclaimed God as the One who solves *han* in the present and declared a future life.[90] Balanced spiritual experience, the prayer movement, the cell structure, and lay activities have made it possible for the Holy Spirit movement of the YFGC to take root in Korean culture.[91]

Summary

The Pentecostal movement as led by Cho, often called the Full Gospel movement, may be positively evaluated in connection with the indigenization of the Holy Spirit movement in Korea. His message has brought hope and joy to the poor and oppressed. Speaking in tongues has contributed greatly to release the *han* in them. By appointing women leaders in the cell-unit system, Cho has acknowledged their capability and thus raised the position of women in society. He has also brought spiritual renewal while most churches have been institutionalized.

This Holy Spirit movement may be viewed as a synthesis of the various Holy Spirit movements of Korean church history. Cho's emphasis on prayer and the second coming of Jesus Christ follows the tradition of Sun-joo Gil's

---

[86] Robert H. Schuller, *Your Church Has a Fantastic Future* (Ventura: Regal, 1986), 76.

[87] Sung-hoon Myung, *Church Growth and Sermons* [in Korean] (Seoul: Seoul Books, 1992), 70-71.

[88] 'Tochakhwa' [indigenization], in Young-je Han (ed.) *One-Volume Christian Encyclopedia* [in Korean] (Seoul, Christian Literature, 1992), 1446.

[89] Bong-bae Park, 'The Indigenization of Christianity in Korea' [in Korean], *Christian Thoughts* (Jan. 1971), 81.

[90] ITI, *The Influence of the Pentecostal Movement on the Korean Church* [in Korean] (Seoul: ITI, 1993), 69.

[91] ITI, *The Influence of the Pentecostal Movement*, 52.

Holy Spirit movement; his emphasis on mystical experience through the cross is in line with Yong-do Lee's Holy Spirit movement; and his emphasis on healing was also noted in Ik-doo Kim's Holy Spirit movement. Cho's Holy Spirit movement has made the most of the shamanistic background of Koreans to bring rapid church growth. He avoids syncretistic shamanism by adhering to the principles of the Bible.

The Yoido Full Gospel Church and Cho have grown steadily in their fifty years' history. During this time the YFGC has been well organized. Harvey Cox points out that order, authority and responsibility should be emphasized in order to continue growth in an organization. However, this brings with it the danger of lessening spirituality, as he warns.[92] Furthermore, Cox suggests that the Korean church may lose its power of ethical critique against Korean society if it takes too much interest in organization.[93] This presents a critical task for Pentecostals: how to balance the work of the Holy Spirit and the operation of organizations.

It is possible to maintain balance only when quantitative growth is accompanied by qualitative judgment. This means that the YFGC must broaden its interests to include wider social concerns and social reforms. Previous Holy Spirit movements have been more concerned with personal salvation and church growth, and the YFGC will have to make a critical choice for its own future.

The Pentecostal Movement and Shamanism

Many scholars view the explosive growth of the Korean church, especially the Pentecostal churches to be the result of shamanistic influences. Some even make the criticism that the pastors of the Pentecostal churches have the same function as shamans.[94]

Shamanism has been handed down in the 5,000 years of Korean history and it has critically influenced Buddhism and Confucianism to produce the Buddhist and Confucian ceremonies that have shamanistic aspects. It has also influenced Christianity—both directly and indirectly. Many Christian scholars continue to engage in research on this subject.

What is interesting is that many outstanding scholars, especially foreign ones, discuss the enormous influence of shamanism on Korean Christianity in relation to the growth of the Pentecostal churches of Korea. Mark Mullins has said that although Pentecostal church leaders would deny the influence of 'pagan religion', many scholars agree that shamanism has been the central

---

[92] Cox, *Fire from Heaven*, 236–37.

[93] Cox, *Fire from Heaven*, 237.

[94] Boo-woong Yoo, 'Response to Korean Shamanism by the Pentecostal Church', *International Review of Mission* 75 (Jan. 1986), 70–74.

force shaping the development of Korean Pentecostalism.[95] Harvey Cox deals with the Pentecostal movement of the Korean church in the eleventh chapter of his book *Fire from Heaven* and its relation with shamanism. He speaks positively of the influence of shamanism on the Korean Pentecostal movement and answers affirmatively to the question of whether there can be a Christian shamanism.[96] Speaking of shamanism and Christianity in Korea, Cox states that he had difficulties in understanding the Korean church, for he had used cassette tapes and material written in English only when he wrote *Fire from Heaven*, without ever going to Korea.[97]

In 1982 several Korean scholars published *A Study of the Pentecostal Movement in Korea* as a joint research project.[98] Gwang-il Kim, a medical doctor and professor of Hanyang University, employed a psychological approach to Christian healing while Gwang-sun Suh, a Christian scholar and professor of the Department of Christian Studies at Ewha Women's University, used a theological approach in his study of exorcism. They concluded that the Korean Pentecostal churches were greatly influenced by shamanism.

Gwang-il Kim took Gi-dong Kim and the Sungnak Baptist Church as an example. The church is well-known for its unique forays into demonology and he claimed that Gi-dong Kim's exorcisms were exactly the same as that of *gut* (a ritual ceremony of shamanism). There are three steps in the ceremony of *gut*: demon calling, demon treating, and casting out demons. Gi-dong Kim's case eliminates the second step of treating the demon. Kim calls out the demon by saying, 'Who are you?' and then shouts 'Come out' and casts it out. The names of the demons, without exception, are exactly the same as those in shamanistic society.[99] So is the nature of the demons in that they are the spirits of those who died unfairly; they are real beings with personalities; and they enter and possess human bodies and cause diseases. Some say that only Kim and his best disciples can cast out demons and this coincides with the concept of the shamanistic world in which only the most powerful shamans can cast out demons. In regard to the methods of exorcism, they are the same: Kim yells, 'You, demon, go away', and shamans yell, 'You, demon, eat this and go away'. The only difference between them is that Kim eliminates some symbolic procedures. Ok-gil Oh of the Martyrdom Gospel Center, according to Gwang-il

---

[95] Mark Mullins, 'The Empire Strikes Back: Korean Pentecostal Mission to Japan', in Karla Poewe (ed.) *Charismatic Christianity as a Gospel Culture* (Columbia, SC: University of South Carolina, 1994), 92.

[96] Cox, *Fire from Heaven*, 228.

[97] Cox said this in the foreword of the Korean translation of his book. Harvey Cox, *Fire from Heaven* (trans. Ji-hwang You; in Korean; Seoul: Dongyun, 1996), 5–7.

[98] David Gwang-sun Suh, et al. *A Study on the Pentecostal Movement in Korea* [in Korean] (Seoul: Korea Christian Academy, 1982).

[99] Gwang-il Kim, 'Psycho-Medical Research on Christian Healing', in *A Study on the Pentecostal Movement in Korea*, 267.

Kim, takes all of the three steps of calling, conversing, and casting out demons. Oh's case is not different from the *gut* ceremony.[100]

One thing that should be mentioned here is the fact that Gi-dong Kim and Ok-gil Oh are not recognized by the majority of Korean Christians. Gi-dong Kim was judged to have doctrines with 'heretical tendencies' by the Baptist Church for his demonology that has no biblical basis. Kim asserts that, when a person dies short of the full span of life, he or she becomes a demon and wanders around until it finds a place to stay in a human body.[101] Kim was condemned by Baptists and expelled from the denomination. The Presbyterian and Methodist churches have also judged Kim 'heretical' and have no co-operative work with him. Kim's demonology remains a controversial issue. His church places primary concern on exorcism, which attracts a great number of people to his church. This shows certainly the shamanistic influence. The success of such exorcism is the result partly of the Korean church's disinterest in such things and that it has either failed in theological research or in providing correct doctrinal guidelines.

There has been much discussion of Christian healing in relation to exorcism. Is healing Christian or shamanistic or a mixture of the two? Divine healing, as well as baptism in the Holy Spirit, is one of the principal doctrines of the Pentecostal movement. Gwang-il Kim states that the Christian healing ministry has positive effects as it works as an anxiety-relieving system to hopeless patients and helps in the work of Christian evangelization.[102]

Yonggi Cho of the YFGC follows the tradition of Pentecostalism and prays for divine healing at every service after delivering a sermon. He sometimes calls out the kind of disease and announces its healing. He stresses that healing was one of the major public ministries of Jesus. He also asserts that Jesus solved the problems of sins, physical diseases, and curses of one's life circumstances when He said, 'It is finished', on the cross. Based on this belief, when Cho prays for the divine healing he emphatically quotes Isaiah 53, 'With his stripes, we are healed' (KJV). His healing ministry played an important role in the YFGC's becoming the world's largest church.[103]

We find in the history of the Korean church that the healing ministry of Ik-doo Kim, a Presbyterian minister under the Japanese occupation, was an integral part of his ministry. The healing ministry has been rather ignored in Korean churches since the Olive Tree Church of Tae-sun Park was condemned as heretical and expelled from the Presbyterian Church Council. The reason is that Park had caused serious problems by faking healing and thus turned the mind of Korean church leaders away from such supernatural phenomena. Nonetheless, the poor who were still under shamanistic influence longed for

---

[100] Kim, 'Psycho-Medical Research', 268.
[101] ITI, *When the Holy Spirit Comes Upon You*, 155.
[102] Kim, 'Psycho-Medical Research', 191–92.
[103] ITI, *When the Holy Spirit Comes*, 145–46.

healing. It was then that the YFGC emerged and placed stress on divine healing. People rushed to the YFGC and made the church grow rapidly. The general problem of the healing ministry lies in people's shamanistic tendency, seeking healing rather indiscreetly. In fact, Cho tries to watch out for the influence of shamanism on this ministry and stresses that healing is biblical and is a duty of Christian churches. However, many people are not interested whether healing is biblical or not—they are only concerned about healing itself. Therefore, it remains a major task for Pentecostal churches to guide and educate these people correctly.[104]

The next problem of Pentecostalism in regard to the shamanistic influence is its doctrine of prosperity.[105] Yonggi Cho emphasizes 3 John 2 and speaks of the threefold blessing. In other words, he claims that, if the spirit goes well, a Christian will get along well in every way and will enjoy health and prosperity. Dong-sik Ryu warns that this claim, if misused, is likely to lead people to focus only on material blessing in the present life and healing from diseases. According to Ryu, this claim may not be freed from a shamanistic structure.[106] In fact this problem has been a burning issue in America where the Pentecostal movement of the twentieth century was born. Conservative scholars with a Puritan background strongly oppose the 'prosperity theology' that some of the Pentecostals emphasize. We find a typical example of the problem of misinterpreting prosperity theology in the Jim Bakker case.[107] Bakker used to overemphasize material property but, ironically, this was one of the causes of his downfall. The downfall of Jim Bakker's ministry shocked America.

Cho responded to the situation in an interview saying that he was sick of hearing testimonies such as, 'I am very lucky to find a good job after giving a big offering to the Lord' or 'I am blessed that I now receive a higher salary than before in return for my offering'. He said that this attitude cheapens the grace of God by treating it as an object for commercial transaction.[108]

Yonggi Cho tries to overcome this weakness by becoming involved in social concerns. He supports and trains the poor and underprivileged by building a welfare town for them, encourages blood donation, offers free cardiac operations to children with congenital heart diseases, and sends relief funds to

---

[104] The YFGC offers various levels of Bible study classes to resolve these problems and urges its members to read through the Bible once a year. The YFGC published *One Year Reading Bible* [in Korean] as a guide and help for reading through the Bible.

[105] See Young-hoon Lee, 'Biblical Teachings on Prosperity Theology' (A paper presented at the World Evangelical Fellowship Theological Commission Conference, Seoul, Korea, 1995). See also *Evangelical Review of Theology* 20 (Jan. 1996).

[106] Ryu, 'Korean Church and the Holy Spirit Movement', 20.

[107] Jim Bakker is a former Pentecostal television evangelist who was disgraced by scandals involving the embezzlement of funds and other charges.

[108] 'Cho's Problem with Prosperity', *Chrisma & Christian Life*, March 1988, 70.

the third world.[109] As stated earlier, the Minjung theology movement also is concerned about the poor and the oppressed. However, the social activities of the Minjung movement and the YFGC are quite different. The former focuses on social participation and the reform of society like the liberation movement, while the YFGC is more concerned about charity and the direct relief for the poor.

How to overcome the negative influence of shamanism is an important task of the Holy Spirit movement.

The Pentecostal Movement and Social Engagement

As the churches obtained a degree of growth and influence in society, there was a growing expectation for the churches to take an active step toward social needs and issues. This was particularly evident toward the large churches such as the YFGC. It is true that a local church itself had been a social network providing a safety net for the socially marginalised. For example, the Korean church had long practised what is called 'love rice' (or *sungmi*). When cooking any meal, most Christian women set aside a small amount of rice for those who were needy. Once a week, the rice was brought to the church for the use of the needy within the church as well as for the local community.

This section looks at the YFGC's ministry of social service, as the best representation of the Holy Spirit movement in Korea. The opening of the Elim Welfare Town (1986) by the YFGC was hailed as a ground-breaking step toward social care. The Town was another example of a partnership between the church and the local government. The facility has provided skills training for the youth. The ministry soon expanded to the establishment of the Elim Welfare Association in the same year to provide a shelter and nursing facility for the elderly without children. Later the church added the Canaan Silver Town and the feeding programme for the elderly in 1994. The church's social care ministry included their attention to the physically and mentally handicapped. The church started programmes like the 'Class of Love' (1987) and rehabilitation facilities such as 'House of Hope'. Also significant is a continuing campaign to assist children with heart diseases. The programme which began in 1984 has so far assisted more than four thousand surgeries. Disaster relief has become a regular part of its social ministry, such as the care for flood victims.

The publication of the *Kukmin Ilbo*, a Christian daily newspaper, in 1987 was viewed not only as a courageous but also as a risky enterprise. Financial resources to sustain such an operation have been borne by the church until now, and this demonstrates a role for mega-churches in society. Considering the

---

[109] At a plenary session of the Second World Assemblies of God Congress in September 1995 held in Jerusalem, Cho emphasized that 'the work of the fullness of the Holy Spirit is to participate in the suffering of the cross'.

powerful influence of the mass media in modern life, the newspaper has brought Christian opinions and influences into mainstream society.

The church, like the rest of the country, participated in the nation's effort to counter the deep economic recession during the Asian economic crisis. Not only instituting a series of prayer programmes, the church also began an austerity campaign. The church ground became a recycling centre as members diligently brought recyclable items to the church. The proceeds were donated to the needy, particularly those who had lost their jobs, in the long tradition of 'love rice'. This neighbour-care movement also includes many rural churches which struggled to maintain its pastors and ministries. Large urban churches took note of this difficulty and extended their assistance to many struggling churches. Also noted is the church's participation in the nation-wide campaign to collect gold. When the economic crisis hit the nation, the national economy badly needed short-term international loans, and the entire system came under the supervision of the International Monetary Fund (IMF). Koreans remember this as an 'IMF crisis'. As the country struggled to service its mounting debt with its hopelessly devalued currency, in 1997 the government pleaded to the nation to donate or sell their gold to the government. Gold became an important new currency to service the debt, as the price of gold in Korea was not as seriously affected by devaluation as the national currency. The YFGC ran a large-scale campaign as part of its 'prayer' for the nation. As the result of such a nation-wide participation, coupled with the restructuring of the financial and business sectors, Korea was able to 'graduate' under the IMF supervision earlier than predicted.

Summary of the Period

This period marks a significant change for Korean Christians in general and Pentecostals in particular. Korean Christians with their active social engagement, particularly in view of other traditional religions such as Buddhism, have changed the role of Christianity (and of religion for that matter) from the private to the public arena. This is first of all attributed to the phenomenal numerical growth of Christians, in which the Pentecostal churches took the lead, including the founding of the mega-church movement. However, this also resulted in criticisms from society, as the churches were expected to provide higher moral standards and social services. This led the Korean churches to pay attention to care ministries, where the YFGC's feat epitomized this change. At the same time, the slowing of church growth has compelled Korean Christianity to rethink its reason for existence in society. It is true that the churches continued to try hard to recover the old days of explosive growth, but it appears also evident that, owing to the changing social milieu, the church would need to discover a new meaning and role within society and the global scene.

This was also an important maturing period for the Pentecostal-charismatic communities in Korea. Now widespread across the denominational and confessional boundaries, the Pentecostal churches faced a serious social challenge. Coupled with growing economic affluence, the traditional emphasis on the theology of blessing did not have as strong appeal to the newer generation as it once to the older generation who had gone through poverty and colonial oppression. This challenging context was particularly felt in the theological world. The simple replication of Western originated theological thinking will not serve the unique socio-cultural needs which are changing rapidly. The struggle of the church, from explosive growth to stagnation in less than a generation requires a serious engagement of theological minds in service of the church. The Pentecostal movement should be encouraged to pay additional attention to the socio-cultural context.

In the same period, the growth of the Korean church began to attract international attention, especially among mission scholars. The YFGC was often featured as a shining example of the missionary work of the Western church. The church growth movement also paid much attention to the mega-church movement. Naturally the YFGC and Yonggi Cho were often viewed as the epitome of church growth and mission studies. Cho's extensive worldwide evangelistic ministry has led his church and the Korean Pentecostals to a global vision. The new missionary movement among Korean Christians also added an international dimension to their Christian life.

Although the chapter highlights a single congregation, the YFGC, this does not imply that all Pentecostal churches were mega- or large churches. There are many struggling small congregations in urban centres as well as rural areas throughout the country. Their members also came from struggling social classes. Nonetheless, the general theological trends of these churches were not significantly different from the YFGC's. In fact, emphases on healing, the supernatural intervention of God for daily human needs, and the goodness of God were found in most churches, including "Pentecostalised" mainline and evangelical churches. While this widespread Pentecostal type of worship and theology is commendable, the Pentecostals are called to continue their cutting-edge spiritual leadership in the coming years.

Chapter 8

The Sixth Period (2000–)

Social Context

Inter-Korean Relations

As in many parts of the world, the beginning of the third millennium saw many changes in Korea. On the national scene, the beginning of the millennium marked a rapid development in South-North Korean relations. After the Cold War era Korea has remained as the only divided nation that is still in a state of military conflict. The election of president Dae-jung Kim, a long-time opponent of the military rule in the 1960s and 1970s, marked a radically new era for the two-Koreas relationship. Some of his predecessors often used the military and political tension between the demilitarized zone (DMZ) which divides the Korean Peninsular into two, as a pretext for dictatorial leadership. Kim's 'Sunshine Policy' toward North Korea during his term (1998-2003) brought a steady stream of contacts and exchanges, not only on the governmental level, but more so in the non-governmental sectors. This frequent exchange resulted in the opening of the famous Keumkang Mountain to South Korean tourists. More importantly, the reunion meetings of families separated for more than half a century stirred the nation's emotions. Before his term ended, Kim made a historic state visit to North Korea for a summit, for which he won the Nobel Peace Prize with his North Korean counterpart Jung-il Kim. This open-door policy was succeeded by the next president Moo-hyun Roh (2003-2008). He also ended his term with a state visit to North Korea. During his term, a railroad was reconnected across the DMZ, and a daily freight train now operates between Seoul and Gaesung, a North Korean city where South Korea has developed an industrial complex. At the same time, a steadily increasing number of North Korean defectors have arrived in South Korea, creating a new challenge for South Korean society. Internally what has become quite evident is a large ideological divide between the older generation that experienced the Korean War, the Vietnam War and an anti-communist orientation, and the younger one that does not know such struggles. The divide is further deepened by their different social and economic orientations: post-war poverty contrasts with a relatively prosperous economy in latter-day South Korea. Any naïve approach to the issue of national reunification has proven to be far from the reality of ideological divisions. Difficulties surrounding the six-party talks for nuclear disarmament are just one example, and so are recent tensions across the border since the inauguration of a conservative government after the ten-year governments which supported what is called the 'Sunshine Policy'.

In several ways, the church in South Korea has been affected by and responded to this rapid social change after five decades of total hostility. The first is the church's role in facilitating the ideological shift at the social level. The government initiated various media campaigns to revise the entire country's attitude toward North Koreans, from the arch-enemies to 'brothers and sisters'. The church is the best agent to bring about this change, as love is its cardinal teaching: not only of neighbours but also of enemies. The second is its active participation in inter-Korean exchanges. In the wake of North Korea's chronic starvation, along with the governmental agencies and business communities, churches provided substantial humanitarian aid. The third is the care for North Korean defectors, specifically helping them to be assimilated into South Korean society. Again, the church is the best qualified social network to provide such vital assistance.

In this discussion, our attention will be focused on the YFGC as the representative of the Pentecostal movement in Korea. It is noteworthy that Pentecostal-type of worship and preaching has become more common in the new millennium, especially as the entire Korean church pays much attention to the celebration of the centennial of the Pyongyang Great Revival in 2007. The emphasis on spiritual gifts, terminologies such as 'baptism in the Holy Spirit', 'prayer for healing' and the like have become household names for Christians regardless of their denominational affiliations. People observe that some traditional, and, therefore, non-Pentecostal churches have become more 'Pentecostal' in worship and preaching, while some Pentecostal churches have adopted a more traditional form of worship.

The Church's Social Responsibility

In the beginning of the new millennium, the church faced new challenges. First, the acclaimed church growth from the 1970s began to even out in the early 1990s, and its stagnation has continued since then. This disappointing phenomenon has much to do with the economic development of the country. The most appealing message from Cho was God's power to undo the curses which human sins brought into the world. Therefore, "salvation" through the work of Christ extends to every aspect of life, including physical and material well-being. His message of healing and material blessing had such a powerful appeal to those who struggled for their daily existence. The relative economic prosperity of the nation simply reduced the "demand" of such uplifting power, and it was generally felt in every church. In another way, this 'church slowth' has manifold implications for Pentecostal churches, especially for those in the

YFGC's network that had been the main powerhouse for church growth. Under Cho's leadership, more than a dozen large churches were born in the last quarter of the twentieth century, while a massive church planting programme was initiated by Cho in the late 1990s. While the churches struggle to revive their growth momentum, two things have been observed: the surprising growth of the Roman Catholic Church and the explosive growth of overseas mission activities. The growth of the Catholic Church is largely attributed to their focus on social services.

Second, unlike the previous decades, the presence and impact of Christianity in South Korea has been felt throughout society. The strict "privatization" of religious matters is no longer the norm. Several public media systems were established by religious entities, such as TV, radio and newspapers. The appearance of the *Kukmin Daily Newspaper* by the YFGC was the most visible demonstration of such a development. It was followed by another daily paper by the Unification Church, but its religious ownership has been rather concealed. Also the public role of religion was felt in high-ranking government posts, such as the presidency. In major social sectors such as the government, the military, education, business, the arts and culture, the proportion of Christian leaders is higher than the average for the nation. The recent election of a Christian president in 2008 with a large measure of support from Christian communities demonstrated the increasing Christian influence in society.

At the same time, religious matters began to receive secular media attention that was often extremely critical in their coverage. This is an indication of the increasing social impact of religion, and also the public's general expectation of the religious groups to provide moral guidance. In a secular TV station, some comedy programmes cynically feature a mega-church pastor. With the growing social consciousness toward the socially marginalized, religious groups are expected to be more than self-serving. The prime target has been the mega-size churches and their leaders, which have embraced Pentecostal and charismatic forms of church life and leadership.[1] The common allegation has been against the churches' self-serving attitude, their moral and financial abnormalities, and the hereditary leadership succession of several large churches. A criminal charge against a mega-church pastor epitomized this public scrutiny.

With this increasing social pressure, coupled with the stagnation of the church's growth, Christians pay heed to several potential solutions. One is the inner renewal of the church. With the centennial celebration of the 1907 Pyongyang Revival, the nation's Christian community joined together to mark the centenary, and committed itself in prayer to work for the renewal of the

---

[1] Young-gi Hong, 'Social Leadership and Church Growth', in Wonsuk Ma, et al. (eds.), *David Yonggi Cho: A Close Look at His Theology and Ministry* (Baguio, Philippines: APTS Press, 2004), 221-51.

church. Its theme of 'Transformation' epitomizes this desire. The other is an active social service and engagement, a trend that began in the previous period. Churches are now providing a substantial amount of social assistance: from feeding centres and medical assistance to the poor, to reconciliation initiatives among Christians and across the DMZ. Also a recent addition is the emphasis on environmental responsibility.

Globalisation of Christian Mission

The steady growth of mission awareness and engagement among the churches in the global south has been noted by mission observers both in the West and the rest of the world. Among such emerging mission forces in the non-western world is the Korean church. It is important to acknowledge that the Pentecostals are not always in the forefront of mission leadership whether in terms of numbers or historical chronology. However, there are two specific areas where a distinct Pentecostal contribution to the mission movement can be justified. Firstly, regardless of theological and ecclesiastical affiliations, the Korean church in general has at the least been open to, or more appropriately has adopted, Pentecostal-charismatic aspects of Christian life and experience. The majority of Korean field missionaries, for example, regularly pray for divine healing without much hesitation, although not everyone would pray for baptism in the Spirit with speaking in tongues as a sign. Secondly, although not much known outside the Yoido church circle, David Yonggi Cho has epitomized Korean mission engagement through his massive evangelistic crusades not only in traditional 'mission fields' such as Asia, Africa, Latin America and Eastern Europe, but also in 'mission centres' such as Europe and North America. To date, Cho is the only Korean who has realised the mission potential of the Korean church in the international arena. Although some others have followed his example, they are limited to one or two locations, e.g. Japan and China. This shows not only the unprecedented success of Cho, but also his vision and confidence in the missionary call of the Korean church.

Just as the Korean church in general, the Pentecostal church has arrived at a point where its missionary success is seriously tested especially on several issues: the rethinking of missionary engagement and global mission leadership. In missionary engagement, the Korean church in general has narrowly focused its missionary efforts on evangelism and church planting. Theological education and social service such as relief efforts are all means to support this evangelism-church planting mode of mission. However, in several important ways, the Korean Pentecostals, especially the YFGC, has consistently expanded its mission scope to include social engagement as a valid mission operation. This move aligns with the spirit of the Lausanne Covenant,[2] which defines evangelism and social service as two partners of mission. However, Pentecostals are called to do more than providing care for victims: they are to deeply engage with social structures and systems which often cause evil and suffering.[3] How Pentecostals will develop their holistic mission theology and praxis will be a critical contribution to the global mission world.

In the area of global mission leadership, the timing cannot be more critical than now. With close to 20,000 cross-cultural mission workers, the Korean church is the second largest missionary-sending body, having overtaken the United Kingdom some time ago. The new century Christian mission is predicted to see emerging mission forces from the global south, and the Korean church has been charged with providing critical leadership for the new missionary era. Timing cannot be more critical as the world is to celebrate the centenary of the watershed Edinburgh Missionary Conference of 1910. Some of its published documents call for humility from the western church for its unhealthy attitude toward mission and the mission field while urging it to go forward with hope with the new strongly emerging mission players.[4] As in the 1910 conference, the centenary plans to produce another set of mission documents which will guide the next generations of Christian missions. How to encourage new mission voices from the emerging mission church in the global south will take not only the mindful consideration of the organizers but also the active championing of the emerging churches. The Lausanne movement also expects new global mission partners to play a critical leadership role at its third international congress in Cape Town, South Africa in 2010. This outcry for global mission leadership from the emerging mission churches like the Korean church reflects the radical change in mission thinking, in its paradigms and engagements. Considering that global mission discussions are still heavily influenced and led by the western church, this is where global mission leadership is essential from the global south and the Korean church has raised such expectations in the world church. It will, however, take more than an impressive number of mission workers for it requires a credible and competent group of mission leaders. For this reason, the efforts of new Pentecostal leaders in Korea are encouraging. One example will be the International Symposium on Global Christianity in 2009 where the role of the 'Southern Church' in global Christianity is to be explored. There is already a strong desire for such a

---

[2] The document is found in various places, e.g. the website of the Lausanne Committee for World Evangelization, 'The Lausanne Covenant' (http://www.lausanne.org/lausanne-1974/lausanne-covenant.html).
[3] Wonsuk Ma, 'The Third Ripple: Deeper and Wider Mission Engagement', *Lausanne World Pulse*, www.lausanneworldpulse.com/themedarticles.php/926: April 4, 2008.
[4] Kenneth R. Ross, 'Towards 2010', *International Review of Mission* 95 (Jan-Apr 2006), 376-377.

forum to be an annual event to encourage the world church to redefine the role of the emerging churches. The Pentecostal church in Korea has this leadership mandate not only for the sake of the Korean church, but also for the explosively expanding Pentecostal-charismatic type of churches in the South.

Emerging Pentecostal Trends

As the largest single congregation in the country as well as in the world, the YFGC developed numerous programmes to address the emerging issues in society. Although social care and service began in the 1990s, there has been a drastic change in its attitude toward social needs and issues. This does not mean that the traditional spiritual emphasis was abandoned: in fact, from year 2000, a concerted effort was made to establish new churches throughout the country. Out of the goal of 500 new churches, 280 have been established by early 2008.

Social Engagement

Cho and the YFGC have had been deeply involved in a social service ministry as an important part of the church's programme, particularly from the 1990s. However, the beliefs and ethos of Pentecostalism have provided a unique social uplift. D. Martin's sociological analysis of Latin American Pentecostalism demonstrated the empowering impact of Pentecostals that results in upward social mobility.[5] Cho's message of a 'good God' has produced a similar upward social movement. He appointed thousands of lay women to head their home groups, and this contributed significantly to the improvement of women's role in the traditionally male dominant society. Care of the needy through its extensive cell network has been a hallmark of the church.

The new period has seen more intentional efforts to strengthen the church's role and responsibility in society. To systematically co-ordinate such efforts, and also to avoid overt religious identity, the 'Good People' a non-governmental organization (NGO) was established in 1999. The activities of the Good People in its less than a decade's history are impressive. Some of

---

[5] For Cho's theology of 'good God', see Rodrigo D. Tano, 'Dr. Yonggi Cho's Theology of Good God' (I, 17-30); Donald W. Dayton, 'The "Good God" and the "Theology of Blessing" in the Thought of David Yonggi Cho' (I, 31-56); Young-hoon Lee, 'Influence of Dr. Cho's "God is so good-faith" in the Korean Churches' (I, 57-80); Yeol-soo Eim, 'The Influence of Dr. Cho's Goodness of God Theology upon His Ministry' (I, 81-104), all in Youngsan Theological Institute (ed.), *Dr. Yonggi Cho's Ministry and Theology* (Goonpo, Korea: Hansei University Logos, 2008). For the Latin American case of Pentecostal social upward mobility, see David Martin, *Tongues of Fire: The Explosion of Pentecostalism in Latin America* (Oxford: Blackwell, 1990).

their highlights include: a hospice ministry among terminal cancer patients (from 2001); relief activities for flood victims in Pajoo and Gosung (1999, 2003); feeding programmes for school children; care for the homeless through feeding (twice per week for an average of 500 each time) and medical service (monthly); the establishment of a Good People's Home as a shelter and recreation facility for the homeless; the establishment and management of the Silver Center for the elderly; a heart surgery programme for young patients; a Habitat-like programme to supply low cost housing for the poor; a cataract surgery programme for the poor and many others. The international activities of the Good People include: three refugee centres; a tuberculosis programme in the Philippines and many countries; a livelihood project (Philippines); the establishment and management of orphanages and vocational schools (Sri Lanka); the opening of a vocational school for textile workers (Bangladesh); an elementary school ministry (Indonesia); the opening of a computer centre for a youth vocational school (Vietnam); a medical ministry (Afghanistan); the establishment of a child care centre (Vietnam); a potable water project (Vietnam); and a cataract surgery programme in many countries. Equally significant is the construction and management of a Christian correctional institution (prison) under the auspices of the Christian Council of Korea (CCK). However, the church's social engagement goes beyond care for the needy. Deeper engagement should include human rights issues and structural evils. For this reason, the YFGC's active involvement in some human rights issues, such as those of foreign immigrant workers, is noteworthy.

In fact, Cho publicly announced that he would commit himself to social service ministry after his formal retirement in 2008. To facilitate his concentrated social service, a charity body called the Foundation of Sharing Love and Happiness has been registered in 2008. According to him, sharing love and happiness is the spirit of the early church. He is going to provide leadership over this new ministry as president, extending God's grace not only to fellow humans but also to the environment.

Leadership Succession

As much as the rise of mega-churches was hailed as a symbol of the most visible sign of Korean church growth, challenges they pose to society have been of great concern to observers. When several mega-churches began their well-laid plans of hereditary succession, its ethical propriety has become a serious question not only within Christian circles but also in society. With the YFGC as the largest church in the country, and with Cho reaching his near-retirement point, much attention has been given to the issue of succession. The charismatic style of Cho's leadership made succession an extremely difficult question.[6]

From 2005, in a series of interviews and statements, Cho publicly announced his retirement in 2008. He also declared that the process would be open for a wider input. In 2006, his successor was elected in the elders' council through a secret ballot. Cho, who did not participate in the process so as not to influence the outcome, expressed his full support for the newly elected candidate. The formal retirement of Cho, and the installation of Young-hoon Lee took place in May 2008. This process of succession has been widely acclaimed by the public, both Christian and secular. Many expect that this has drastically improved the general perception of the public toward mega-churches, and will influence successions of other large and mega-churches in Korea. As a side effect, it is also responsible for a shift in existing views: a large church does not necessarily require a charismatic type of leadership. For this reason, the successful transition of the succession process will have major implications for Korean Christianity.

Reconciliation and Christian Unity

National Reconciliation

The close connection between patriotism and Christianity has been a long tradition as Korean Christianity grew in its formative stage under the harsh colonial rule of the Japanese. The church was the breeding ground for independent movements, while providing an education space for Korean culture and language, when the use of the Korean language was forbidden by the colonial authorities. This link continued during the inter-Korean conflicts. The new development in the inter-Korean relations has been understood within this large context, and it called for the YFGC to actively participate in this process of national reconciliation. The first response was to pray for national unity and reconciliation, and to participate in the humanitarian assistance

 programme of the Christian Council of Korea. The CCK also began a campaign to restore churches in North Korea that had been destroyed or closed down. Providing assistance to North Korean defectors to settle in South Korean society has been another programme under the auspices of the CCK. This includes the orientation process for the

---

[6] See Hong, 'The Backgrounds and Characteristics of the Charismatic Mega-Churches', 117.

North Korean settlers in South Korea through the Free Citizen's College.

This indirect participation soon grew into a direct ministry of the YFGC. The projects include the opening of a soya bean processing factory in 2005 to produce soya oil and soya power. To counter the chronic food shortage of North Korea, the 'Bread of Love' campaign was set up in the YFGC to donate food to the needy. The church also opened a hospital in north China close to the North Korean border, while assisting 50 eye surgeries in Yenben, the major city of northern China where the Korean-Chinese population is concentrated. This medical assistance underwent a major development in 2007 with the construction of Choyonggi Cardiac Hospital in Pyongyang (photo: an artist's rendering). Cho made a visit to commence the construction of the facility in the same year.

Church Unity

Ecumenical initiatives of the YFGC and Cho should be understood in the same light of 'reconciliation'. It is demonstrated in two specific areas: unity from within and unity without. Over the last three decades in the twentieth century, the Korean Assemblies of God was split into four groups. The major schism in 1981 resulted in the division between the (Seodaemun) Korean Assemblies of God, the major group, and the (Banpo) Korean Assemblies of God. The latter further split into two: the (Banpo) Korean Assemblies of God and the (Jesus) Assemblies of God in 1985. The (Jesus) Assemblies of God was initially headed by Young-mok Cho, Cho's younger brother. After a series of attempts two large groups (the Seodaemun group and the Jesus Assemblies of God group) agreed to bring both divided bodies together in October 2007. During this process, many churches of the other two smaller groups joined the merger, so accomplishing an unprecedented church unity.

Equally important is the YFGC's role in inter-denominational programmes. As Cho encouraged the Korean Assemblies of God, to which the YFGC belonged, to become a member of the National Council of Churches in Korea (NCCK) in July 1996, in addition to its membership with the CCK, an evangelical national body, the YFGC's influence has been greatly enhanced. The church's participation in the CCK's social care programmes and the NCCK's human rights projects are some examples.

Also significant is the YFGC's international ecumenical contribution. The first is the international ministry of David Yonggi Cho. He has been conducting evangelistic crusades in many countries from 1964, and all the crusades have always been inter-denominational. His crusades have drawn churches from different confessions and traditions together to reach the nation with the Christian message. In a more intentional way, the church has played an important role in ecumenical activities at the international level. In several international ecumenical dialogues, representatives of the YFGC participated. One example was the hosting of the ecumenical dialogue between the World Alliance of Reformed Churches and Classical Pentecostals in May 1999. The fourth meeting of this annual ecumenical dialogue was held at the church's ultra-modern communication centre enjoying the hospitality of the church. Around the year's theme 'The Holy Spirit, Charisma and the Kingdom of God', ten theologians from each side engaged in a profound dialogue over the presented papers to identify the convergences and differences between the two traditions. The hosting of this week-long intensive programme testified to the ecumenical commitment of the church. Around the same time, the church participated in the formation of the Global Christian Forum, a new international ecumenical initiative to 'provide a neutral space for fellowship and partnership across the confessional and denominational divides.[7] Its first international conference in Nairobi in 2007 was the fruit of such ecumenical engagements.[8]

Environmental Stewardship

Environmental stewardship has become another important area of ministry. Cho and the YFGC have recognized the need for an environmental stewardship ministry. During the New Year special worship service on January 4, 2005, Cho issued a call for Christian intervention for the restoration of the broken relationship between God and his creation as the first step in facing environmental problems.[9]

> Just recently I found out many insufficiencies of myself in the forty-seven years of ministry. The Bible says, 'For God so loved the world that He gave His son and only Son, that whoever believes in him shall not perish but have eternal life'. However, I misinterpreted it; I understood that God so loved 'humans', not 'the world', that He gave His one and only Son. What is the world? In the world, there are all things such as people, society, sky, land, ocean, plants, insects and animals. The Bible says that God so loved 'the world' that He gave His only Son; it does not limit and say that God so loved 'humans' that He gave His only Son.
>
> We are responsible for nature. When Jesus died upon the cross, he redeemed for nature also. Even though nature carried a curse because of fall of Adam, the power of blood that Jesus shed on the cross saves nature. We should pray for nature. Even a bug and a worm, all is God's creation. They suffer living in this corrupt state. We have to stop damaging nature. We should pray for and bless

---

[7] Richard Howell (ed.), *Global Christian Forum: Transforming Ecumenism* (New Delhi: Evangelical Fellowship of India, 2007) reports this new ecumenical process. The representative of a Korean Pentecostal has been present from the beginning.

[8] For its conference message, see Global Christian Forum, 'Message from the Global Christian Forum to Brothers and Sisters in Christ throughout the World' (www.globalchristianforum.org, 2007).

[9] Muncheol Shin, 'Eco-theology of Young-san' [in Korean], *The Holy Spirit and Theology* 22 (2006), 115.

nature. Humans can live when nature lives. We should develop such a movement.[10]

This sermon represents Cho's theological understanding of nature and the environment. He sees the fall of Adam as a triple corruption which polluted the spirit, the body, and environment. As Adam sinned, all humankind was condemned to spiritual death. In the same way, there occurred the environmental curse (Genesis 3:17-18) and physical death (Genesis 3:19); this is the threefold fall.

However, God sent us his Son Jesus Christ to redeem our sins which were handed down through generations after the first sin of Adam (Matthew 1:21; John 3:16). Jesus made atonement for our sins through his death on the cross and his resurrection from the dead. Through the redemptive work of Jesus our sins were cleansed away, thus recovering the image of God in Jesus Christ (Romans 8:29). Having recovered the pure image of God through Jesus Christ, humans now become a new creation so that we can 'enjoy good health and that all may go well, even as our soul is getting along well' (3 John 2). This is the threefold blessing that is for us.

Cho has recognized that the redemptive work of Jesus Christ brings three-fold redemption. Jesus' redemption carries our curse, but blesses our spirit and our environment, takes away the physical curse of illness and death, but gives us the right to health and divine healing. Just as the fall of Adam is the threefold fall, so the redemption of Jesus Christ extends even to nature. As a result, humans, the environment, and all creation should have a relationship of care and love. Having this belief, Cho has been increasingly committed to bring justice to nature and the environment.[11] His participation with his associates in the clearing campaign of the oil spill in the Tae-an Peninsular in 2007 (photo) exemplified his and the church's commitment to environmental stewardship.

Towards the Future

We have seen less than half of this period and the radical rate of social change will also require an accelerated engagement of Korean Pentecostals with social, missional and global issues. The YFGC is called to continue at the cutting edge of mission engagement as part of the church's mandate. The development of

---

[10] Yonggi Cho in an untitled sermon (Yoido Full Gospel Church, Seoul, Korea on Jan 4, 2005).

[11] Shin, 'Eco-theology of Young-san', 99-100.

the first decade of the new century, however, suggests that the church will enhance its social role. The new younger leadership is expected to bring a new response to changing social contexts while remaining deeply rooted in Pentecostal spirituality.

The public through its secular media will continue to scrutinize the churches, especially the large ones. This also strongly implies that such churches now under younger and new leadership have an unprecedented opportunity to lead Korean Christianity into a new level of social commitment and leadership. This will require a voluntary networking among such leaders. The public role of religion, including Christianity, is a general trend throughout the world, and the group of new leaders needs to discern such a development. The YFGC has already developed such a network among its daughter- and sister-churches, and its expansion will naturally enhance Christianity's social impact.

It is also imperative to intentionally review its traditional theological emphases. The person and work of the Holy Spirit, as Cho's foundational theological basis, should continue as the theological characteristics of the YFGC. In fact it will be critical to theologically ground the recently developed mission and social engagements securely in the distinctly pneumatological emphasis of Cho and the church. In order to develop such a pneumatic mission basis a serious theological exploration is necessary. In the past the YFGC has provided a distinct theological guidance to the Korean church. The growing emphasis of the work of the Holy Spirit in the Korean church regardless of denominational affiliation is a good example. [12] Prayers for healing and miracles were the practical outgrowth of such a theological influence of the church. Another theological influence is what is called the 'theology of blessing'. Cho's emphasis on God's immanence has turned other-worldly oriented Korean Christianity into a dynamic social entity. At the same time, this teaching has often been accused of being 'shamanistic'. [13] While this theology is well justified biblically and contextually, there is a clear need to safeguard this theological argument so that it will be more than self-serving.

The growing expectation regarding the Korean church for global leadership will inevitably draw attention to large churches that are characteristically charismatic in nature. [14] The YFGC, as the largest in Korea as well as in the world, is expected to pioneer new ways to demonstrate the leadership call of the Korean Christians, including Pentecostals. Cho was able to conduct large

---

[12] Sometimes it is called 'Pentecostalisation'. See Chang-sup Shim, 'Assessing the Impact of Pentecostalism on the Korean Presbyterian Church in Light of Calvin's Theology', *Chongshin Theological Journal* 3 (1998), 115-31.

[13] E.g. W.J. Hollenweger, *Pentecostalism*, 100, n. 2 calls Cho 'a Pentecostal Shaman par excellence'.

[14] Hong, 'The Backgrounds and Characteristics of the Charismatic Mega-Churches in Korea', 99-118.

crusades with his popular delivery of a message of hope, but the next generation leadership will come with a different set of gifts. It is then imperative for the new leadership to explore meaningful and significant ways to contribute to world Christianity. For the new generation it will take different forms to provide the leadership for global Christianity, perhaps less through personal charisma, but more through co-operative and systematic approaches. There is no reason why, for example, a theological foundation is established in honour of David Yonggi Cho to make a decisive contribution in raising world-class Pentecostal leaders from the global south, just as John Stott achieved through his Langham Partnership International.

The rest of the period is still a blank sheet of paper and the role of YFGC to Korean Christianity will be paramount.

Chapter 9

Conclusion

Summary

The Korean Protestant church has grown and developed rapidly enough to receive worldwide attention in its short history of a century or so. The Holy Spirit movement of the various Korean churches may be responsible in good part for such growth. The history of the Korean church can be divided into six periods of twenty years each. The Holy Spirit movement in the Korean church generally shows unique features in each period which are related to the political, social and religious background of the period.

The first period is from 1900 to 1920, when Korea was succumbed to Japanese occupation. It was a time of chaos both politically and socially and can be considered as a period of a religious vacuum. Since many Koreans had lost direction in life, they sought hope in Christianity. The Great Revival of 1907 that took place in Pyongyang, the then capitol of North Korea, had a significant influence on the life-style of Korean Christians. The revival started in a Bible study and prayer meeting that was primarily led by a Methodist missionary. It reached its peak at Pyongyang and then spread throughout the country. The outstanding characteristic of this revival was repentance on the model of the early church as described in the New Testament.

Sun-joo Gil, a Presbyterian minister, was one of the outstanding leaders of this movement. The main focus of Gil's theology was on eschatology. Gil emphasized the second coming of Jesus Christ and life after death. As a result of this emphasis in preaching, Korean Christians of the period tended to be concerned chiefly with the future life and personal salvation.

Influenced by this revival, Bible study and prayer became integral parts of Korean Christian life. The repentance movement chiefly stressed personal salvation and personal experience, and for that reason was largely lacking in social concern. This tendency has passed into the mainstream of Korean church life.

The second period (1920–1940) was a time when Korea was under Japanese occupation. Since Christians had played the major role in the Declaration of Independence of 1 March 1919, the Japanese began to persecute the Korean churches. In the midst of this devastating situation Korean Christians were comforted by the Holy Spirit movement and, as a result, became interested in having what they called mystical experiences. The Christian leaders of the Holy Spirit movement at this time were Ik-doo Kim, a Presbyterian, and Yong-do Lee, a Methodist. Ik-doo Kim emphasized and practiced divine healing, while Yong-do Lee stressed the mystical union with Christ. Although Yong-do Lee's ministry was brief, his theology and faith made a great impact on the Korean church. Since both these leaders, Kim and Lee, emphasized personal religious experiences, the Korean church in this period, being more concerned about individual faith, tended to emphasize empiricism.

The third period, between 1940 and 1960, is considered in retrospect a period of confusion. During this time Korea was liberated from Japanese occupation. A few years after liberation communist North Korea invaded South Korea, and the war, which lasted three years, caused much confusion. The Korean churches, which up to then had been forcibly unified by the Japanese, began to divide by denomination. In almost all denominations now, after a series of divisions, two groups—conservative and liberal—co-exist. Theological differences and conflicts between these two groups in each denomination also caused continuous divisions. The church lost the force of its leadership in society due to these constant divisions. The various churches became legalistic in orientation and in good measure ignored the spiritual needs of the people. This situation brought about the rise of Spirit-oriented movements such as the Olive Tree Church and the Unification Church. Against this background, the preparation for the Pentecostal movement was in the making.

The fourth period (1960 to 1980) was a time of explosive growth and the revival of the Korean church. Student demonstrations and military coups created an insecure atmosphere in Korean society where people began to find comfort in Christianity. The Holy Spirit movement of the Evangelicals and the Pentecostals manifested in large-scale crusades, thanks to the united efforts of many churches of different denominational backgrounds. This movement contributed at the same time to the growth of the individual churches. As the military government continued to assume power over a long period, liberal groups of church leaders rose up in protest. One outcome was Minjung theology, a unique indigenized Christianity of the Koreans. The Minjung theology movement, which was advocated by learned liberal Korean Christians, was well received by the world Protestant churches.

In the fifth period (from 1980 to 2000), the Holy Spirit movement has spread throughout all the Christian denominations in Korea. Influenced in good part by the YFGC, the Pentecostal/Charismatic movement spread rapidly in all denominations. The churches involved in this charismatic movement have achieved remarkable church growth, which has brought them to the attention of the world churches.

During this period, the leaders of the Holy Spirit movement broke new ground for mission and social engagement. Unlike the previous period where

Korean Christianity was sharply divided as to how to engage with social issues, there was a general consensus toward the church's role in society.

The last period (from 2000 onwards) in some ways continues the trends of the previous period. However, the churches are now seriously challenged to grapple with a more affluent social setting and the development of inter-Korean relations. Also in this period, Korean Christianity begins to witness the emergence of a second generation of mega-church leaders. This changing social context has called the churches to the caring for the socially marginalized, while actively participating in the nation's efforts to facilitate the process of national reunification.

Also noticeable is the Pentecostal and charismatic churches' active participation in the ecumenical movement as part of their self-understanding in playing a reconciliation role. The new cutting edge social issues include environmental stewardship and a 'deeper' engagement of the church with structural evils. Also significant is their struggle with the negative influence of shamanism. One of the greatest challenges for the Holy Spirit movement is to craft its unique mission approaches based on its unique spiritual resources. So far, its missional engagement has not been much different from that of the non-Pentecostal and non-charismatic churches.

Unique Features

The Korean Holy Spirit movement is, in some aspects, unique. In the various periods demarcated above, it has been characterized by unique features, depending on the political and social situations of each period. It started as a repentance movement and developed into a movement of mystical union with Christ. It then became a recognizable evangelical movement with large-scale crusades, and then after encountering Minjung theology, transformed into Pentecostalism, and finally into a charismatic movement. The different features of the Holy Spirit movement in these periods co-exist syncretically in the Korean churches. It is special to this country that the Holy Spirit movement started at almost the same time as the world Pentecostal movement, without any apparent connection or influence between the two. On the other hand, just as with the first Pentecostal movement that took place in the United States, the movement in Korea was originated by a Methodist minister through Bible study classes and prayer meetings. In addition to these similarities, the Holy Spirit movement planted its roots in Korea as a repentance movement, which was then formulated in a traditional Korean, Christian-faith style.

This kind of revival movement developed independently under the leadership of the three largest denominations in Korea—Presbyterian, Methodist, and Holiness churches—until the Yoido Full Gospel Church, a Pentecostal church, took the lead in the 1970s.

Another feature of the Korean Holy Spirit movement is the house church movement that is called the 'cell group meeting movement'. The YFGC attained 20 to 30 per cent annual growth rate during the first three decades by its well-structured cell group ministries. Most Korean churches have adopted this system and employ the cell-group system as a fundamental source of church growth. This is a house-to-house ministry which reminds us of the early Jerusalem community described in the Acts of the Apostles.[1]

A unique feature of the Holy Spirit movement in Korea lies in its diversity. The movement has both conservative and liberal wings. The Confucian tradition of ancient Korean society and American Puritanism worked together to form the conservative and evangelical characteristics of the Holy Spirit movement. Not only that, the liberal tendencies of the Holy Spirit movement and its own uniqueness have come together to produce Minjung theology, which may be described as a 'Koreanized' Holy Spirit movement. Such variety in the movement opens itself to the possibility of furthering the ecumenical movement. Since the Holy Spirit movement has spread through almost all the Protestant churches of Korea and among many Catholics as well, this breadth gives it an important position in the ecumenical movement in Korea.

Reasons for Its Success

Rich Religious Soil

Koreans are known to be a religious people, which is to say that most of their lives have been based on some kind of religious belief. Shamanism, with 5,000 years of Korean history, has been a fixture in the mental structure of Korean consciousness. Buddhism, with 1,500 to 1,600 years of history, has also taken root in Korea because of the religious character of the people. This background of the Korean spirit is surely one of the reasons why there have been so many converts, without a strong opposition, from the time the Holy Spirit movement was planted.

The influence of the shamanistic nature of the old Korean religion should not be overlooked. Because of it, the successes of the Holy Spirit movement would be often associated with it since both appear to be quite emotional on the surface. The leaders of the Holy Spirit movement try to go beyond this criticism, however, by disciplining their members with intensive Bible studies and by turning their interests to social concerns. Theologians and scholars must continue their explorations and research on this subject while the leaders of the churches need to work diligently to maintain sound doctrines.

---

[1] Acts 2:42-47

Cultural Background: Ignorance of Spiritual Needs

Confucianism is the dominant ethos in the structure of consciousness of the Korean people. Influenced by Puritanism and Confucianism, the Presbyterian, Methodist, and Holiness churches all have the tendency to emphasize reverence and solemnity. This has given Korean Christianity something of a legalist and authoritarian cast. As an inevitable result, the major leading Christian denominations have to a certain extent ignored people's spiritual needs. Spirit-oriented movements rose among the people in order to fulfil this need. However, these movements caused many problems in society and soon they were judged 'heretical' by the major Christian denominations. It is from this background that the Pentecostal and the Charismatic movements emerged. After the 1970s, the Charismatic movement has spread widely to all denominations in Korea.

Unstable Society

Since the introduction of Protestant Christianity into Korea in the late nineteenth century, the country has gone through a period of enlightenment, a colonial period, national liberation, the Korean War, student revolts, and a military coup and dictatorship. As a result of a series of such events, Korean society became unstable in many aspects. The people could not turn to and depend upon the traditional religions. In this situation, Christianity exerted a powerful influence on Korean society.

The instability of Korean society has been a factor leading people to accept the Holy Spirit movement in their search for stability and the spiritual satisfaction they needed so desperately. Christianity is developing rapidly in Korea, even now, centered on the Holy Spirit movement. In a way, the church's growth can be adversely affected by a more stable social situation, and this is what has happened in the last decade or so.

Its Influences

There are several areas where the influences of the Holy Spirit movement are most felt, the first being spiritual awakening. Passing through the five periods of one hundred and ten years of Korean Protestant church history, we have seen the Holy Spirit movement playing a major role in awakening the spiritually powerless Korean churches in all periods. The Holy Spirit movement encourages people to realize the importance of spiritual experiences. By encouraging passionate faith, the Pentecostal Holy Spirit movement revitalized the Korean church which had tended to be intellectual, rational and formal in its outlook. Thus such a movement changed people's faith from understanding the word of God intellectually to understanding the words through experience. Also, Pentecostals broke away from formal conventional worship heavily dominated by clergy in the pulpit, and radically transformed worship to be a place where people in the pews actively participate in the service with praise and prayer. As a result, worship changed from an occasion of solemnity to a celebration with the full participation of everyone present. Lively modern Christian songs, or 'gospel songs', frequently sung by Pentecostals, have made the church more friendly and accessible to non-Christians. Consequently, Christians regularly invite their family members and friends to worship. Moreover, Pentecostals believe not only that the kingdom of God will be realized in heaven by the Second Advent of Christ but also that the kingdom of God will be realized on earth.[2] Such concern is not irrelevant to the healing ministry of Jesus in the early church.[3] Spiritual experience gives confidence in the Christian life, helps Christians dedicate themselves to the glory of God, and encourages them actively to spread the gospel.

Second, the ecumenical movement is another area of influence. After the Korean Holy Spirit movement started at Wonsan by the repentance of a Methodist missionary, Presbyterian missionaries at Pyongyang invited the Methodist missionary as a speaker, held a Bible class, and shared the grace of God. Such inter-denominational crusades were followed by the Pyongyang Revival movement in 1907. In the 1970s, many crusades were held in Korea: Billy Graham's evangelism crusade in 1973, the Explo crusade in 1974, the National Propagation of the Gospel crusade in 1977, and other large crusades.[4] The large inter-denominational crusades in the 1970s showed that the ecumenical movement is possible only through the Holy Spirit movement. This brought about a remarkable church growth in the 1970s. As a result, the Holy Spirit movement has currently spread to almost all denominations.

Third, it has led the church growth movement. The Holy Spirit movement is the most crucial factor in the growth of a church. The prayer movement and the house church movement (cell group movement) are becoming the most important factors in church growth. We can find a perfect example of this in the Yoido Full Gospel Church.

Its Challenges

The Holy Spirit movement in Korea is open to the following challenges:

The first is sectarianism. Until the early 1980s the Korean Pentecostal churches have had no close relations with other churches and for this reason have been criticized for being anti-ecumenical. Since most of the churches that are involved in the Holy Spirit movement belong to the conservative wing,

---

[2] George E. Ladd, *A Theology of the New Testament* (Grand Rapids: Eerdmans, 1983), 69.

[3] Young-hoon Lee, 'The Influence of the Pentecostal Movement on the Korean Church', *International Theological Institute* (1993).

[4] Lee, 'The Influence of the Pentecostal Movement', 118.

dialogue between the conservative and the liberal groups is not actively encouraged.

Second, it generally lacks social concern. The Pentecostal-oriented churches are criticized for their biased emphases on personal salvation and spiritual expcricnces. Since many churches that have participated in the Holy Spirit movement did not show much interest in social justice and ignored the requests of society, the influence of this movement on society has decreased. For this reason, the recent change among the Pentecostal-charismatic churches toward social engagement is encouraging.

Third, also significant is the lack of doctrinal standards. The Holy Spirit movement may have achieved quantitative success in its rapid growth, but this has not been accompanied by qualitative advancement. This calls for systematic theological education. A correct and sound doctrinal understanding of the action of the Holy Spirit in the life of the church is needed. Since each denomination of the Korean church has a different understanding of the Holy Spirit, it is urgent to establish a unified pneumatology through continuous theological research and dialogue.

Fourth, an emotional tendency in Christian faith is another weakness. Since the Holy Spirit movement emphasized spiritual experience, it was inevitable that it had emotional tendencies. This tendency should be balanced to avoid an unstable and biased faith. Many people became over-emotional, emphasizing spiritual experiences while remaining ignorant of basic biblical doctrines. From this weakness of the Holy Spirit movement, many heretical tendencies have appeared. Therefore, it is urgent to establish a sound doctrine of faith with balanced spiritual experience and biblical knowledge. In addition to this, a clear distinction must be made at all points between the negative influences of shamanism and the Holy Spirit movement.

Suggestions for the Future

A study of the Holy Spirit movement would be incomplete if it did not direct our attention to lessons and suggestions for the future. There should be no end to research in the Holy Spirit movement, since there cannot be an end to church growth or to the development of a theology of the Holy Spirit movement.

Concluding this study on the historical and doctrinal development of the Holy Spirit movement in Korea, the following discussion may guide reflections on the future of the Korean Holy Spirit movement.

Theological Issues

The unique theological contribution of the Korean Pentecostal movement and particularly that of Cho have been consistently explored, largely to the credit of

ITI and Youngsan Theological Institute of Hansei University.[5] There are several areas which demand a continuing theological work.

First, the traditional emphasis on the person and work of the Holy Spirit among the Pentecostals should continue, but in the healthy and wider context of Christian theology. Its theological standards should derive from a theory of the Holy Spirit without neglecting the other great mysteries such as the incarnation, the divine Trinity, the church, and the life of grace. It is, therefore, critical to nurture younger theological minds to be able to articulate pneumato-centric theology in a changing social and cultural context.[6] This can be significantly facilitated not only through formal theological education but also informal and non-formal theological discussions, forums and exchanges. Equally critical is that such theological minds should ground their theological exploration on their personal spiritual experience unique to the Holy Spirit movement. They include 'baptism in the Holy Spirit', deep commitment to the authority of the scriptures, devoted prayer life often accompanied by fasting, and openness to the supernatural work of the Holy Spirit, such as healing and miracles. By nature, Pentecostal theologians need to be reflective practitioners, and, therefore, their theological work should reflect their theological knowledge and personal experience.

Second, it is also important to draw upon the unique features of the Korean Holy Spirit movement from the Pyongyang Great revival, and continuing through various individuals and communities. One important locus in fostering the uniquely Korean form of spirituality has been the prayer mountain movement. While the mainline churches, especially their theologians and ecclesiastical leadership, were reluctant to recognise the growing influence of Pentecostal-charismatic type of Christianity, it was the prayer mountains, often distant from the mainstream ecclesiastical authority, which nurtured the Pentecostal-type spiritual practices. Integrated in the emphasis of prayer and fasting, many devoted Christians have made their prayer mountain retreat as part of their spiritual exercise. Often motivated by a dire sense of physical, mental, economic or spiritual needs, the Korean spiritual tradition is naturally expressed in the expectation of personal encounters with God's reality and power. Naturally, beliefs in baptism in the Spirit, healing, personal renewal,

---

[5] In addition to the latter's annual theological symposium, see the recent publication of *Dr. Yonggi Cho's Ministry and Theology*, 2 vols. (Goonpo, Korea: Hansei University Logos, 2008).

[6] Examples are: William W. Menzies, 'David Yonggi Cho's Theology of the Fullness of the Spirit' (II: 175-192); Mun Hong Choi, 'Dr. Yonggi Cho and the Holy Spirit' (II: 193-224); Allan Anderson, 'The Contextual Pentecostal Theology of David Yonggi Cho' (II: 281-308); Myung Soo Park, 'David Yonggi Cho and International Pentecostal/ Charismatic Movements' (II: 309-335), in *Dr. Yonggi Cho's Ministry and Theology* (2008); and Hwa Yung, 'The MIssiological Challenge of David Yonggi Cho's Theology', in *David Yonggi Cho*, 69-93.

miracles and other supernatural experiences were part of a common spirituality.[7] They have been the main expressions of a Pentecostal-charismatic type of spirituality in many established churches. Such 'back-door spirituality' found its outlet during the annual revival week of almost every church in Korea. Typical revivalists have introduced rather controversial teachings such as healing under the sanction of the annual revival. In some ways it was such popular acceptance of a Pentecostal-type of spirituality that gradually influenced the clergy and ecclesiastical leadership as well as the theological communities. Therefore, it is essential to consciously identify the spiritual resources of the Korean Holy Spirit movement, while appropriating outside influences with discernment.

Third, the Holy Spirit movement should become vigilant and discerning to guard itself against social and religious currents, indigenous as well as foreign. For example, the extent of the influences of shamanism on Korean Pentecostal Christianity has been a matter of debate. The issue, at least within Korea, was motivated by the seemingly self-serving attitude of some Pentecostal Christians, especially around the idea of 'blessing'.[8] Also serious were new Christian ideas and practices introduced into Korean Christianity, such as territorial spirits, inter-generational curses, and inner healing. Without a serious theological screening and evaluation, an uncritical acceptance of questionable teachings and practices can do more harm than good to the Holy Spirit movement. At the same time, it is equally necessary to re-evaluate some Korean traditional religious spiritualities and traditions that can be positively adapted into Christian thinking and practice. In a way, the strong emphasis on prayer and fasting among Korean Pentecostals may be attributed in part to the influence of some non-Christian Korean religions.

Fourth, it should chart a clear theological path for the powerful influence of the theology of blessing, which has been popularly associated with Pentecostal-charismatic theology.[9] In the past two decades, Korean Pentecostals have often

---

[7] There are extensive studies on healing in Korean Pentecostal thinking: e.g. Vinson Synan, 'Roots of Yonggi Cho's Theology of Healing' (I: 263-310); Sang Bok Lee, 'Dr. Yonggi Cho's Theology of Healing and Neuroscience' (I: 311-344); and Pan Ho Kim, 'Paul Tillich and Dr. Yonggi Cho: A Dialogue between Their Perspective Theologies of Healing' (I: 345-373); Thomas K. Mathew, 'Oral Roberts and David Yonggi Cho: A Comparative Evaluation of Their Theologies of Healing' (I: 263-294), all in *Dr. Yonggi Cho's Ministry and Theology* (2008).

[8] E.g. Gwi Sam Cho, 'The Missional Contextualization of Bok (Blessing) in Korean Religious Mentality Based on Cased of Yoido Full Gospel Church', in *Dr. Yonggi Cho's Ministry and Theology* (2008), I: 215-234.

[9] For some studies, see Wonsuk Ma, 'David Yonggi Cho's Theology of Blessing: A New Theological Base and Direction' (I: 179-200); Sam Hwan Kim, 'The Question of Good and Evil in Full Gospel Faith: A Study of Theological Foundation for the Threefold Blessing of Yonggi Cho' (I: 201-214), all in *Dr. Yonggi Cho's Ministry and Theology* (2008).

been perceived as socially unconcerned, while pursuing individual well-being. It can be argued that the mass Holy Spirit movement created a social uplift or upward social mobility among its adherents. As the Spirit is God's life-giving agent, the legitimacy of such a theological argument is biblically grounded. Therefore, it is important that Korean Pentecostals reflect on and articulate the biblical and theological perspective of this belief into a balanced missional expression.[10] This will keep them from confusing the means with the end: material and physical blessing is to be part of God's empowerment for witnessing.[11]

Practical and Missional Issues

First, the movement should create a way forward for national reconciliation and church co-operation. As an inter-Korean relationship develops, the church will be expected to continue its active contribution to and engagement with the process. Ecumenism is another area of reconciliation. Recent discussions on ecumenism have opened a new ground for the traditionally excluded churches to participate in ecumenical discussions and efforts. Through the serious evaluation and criticism of the organized ecumenical movement, such as that of the World Council of Churches, now non-western churches and evangelical and Pentecostal churches are urged to make an important contribution to the process. Empirically many are convinced that the Holy Spirit movement can fulfil the ecumenical movement in Korea and the world. While actively participating in such initiatives, how Korean Pentecostals can forge their own theological reflections and contribute to the wider ecumenical process is critical, based on their unique historical and spiritual experiences. The same applies to the inter-Korean issues. Such reflections and experiences will in turn facilitate churches elsewhere that are struggling in the midst of a racial conflict.

Second, it should develop the theological means for social engagement among the Pentecostal-charismatic churches and believers. Religious communities in Korea have been called to provide their distinct service to society. Due to its much publicized growth, Christian churches in general and large Pentecostal-charismatic type churches in particular, have been challenged, and have developed their social programmes. When the Holy Spirit movement loses its interest in social justice and in people who are oppressed and neglected, it will lose its influence on Korean society. A serious question is if there is any uniquely Pentecostal theological resource to inform

---

[10] The kingdom of God has been proposed as a useful theological context for Pentecostal thinking. See, e.g. Leslie C. Allen, 'The Kingdom of God in Psalms' (II: 75-100); Hee Sung Kim, 'Rev. Yonggi Cho's Kingdom of God' (II: 101-126); Christoph Schwöbel, 'The Kingdom of God and the Trinity' (II: 127-146), all in *Dr. Yonggi Cho's Ministry and Theology* (2008).

[11] Wonsuk Ma, 'Tasks and Challenges for Korean Pentecostal Churches in the Twenty-First Century', *Australasian Pentecostal Studies* 5-6 (2001), pp. 63-94.

and resource their social approaches. The Spirit's empowerment is often found in the context of socially and spiritual marginality (e.g. Luke 4:18-19), while the same Spirit draws diverse people into a common household of God. Korean Pentecostals can provide a significant theological basis for their social work and an even deeper social engagement.

Third, for decades the Korean church was hailed for its exponential church growth to which the Holy Spirit movement has been the most significant contributor. Consequently 'church growth' has continued to be a popular topic in Korea. However, it is also noticeable that the concept of church growth has gradually acquired a negative connotation over the years particularly in the West. Whereas the North American church growth movement flourished for about a generation, Korea may be one of just a few places where 'church growth' is still actively discussed. However, its true legitimacy and usefulness may be found in the mission context, as Donald McGavran might have had in mind when he began the School of World Mission and Church Growth in 1965 at Fuller Theological Seminary. Therefore, Korea may be able to claim its unique global leadership in church growth studies, precisely because it represents a church within a non-Christian mission context. With its unique cell group system, churches like the YFGC will be able to develop a healthy theology of church growth based on its theological grounding of empowerment. For this reason, even after Cho's era, his internationally acclaimed Church Growth International should continue to increase its influence on the world.

The fourth is its missionary commitment. Although the Korean Holy Spirit movement, due to its historical context, has focused itself on immediate social issues, the Pentecostal movement has been traditionally mission-oriented. The substantial part of the movement's growth is attributed to western missionary efforts. As early as the 1960s, the YFGC began its international mission by sending its missionaries initially to western countries where Korean immigrant communities were concentrated, and through Cho's international ministries. From the 1980s, cross-cultural missionaries were sent to many parts of the world. Pentecostal theology is by nature a mission-oriented theology through the empowerment of the Holy Spirit. The early decades of the Pentecostal movement in North America and Europe testify to this conviction. While Pentecostal churches in Korea continue their missionary expansion, it is important to develop their unique mission theology and approaches.

The Global Call

With the southward shift of the centre of global Christian gravity, the critical role of the churches in the global south (provisionally called 'southern churches') is consistently recognized. A century after the Edinburgh Missionary Conference in 1910 this awareness is becoming even more apparent. Within this unique context, the Korean churches and particularly the YFGC will influence the other 'southern churches' and world Christianity, both positively and negatively. For this reason, the unique global influence and even the leadership of the Korean Pentecostal churches over the rest of the world cannot be ignored. This requires them to be particularly aware of their potential and opportunities.

One area of particular influence is the theological leadership of the Korean Pentecostal church, especially for the growing 'southern churches'. As the world's second largest missionary-sending church, the Korean church has demonstrated its resourcefulness and global potential. The development of a healthy contextual or local theology is an urgent task in many developing churches, and the Korean Pentecostal churches can provide valuable assistance. This will also require the Korean church to 'think and live globally'.

They can also invite other 'southern churches' to join a creative missionary exploration with approaches uniquely appropriate to churches that may not have financial resources, but are rich in their commitment to mission and in their contextual experiences as Christians. With the constant decrease of western missionary influence and leadership, this will require the Korean Pentecostals to strengthen their infrastructure in theological education and mission research.

The global challenge is unique, particularly for the YFGC as much of its global ministry has been centred on Cho's vision and leadership. It will have to take different forms as the make-up of the next generation of church leadership will come with a different set of gifts. Its attention to a global contribution will provide an important leadership to the entire Korean church and also to the emerging 'southern churches'.

As the Lord tarries, the Holy Spirit movement of Korea will need to revisit its missionary calling in its changing local and global context. Its main resource is the empowering presence of the Holy Spirit, and how it lives this missional life with its creative expression will be an on-going challenge. Nonetheless, the missionary bidding of the Lord remains unchanged:

> But you will receive power when the Holy Spirit comes on you; and you will be my witness in Jerusalem, and in all Judea and Samaria, and to the ends of the earth.[12]

---

[12] Acts 1:8

BIBLIOGRAPHY

Studies on Pneumatology and Pentecostalism

Adams, D.L. 'Calvin's Understanding of the Holy Spirit and the Contemporary Church'. *Taiwan Journal of Theology* 11 (1989), 83–106.

Alexander, D.L. *Christian Spirituality: Five Views of Sanctification* Downers Grove, IL: Inter-Varsity, 1988.

Anderson, Allan. *An Introduction to Pentecostalism.* Cambridge & New York: Cambridge University Press, 2004.

Anderson, R.M. *Vision of the Disinherited: The Making of American Pentecostalism.* New York: Oxford University, 1979.

Bennett, Dennis J. *Nine O'clock in the Morning.* Plainfield, NJ: Logos International, 1970.

Bartleman, F. *Azusa Street.* Plainfield, NJ: Logos International, 1980.

Binyon, P.M. *The Concepts of 'Spirit' and 'Demon': A Study in the Use of Different Languages Describing the Same Phenomena.* Frankfurt-am-Main: Peter Lang, 1977.

Bloch-Hoell, N. *The Pentecostal Movement: Its Origin, Development and Distinctive Character.* New York: Humanities, 1964.

Blumhoffer, E.L. and B. Randall (eds.) *Modern Christian Revivals.* Urbana, IL: University of Illinois, 1993.

Brumback, C. *What Meaneth This?* Springfield, MO: Gospel Publishing House, 1947.

Bruner, F.D. *A Theology of the Holy Spirit: The Pentecostal Experience and the New Testament Witness.* Grand Rapids, MI: Eerdmans, 1970.

Burns, J.P. and M.F. Gerald. *The Holy Spirit: Message of the Fathers of the Church.* Wilmington, DE: Michael Glazier, 1984.

Calley, M.J.C. *God's People: West Indian Pentecostal Sects in England.* London: Oxford University, 1965.

Carlson, G.R. *Our Faith and Fellowship.* Springfield, MO: Gospel Publishing House, 1977.

Carter, C.W. *The Person and Ministry of the Holy Spirit: A Wesleyan Perspective.* Grand Rapids, MI: Baker, 1974.

Chan, Simon K.H. 'Evidential Glossolalia and the Doctrine of Subsequence'. *Asian Journal of Pentecostal Studies* 2:2 (1999), 195-211.

Chinnici, J.P. (ed.) *Devotion to the Holy Spirit in American Catholicism.* New York: Paulist, 1985.

Clark, M.S. *Spiritual Dynamics: The Holy Spirit in Human Experience.* Springfield, MO: Gospel Publishing House, 1976.

Clark, Mathew S. 'Initial Evidence: A Southern African Perspective'. *Asian Journal of Pentecostal Studies* 1:2 (1998), 203-217.

Clark, M.S. et al. *What Is Distinctive about Pentecostal Theology?* Pretoria: University of South Africa, 1983.

Congar, Y.M.J. *I Believe in the Holy Spirit.* Vol. 1: *The Holy Spirit in the 'Economy', Revelation and Experience of the Spirit.* Tr. David Smith. New York: Seabury, 1983.

_____. *I Believe in the Holy Spirit.* Vol. 2: *He Is Lord and Giver of Life.* Tr. David Smith. New York: Seabury, 1983.

_____. *I Believe in the Holy Spirit.* Vol. 3: *The River of the Water of Life (Rev. 22:1) Flow in the East and in the West.* Tr. David Smith. New York: Seabury, 1983.

Cox, H.G. 'Why God Didn't Die: A Religious Renaissance Flourishing around the World-Pentecostal Christians leading the Way'. *Nieman Reports* 47 (1993), 6–8, 47–49.

_____. *Fire from Heaven: The Rise of Pentecostal Spirituality and the Reshaping of Religion in the Twenty-first Century.* Reading, MA: Addison-Wesley, 1994.

Crowe, T.R. *Pentecostal Unity: Recurring Frustration and Enduring Hopes.* Chicago: Loyola University, 1993.

Culpepper, R.H. *Evaluating the Charismatic Movement.* Valley Forge, PA: Judson, 1977.

Darrand, T.C. and S. Anson. *Metaphors of Social Control in a Pentecostal Sect: Studies in Religion and Society.* New York: Edwin Mellen, 1983.

Dayton, D.W. 'Pentecostal/Charismatic Renewal and Social Change; Western Perspective'. *Transformation* 5.4 (1988), 7–13.

_____. 'The Holy Spirit and the Christian Expansion in the 20th Century'. *Missiology* 16 (1988), 397–407.

_____. 'The Rise of the Evangelical Healing Movement in the Nineteenth Century America'. *Pneuma* 4:1 (1982), 1–18.

_____. *Theological Roots of Pentecostalism.* Grand Rapids, MI: Francis Asbury, 1987.

Dewar, L. *The Holy Spirit and Modern Thought: An Inquiry into the Historical, Theological, and Psychological Aspects of the Christian Doctrine of the Holy Spirit.* London: A.R. Mowbray, 1959.

Dunn, J.D.G. 'Baptism in the Holy Spirit: 20 Years on'. *Mission and Ministry* 7 (1990), 9–12.

_____. *Baptism in the Holy Spirit.* London: SCM, 1970.

_____. *Jesus and the Spirit.* Philadelphia, PA: Westminster, 1975.

Duquoc, C. and F. Casiano (eds.). *Spiritual Revivals.* New York: Herder & Herder, 1973.

Durasoff, S. *Bright Wind of the Spirit: Pentecostalism Today.* Upper Saddle River, NJ: Prentice-Hall, 1972.

_____. *Pentecost behind the Iron Curtain.* Plainfield, NJ: Logos International, 1972.

Edgar, T.R. 'The Cessation of Sign Gifts: History from Early Church to Present'. *Bibliotheca Sacra* 45 (1988), 371–86.

Flora, C.B. *Pentecostalism in Colombia: Baptism by Fire and Spirit.* Rutherford, NJ: Fairleigh Dickinson University, 1976.

Gaver, J.R. *Pentecostalism.* New York: Awards, 1971.

Gee, D. *Concerning Spiritual Gifts.* Springfield, MO: Gospel Publishing House, 1949.

Gerlach, L.P. and H.H. Virginia. *People, Power, Change Movements of Social Transformation.* New York: Bobbs-Merril, 1970.

Gladstone, Robert J. 'Sign Language in the Assembly: How Are Tongues a Sign to the Unbeliever in 1 Cor 14:20-25?'. *Asian Journal of Pentecostal Studies* 2:2 (1999), 177-94.

Goff, James R., Jr. Fields *White unto Harvest: Charles F. Parham and the Missionary Origins of Pentecostalism.* Fayetteville: University of Arkansas, 1988.

Hamilton, M.P. (ed.). *The Charismatic Movement.* Grand Rapids, MI: Eerdmans, 1975.

Hinn, B. *Good Morning, Holy Spirit.* Nashville, TN: Thomas Nelson, 1990.

_____. *Welcome, Holy Spirit.* Nashville, TN: Thomas Nelson, 1995.

Hoekema, A.A. *What about Tongue-Speaking?* Grand Rapids, MI: Eerdmans, 1966.

Holdcroft, L.T. *The Holy Spirit: A Pentecostal Interpretation.* Springfield, MO: Gospel Publishing House, 1962.

Hollenweger, W.J. 'After Twenty Years' Research on Pentecostalism'. *Theology* 87 (1984), 403–12.

_____. *The Pentecostals: The Charismatic Movement in the Churches.* Trans. R.A. Wilson. Minneapolis, MN: Augsburg, 1972.

_____. *Pentecostalism: Origin and Developments Worldwide.* Peabody, MA: Hendrickson, 1997.

Horton, Stanley M. 'Pentecostal Perspective'. In *Five Views on Sanctification.* Grand Rapids, MI: Zondervan, 1987.

_____ (ed.). *Systematic Theology: A Pentecostal Perspective.* Springfield, MO: Logion, 1994.

_____. *What the Bible Says about the Holy Spirit.* Springfield, MO: Gospel Publishing, 1976.

Howell, Richard (ed.) *Global Christian Forum: Transforming Ecumenism.* New Delhi: Evangelical Fellowship of India, 2007.

Huizing, P. and William, B. (eds.). *Experience of the Spirit.* New York: Seabury, 1974.

Hunter, Harold D. *Spirit-Baptism: A Pentecostal Alternative.* Lanham, MD: University Press of America, 1983.

International Theological Institute. *History of Assemblies of God Church.* Rev. ed [in Korean]. Seoul: Seoul Books, 1993.

_____. *The Holy Spirit around the World.* Seoul: ITI, 1993.

Jongeneel, J.A.B. (ed.) *Experience of the Spirit: Conference on Pentecostal and Charismatic Research in Europe at Utrecht University 1989.* Frankfurt-am-Main: Peter Lang, 1989.

Jorstad, E. (ed.) *The Holy Spirit in Today's Church.* Nashville: Abingdon, 1973.

Keefer, L.L. 'The Spirit of Evangelism: Holy Spirit in the Acts'. *Ashland Theological Journal* 20 (1988).

Kerr, J.S. *The Fire Flares Anew.* Philadelphia: Fortress, 1974.

Laube, R.T. *Pentecostal Spirituality: The Lasallian Theology of Apostolic Life.* New York: Desclée, 1970.

Lederle, H.I. 'An Ecumenical Investigation into the Proprium or Distinctive Element of Pentecostal'. *Theology* 21 (1988), 34–41.

Lederle, H.I. *Treasures Old and New: Interpretation of 'Spirit-Baptism' in the Charismatic Renewal Movement.* Peabody, MA: Hendrickson, 1988.

Lee, P.J. *A History of Pentecostal Movement* [in Korean]. Seoul: Voice, 1985.

Lee, Y. (ed.) *Bibliographies on Pneumatology.* Rev. ed. [in Korean]. Seoul: International Theological Institute, 1995.

Lim, David. 'A Reflection on the "Initial Evidence" Discussion from a Pentecostal Pastor's Perspective'. *Asian Journal of Pentecostal Studies* 2:2 (1999), 223-232.

Ma, Wonsuk. 'A First Wavers Looks at the Third Wave: A Pentecostal Reflection on Charles Kraft's Power Encounter Terminology'. *Pneuma* 19 (1997), 189-206.

Ma, Wonsuk. 'The Third Ripple: Deeper and Wider Mission Engagement'. *Lausanne World Pulse.* www.lausanneworldpulse.com/themedarticles.php/926: April 4, 2008.

Macchia, Frank D. 'Groans Too Deep for Words: Towards a Theology of Tongues as Initial Evidence', *Asian Journal of Pentecostal Studies* 1:2 (1998), 149-173.

MacRobert, I. 'The Birth of a Movement: William J. Seymour and the Azusa Mission'. In *The Black Roots and White Racism of Early Pentecostal Church in the USA.* London: MacMillan, 1988.

Malony, H.N. and A. Adams. *Glossolalia: Behavioral Science Perspectives on Speaking in Tongues.* New York: Oxford University, 1985.

Martin, David. *Tongues of Fire: The Explosion of Pentecostalism in Latin America.* Oxford: Blackwell, 1990.

Martin, D. and M. Peter (eds.). *Strange Gifts? A Guide to Charismatic Renewal.* New York: Basil Blackwell, 1984.

McClung, L.G., Jr. *Azusa Street and Beyond.* South Plainfield, NJ: Bridge, 1986.

McDonnell, K. 'Can Classical Pentecostals and Roman Catholics Engage in Common Witness?'. *Journal of Pentecostal Theology* 7 (1995).

_____. 'Communion Ecclesiology and Baptism in the Holy Spirit: Tertullian and the Early Church'. *Theological Studies* 49 (1988), 671–93.

_____. *Charismatic Renewal and the Church.* New York: The Seabury, 1976.

_____ (ed.). *Presence, Power, Praise: Documents on the Charismatic Renewal.* 3 vols. Collegeville, MN: Liturgical, 1980.

_____. *Toward a New Pentecost, for a New Evangelization: Malines Document I.* Collegeville, MN: Liturgical, 1993.

McDonnell, K. and T. M. George. *Christian Initiation and the Baptism in the Holy Spirit.* Collegeville, MN: Liturgical, 1991.

McGee, G.B. 'The Azusa Street Revival and the Twentieth Century Missions'. *International Bulletin of Missionary Research* 12 (1988), 58–61.

McGee, G.B. (ed.) *Initial Evidence.* Peabody, MA: Hendrickson, 1991.

Menzies, Robert P. *Empowered for Witness: The Spirit in Luke-Acts.* London: T. & T. Clark, 2004.

Menzies, William W. and Robert P. Menzies. *Spirit and Power: Foundation of Pentecostal Experience: A Call to Evangelical Dialogue.* Grand Rapids, MI: Zondervan, 2000.

Miller, Donald E. and Tetsunao Yamamori. *Global Pentecostalism: The New Face of Christian Social Engagement.* Berkeley, CA: University of California Press, 2007.

Mills, W.E. *A Theological/Exegetical Approach to Glossolalia.* Lanham, MD: University Press of America, 1985.

Moltmann, J. *The Spirit of Life: A Universal Affirmation.* Minneapolis: Fortress, 1992.

Morse, C. *Not Every Spirit: A Dogmatics of Christian Belief.* Valley Forge, PA: Trinity, 1994.

Mullins, M. 'The Empire Strikes Back: Korean Pentecostal Mission to Japan'. In *Charismatic Christianity as a Gospel Culture.* Karla Poewe, ed. Columbia, SC: University of South Carolina, 1994.

Nelson, P.C. *Bible Doctrine.* Springfield, MO: Gospel Publishing House, 1948.

Nichol, J.T. *Pentecostalism.* Plainfield, NJ: Logos International, 1966.

O'Connor, E.D. (ed.). *Perspectives on Charismatic Renewal.* Notre Dame: University of Notre Dame, 1975.

Oosthuizen, Gerhardus Cornelius. *Pentecostal Penetration into the Indian Community in Metropolitan Durban, South Africa.* Durban, South Africa: Human Sciences Research Council, 1975.

Oulton, J.E.L. *Holy Communion and Holy Spirit: A Study in Doctrinal Relationship.* London: SPCK, 1954.

PCCNA. 'Constitution and By-law'. http://www.pccna.org/constitution_bylaws200510.pdf, Oct 2005, accessed on 3 Feb 2008.

Poewe, K. (ed.). *Charismatic Christianity as a Global Culture.* Columbia, SC: University of South Carolina, 1994.

Poloma, M. *The Charismatic Movement: Is There a New Pentecost?* Boston, MA: Twayne, 1982.

Quebedeaux, R. *The New Charismatics: The Origins, Development and Significance of Neo-Pentecostalism.* Garden City, NY: Doubleday, 1976.

Rahner, K. *The Spirit in the Church.* New York: Seabury, 1979.

Reynolds, B. *Toward a Process Pneumatology.* London: Associated University, 1990.

Riggs, R.M. *The Spirit Himself.* Springfield, MO: Gospel Publishing House, 1949.

Robeck, Cecil M., Jr. *The Azusa Street Mission and Revival: The Birth of the Global Pentecostal Movement.* Nashville, TN: Thomas Nelson, 2006.

Ross, Kenneth R. 'Towards 2010'. *International Review of Mission* 95 (Jan-Apr 2006), 376-377.

Rossum, J. 'The Johannine Pentecost: John 20:22'. *Saint Vladimir's Theological Quarterly* 35.2–3 (1991), 149–67.

Sandidge, J. 'Roman Catholic/Pentecostal Dialogue: A Contribution to Christian Unity'. *Pneuma* 7.1 (1985), 41–60.

Sarles, K.L. 'An Appraisal of the Signs and Wonders Movement'. *Bibliotheca Sacra* 145 (1988), 57–82.

Sherill, J.L. *They Speak with Other Tongues.* Old Tappan, NJ: Fleming H. Revill, 1964.

Starkey, L.M. *The Work of the Holy Spirit: A Study in Wesleyan Theology.* New York: Abingdon, 1962.

Stephens, B.M. 'Changing Conceptions of the Holy Spirit in American Protestant Theology from Jonathan Edwards to Charles G. Finney'. *The Saint Luke's Journal of Theology* 33 (1990), 209–23.

Stronstad, R. 'The Hermeneutics of Lucan Historiography'. *Paraclete* 22 (1988), 5–17.

_____. 'Trends in Pentecostal Hermeneutics'. *Paraclete* 22 (1988), 1–12.

Suenens, Leon-Joseph. *Ecumenism and Charismatic Renewal: Theological and Pastoral Orientations.* Malines Document II. London: Darton, Longman & Todd, 1978.

Suenens, Leon-Joseph and H.C. Dom. *Charismatic Renewal and Social Action: A Dialogue*, Malines Document III. Ann Arbor, MI: Servant, 1979.

Suurmond, J.J. 'The Meaning and Purpose of Spirit-Baptism and the Charisma'. *EPTA Bulletin* 9:4 (1990), 96–130.

Synan, V. 'Pentecostalism: Varieties and Contributions'. *Pneuma* 9 (1987), 31–49.

_____. *In the Latter Days: The Outpouring of the Holy Spirit in the Twentieth Century.* Rev. ed. Ann Arbor, MI: Servant, 1991.

_____. *The Holiness-Pentecostal Movement in the United States.* Grand Rapids, MI: Wm. B. Eerdmans, 1971.

Thompson, J. *The Holy Spirit in the Theology of Karl Barth.* Allison Park, PA: Pickwick, 1991.

Turner, M. 'The Spirit and the Power of Jesus' Miracles in the Lucan Conception'. *Novum Testamentum* 33 (1991), 124–52.

_____. 'Tongues: An Experience for All in the Pauline Churches?' *Asian Journal of Pentecostal Studies* 1:2 (1998), 231-53.

Vischer, L. (ed.) *Spirit of God, Spirit of Christ: Ecumenical Reflection on the Filioque Controversy.* London: SPCK, 1981.

Wagner, C.P. *Look out! The Pentecostals Are Coming.* London: Coverdale House, 1974.

_____. *The Third Wave of the Holy Spirit: Encountering the Power of Signs and Wonders Today.* Ann Arbor, MI: Servant, 1988.

Watkin-Jones, H. *The Holy Spirit from Arminius to Wesley: A Study of Christian Teaching Concerning the Holy Spirit and His Place in the Trinity in the 17th and the 18th Centuries.* London: Epworth, 1929.

Williams, C.G. *Tongues of the Spirit: A Study of Pentecostal Glossolalia and Related Phenomena.* Cardiff: University of Wales, 1981.

Williams, E.S. *Systematic Theology.* 3 Vols. Springfield, MO: Gospel Publishing House, 1953.

Williams, J.R. *Renewal Theology.* 3 Vols. Grand Rapids, MI: Zondervan, 1988–1992.

_____. *The Gift of the Holy Spirit Today.* Plainfield, NJ: Logos International, 1980.

_____. *The Pentecostal Reality.* Plainfield, NJ: Logos International, 1972.

Wimber, J, and S. Kevin. *Power Healing.* San Francisco CA: Harper & Row, 1987.

Wood, W.W. *Culture and Personal Aspects of the Pentecostal Holiness Religion.* Paris: Moulton, 1965.

Zunkel, C.W. 'Let the Fire Spread'. *Brethren Life and Thought* 35 (1990), 291–97.

Studies on Korean Religion, Christianity and Pentecostalism

Adams, D.L. 'Reflections on an Indigenous Movement in Yoido Full Gospel Church'. *Japan Christian Quarterly* 57 (1991), 36–45.

Allen, Leslie C. 'The Kingdom of God in Psalms'. In Youngsan Theological Institute (ed.). *Dr. Yonggi Cho's Ministry and Theology.* 2 vols. Goonpo, Korea: Hansei University Logos, 2008, II: 75-100.

Anderson, Allan. 'The Contextual Pentecostal Theology of David Yonggi Cho'. In Youngsan Theological Institute (ed.). *Dr. Yonggi Cho's Ministry and Theology.* 2 vols. Goonpo, Korea: Hansei University Logos, 2008, II: 281-308.

Baek, N.G. 'The History of Protestant Missions in Korea 1832–1910'. Ph.D. theses, Yale University, New Haven, 1929.

Baek, Nak-jun George. *The History of Protestant Missions in Korea 1832–1910.* 2nd ed. [in Korean]. Seoul: Yonsei University, 1973.

Biermans, J.T. *The Odyssey of New Religious Movement—Persecution, Struggle, Legitimation: A Case Study of the Unification Church.* Lewiston, NY: Edwin Mellen, 1986.

Blair, W. and H. Bruce. *The Korean Pentecost and the Suffering Which Followed.* Carlisle: The Banner of Truth, 1977.

Bunge, F.M., (ed.) *South Korea: A Country Study.* Washington, D.C.: American University Press, 1982.

Byun, J. (ed.). *Diary of Yong-do Lee [in Korean]*. Seoul: Jang-ahn, 1993.

_____. *A History of the Pentecostal Movement in Korea* [in Korean]. Seoul: Sinsaeng-kwan, 1972.

_____. *Biography of Yong-do Lee* [in Korean]. Seoul: Jang-ahn, 1993.

Byun, S. 'Yong-do Lee and Meister Eckhart' [in Korean]. *Theology and World* 4 (1978).

Chan, Simon K. H. 'The Pneumatology of David Yonggi Cho'. In Wonsuk Ma, et al. (eds.). *David Yonggi Cho: A Close Look at His Theology and Ministry*. Baguio, Philippines: APTS Press, 2004: 95-119.

Chestnut, Arthur B. *Put...Shoes on His Feet*. Tulsa, OK: Christian Publishing Services, 1989.

Cho, Gwi Sam. 'The Missional Contextualization of *Bok* (Blessing) in Korean Religious Mentality Based on Cased of Yoido Full Gospel Church'. In Youngsan Theological Institute (ed.). *Dr. Yonggi Cho's Ministry and Theology*. 2 vols. Goonpo, Korea: Hansei University Logos, 2008, I: 215-234.

Cho, Y. 'The Practical Growth of the Church That I Experience' [in Korean]. *Church Growth* (1990).

_____. *I Preach This Way* [in Korean]. Seoul: Seoul Books, 1989.

_____. *More than Numbers*. Waco, TX: Word, 1984.

_____. *Pneumatology* [in Korean]. Seoul: Young-san, 1980.

_____. *Prayer: Key to Revival*. Waco, TX: Word, 1992.

_____. *Successful Home Cell Groups*. Plainfield, NJ: Logos International, 198.

_____. *The Fivefold Gospel and Threefold Blessing* [in Korean]. Seoul: Seoul Books, 1983.

_____. *The Full Gospel Truth*. 2 vols. [in Korean]. Seoul: Seoul Books, 1979.

_____. *The Holy Spirit, My Senior Partner: Understanding of the Holy Spirit and His Gifts*. Altamonte Springs, FL: Creation, 1989.

_____. *The Threefold Blessing* [in Korean]. Seoul: Seoul Books, 1977.

_____. *Do You Really Want Your Church Growth?* [in Korean]. Seoul: Seoul Logos, 1995.

_____. *Small Group Miracle* [in Korean]. Seoul: Institute for Church Growth, 2004.

'Cho's Problem with Prosperity'. *Chrisma & Christian Life*, March 1988.

Choi, J. 'Intercultural Theology from Perspective of Korean Religions' [in Korean]. *Theological Thought* 82 (1993), 96–128.

Choi, J. 'The Development of the "Three-Religions-Are-One" Principle from China to Korea: A Study in Gang Chungsan's Religious Teachings as Exemplifying the Principle'. Ph.D. theses, Temple University, Philadelphia, 1988.

Choi, J. *Story of Korean Religions*. Vol. 1 [in Korean]. Seoul: Hanwool, 1995.

Choi, Mun Hong. 'Dr. Yonggi Cho and the Holy Spirit'. In Youngsan Theological Institute (ed.). *Dr. Yonggi Cho's Ministry and Theology.* 2 vols. Goonpo, Korea: Hansei University Logos, 2008, II: 193-224.

Christian Press. *The Community with Society: The Truth and the False of Korean Churches I* [in Korean]. Seoul: Cumran, 1993.

Church Growth International. *Church Growth Manual No. 7.* Seoul: Church Growth International, 1995.

Clark, A.D. *History of the Church in Korea.* Seoul: Christian Literature Society of Korea, 1971.

Clark, C.A. *Religion of Old Korea.* Seoul: Christian Literature Society, 1961.

Clark, D.N. *Christianity in Modern Korea.* Lanham, MD: University Press of America, 1986.

Commission on Theological Concerns of the Christian Conference of Asia (ed.) *Minjung Theology: People as the Subjects of History.* Maryknoll, New York: Orbis, 1983.

Covell, A.C. *Ecstasy: Shamanism in Korea.* Elizabeth, NJ: Hollym International, 1983.

Cram, W.G. 'A Genuine Change'. *Korea Mission Field* 3:5 (May 1907).

Davis, D.M. *The Life and Thought of Henry Gerhard Appenzeller (1858–1902): Missionary to Korea.* Lewiston, NY: Edwin Mellen, 1988.

Dayton, Donald W. 'The "Good God" and the "Theology of Blessing" in the Thought of David Yonggi Cho'. In Youngsan Theological Institute (ed.), *Dr. Yonggi Cho's Ministry and Theology.* Goonpo, Korea: Hansei University Logos, 2008, I, 31-56.

Eckert, C.J. et al. *Korea Old and New: A History.* Seoul: Ilchokak, 1990.

Eim, Yeol Soo. 'The Influence of Dr. Cho's Goodness of God Theology upon His Ministry'. In Youngsan Theological Institute (ed.), *Dr. Yonggi Cho's Ministry and Theology.* Goonpo, Korea: Hansei University Logos, 2008, I, 81-104.

_____. 'South Korea'. *New International Dictionary of Pentecostal and Charismatic Movements.* Grand Rapids: Zondervan, 2003: 239-246.

Geum, C. and D. Ryu. *A History of Religious Thought in Korea* [in Korean]. Seoul: Yonsei University, 1986.

Gil, J. *Sun-joo Gil* [in Korean]. Seoul: Chongno, 1980.

Gil, S. *Sun-joo Gil's Works.* Vol. 1. [in Korean]. Seoul: Korean Christian Literature, 1968.

Grayson, J.H. *Korea: A Religious History.* New York:, Oxford University, 1989.

Guisso, R.W.L. *Early Buddhism and Christianity in Korea: A Study in the Emplantation of Religion.* Leiden: E.J. Brill, 1985.

Guisso, R.W.L. and Chai-Shin, Y. *Shamanism: The Spirit World of Korea.* Berkeley, CA: Asian Humanities, 1988.

Han, Chun-geun. *Ik-doo Kim Who Never Perish* [in Korean]. Seoul: Biblical Theology, 1993.

Han, S. 'Research on Yong-do Lee, I' [in Korean]. *Ministry and Theology* (May 1978), 202–13.

_____. 'Research on Yong-do Lee, II' [in Korean]. *Ministry and Theology* (June 1978), 210–21.

Han, W. *The History of Korea* [in Korean]. Seoul: Eul-yoo, 1970.

Hatada, T. *A History of Korea*. Ttr. & ed. Warren W. Smith and Benjamin H. Hazard; Santa Barbara, CA: ABC-Clio, 1969.

Henthorn, W.E. *A History of Korea*. New York: Free, 1971.

Hingeley, J.B. (ed.). *Journal of the Twenty Fifth Delegated General Conference of the Methodist Episcopal Church held in Baltimore MD, May 6–June 1, 1908*. New York: Eaton & Mains, 1908.

Hong, C. 'Han is Minjung Theology' [in Korean]. *Theological Studies* (Spring 1990).

Hong, H.S. (ed.). *Korea Struggles for Christ* [in Korean]. Seoul: Christian Literature Society of Korea, 1965.

Hong, Sung-wook. *Naming God in Korea: The Case of Protestant Christianity*. Oxford: Regnum, 2008.

Hong, Y. *Korea's Self-Identity* [in Korean]. Seoul: Yonsei University, 1973.

Hong, Young-gi. 'The Backgrounds and Characteristics of the Charismatic Mega-Churches in Korea'. *Asian Journal of Pentecostal Studies* 3:1 (Jan 2000), 99-118.

_____. 'The Influence of Rev. Cho's Church Growth on Korean Society'. In Sung-hoon Myung and Young-gi Hong, eds., *Charis and Charisma: David Yonggi Cho and the Growth of Yoido Full Gospel Church*. Oxford: Regnum, 2003, 198-217.

_____. 'Social Leadership and Church Growth'. In *David Yonggi Cho: A Close Look at His Theology and Ministry*, eds. Wonsuk Ma et al. Baguio, Philippines: APTS Press, 2004, 221-51.

Hunt, E.N. 'Moon Sun Myeong and the Tong-Il (Unification Church)'. In David J. Hesselgrave (ed.). *Dynamic Religious Movement*. Grand Rapids: Baker, 1978.

Hunt, E.N. Jr. *Protestant Pioneers in Korea*. Maryknoll, NY: Orbis, 1980.

Hurston, J.W. and L.H. Karen. *Caught in the Web*. Anaheim, CA: Church Growth International and Artco, 1977.

Hurston, K. *Growing the World's Largest Church*. Springfield, MO: Gospel, 1994.

Hwa, Yung. 'The Missiological Challenge of David Yonggi Cho's Theology'. In Wonsuk Ma, et al. (eds.). *David Yonggi Cho: A Close Look at His Theology and Ministry*. Baguio, Philippines: APTS Press, 2004, 69-93.

Institute for Full Gospel Education. *The Holy Spirit*. 3 Vols. [in Korean]. Seoul: Seoul Books, 1979–1983.

Institute of Korean Church History Studies. *A History of Korean Church*. Vol. 1 [in Korean]. Seoul: Christian Literature, 1990.

_____. *A History of Korean Church*. 2 Vols [in Korean]. Seoul: Christian Literature, 1990.

International Theological Institute. *The Influence of the Pentecostal Movement on the Korean Church* [in Korean]. Seoul: ITI, 1993.

___. *When the Holy Spirit Comes upon You* [in Korean]. Seoul: ITI, 1994.

_____. *Yoido Full Gospel Church: Its Faith and Theology.* 2 Vols. [in Korean]. Seoul: Seoul Books, 1993.

Janelli, R.L. and Y.J. Dawnhee. *Ancestor Worship and Korean Society.* Stanford, CA: Stanford University, 1982.

Jeon, T. *The History of Church Development in Korea* [in Korean]. Seoul: Christian Literature Society, 1987.

Kang, Chang-soo. 'Resources for Studies of David Yonggi Cho'. In Wonsuk Ma, et al. (eds.). *David Yonggi Cho: A Close Look at His Theology and Ministry.* Baguio, Philippines: APTS Press, 2004, 273-302.

Kang, W. *Religion and Politics in Korea under Japanese Occupation.* Lewiston, NY: Edwin Mellen, 1987.

Kendall, L. *The Life and Hard Times of a Korean Shaman: of Tales and the Telling of Tales.* Honolulu: University of Hawaii, 1988.

Kim, E. 'The Korean Church under Japanese Occupation with Special Reference to the Resistance Movement within Presbyterianism'. Ph.D. theses, Philadelphia: Temple University, 1966.

Kim, G. 'Psycho-Medical Research on Christian Healing' [in Korean]. In *A Study on the Pentecostal Movement in Korea.* Seoul: Korea Christian Academy, 1982.

Kim, Hee Sung. 'Rev. Yonggi Cho's Kingdom of God'. In Youngsan Theological Institute (ed.). *Dr. Yonggi Cho's Ministry and Theology.* 2 vols. Goonpo, Korea: Hansei University Logos, 2008, II: 101-126.

Kim, Heung-gi. *World Christian History* [in Korean]. Seoul: Yerusalem, 1992.

Kim, I. (ed.). 'The Third Turning-point of Christianity'. *Theological Journal* (January 1931).

Kim, Ig-jin. *History and Theology of Korean Pentecostalism: Sunbogeum (Pure Gospel) Pentecostalism.* Zoetermeer, The Nethelands: Uitgeverij Boekencentrum, 2003.

_____. 'A Prominent Woman in Early Korean Pentecostal Movement: Gui-Im Park (1912-1994)'. *Asian Journal of Pentecostal Studies* 9:2 (2006), 199-218.

Kim, I. *Short Biography of Ik-doo Kim.* 5 Vols. [in Korean]. Seoul: Shinmangae, 1976.

Kim, J. '"Six New Churches Everyday: Korean Church Growth": A Report for the Asian Leaders'. Conference on Evangelism (ALCOE), Singapore, November, 1978.

Kim, J.H. *The History of the Revival of the Korean Church.* Rev. ed. [in Korean]. Seoul: Seoul Books, 1993.

Kim, J.T. *Protestant Church Growth in Korea.* Belleville, Ontario: Essence, 1996.

Kim, M. 'It Is Not a Theological Movement But a Social Movement'[in Korean]. In *Minjung and Church.* Seoul: Inter-Varsity Christian Fellowship, 1983.

Kim, N. *A Study on Korean Sects during Japanese Occupation* [in Korean]. Seoul: Saesoon, 1987.

Kim, Pan Ho. 'Paul Tillich and Dr. Yonggi Cho: A Dialogue between Their Perspective Theologies of Healing'. In Youngsan Theological Institute (ed.). *Dr. Yonggi Cho's Ministry and Theology*. 2 vols. Goonpo, Korea: Hansei University Logos, 2008, I: 345-373.

Kim, Sam Hwan. 'The Question of Good and Evil in Full Gospel Faith: A Study of Theological Foundation for the Threefold Blessing of Yonggi Cho'. In Youngsan Theological Institute (ed.). *Dr. Yonggi Cho's Ministry and Theology* 2 vols. Goonpo, Korea: Hansei University Logos, 2008, I: 201-214.

Kim, S. 'Religious Pluralism and the Question of One and Many: A Study of Sotaesan's Perspective'. Ph.D. theses, Philadelphia: Temple University, 1991.

Kim, S. 'Yesterday and Today of the United Movement of the Korean Churches' [in Korean]. *Christian Thought* 424 (April 1994), 44–51.

Kim, Y. 'Confusion in Own Characteristics of the Church—A Response to Byung-moo Ahn's "Nation, Minjung and Church"' [in Korean]. In *Minjung and Church*. Seoul: Inter-Varsity Christian Fellowship, 1983.

Kim, Y. *Abridged Korean Church History* [in Korean]. Seoul: General Assembly of Korean Jesus Presbyterian Churches, 1962.

Kim, Y. *Ten-Year History of the Liberation of Korean Christianity* [in Korean]. Seoul: Education Department of Presbyterian Council, 1956.

Kim, Yong-bock. *Messiah and Minjung: Christ's Solidarity with the People for New Life*. Hong Kong: Christian Conference of Asia, 1992.

Korean Assemblies of God. *The 30 Year History of Korea Assemblies of God* [in Korean]. Seoul: Jong-ryo, 1983.

Korean National Commission for UNESCO (ed.). *Korean Folklore*. Arch Cape, Oregon: Pace International Research, 1983.

Korean Research Institute for Religion and Society. *Annual Report of Korean Religion*. Seoul: Korean Research Institute for Religion and Society, 1995.

Lee, Chang-ki. *The Early Revival Movement in Korea (1903-1907): A Historical and Systematic Study*. Mission 34. Zoetermeer, the Netherlands: Uitgeverij Boekencentrum, 2003.

Lee, G. 'How the Spirit Came to Pyeng-Yang (Pyongyang)'. *Korea Mission Field* 3.3 (March 1907).

Lee, G. 'Religion' [in Korean]. In Sung-nyong Lee (ed). *Korean Studies Today: Development and State of the Field*. Seoul: Institute of Asian Studies, Seoul National University, 1970.

Lee, G. *A New History of Korea* [in Korean]. Seoul: Ilchokak, 1984.

Lee, H. *Korean Religions and Christianity* [in Korean]. Seoul: Yunhab, 1990.

Lee, J. (ed.). *Ancestor Worship and Christianity in Korea*. Lewiston, NY: Edwin Mellen, 1988.

Lee, J. *Korean Shamanistic Rituals.* Hague, NY: Mouton, 1981.

Lee, J. *The Yesterday and Today of the Korean Church* [in Korean]. Seoul: Korean Christian, 1977.

Lee, M. *Church History of Korea* [in Korean]. Seoul: Evangelical Students Fellowship, 1985.

Lee, P.J. 'Pentecostal Type Distinctives and Korean Protestant Church Growth'. Ph.D. theses, Los Angeles, CA: Fuller Theological Seminary, 1986.

Lee, P.J. *The Holy Spirit and Mission* [in Korean]. Seoul: Voice, 1985.

Lee, S. (ed.). *Korean Studies Today: Development and State of the Field.* Seoul: Institute of Asian Studies, Seoul National University, 1970.

Lee, S. 'A Study of the Relationship of the Korean Church to the Indigenous Culture of Korea'. *Asia Journal of Theology* 9.2 (1995), 230–47.

Lee, Sang Bok. 'Dr. Yonggi Cho's Theology of Healing and Neuroscience'. In Youngsan Theological Institute (ed.). *Dr. Yonggi Cho's Ministry and Theology.* 2 vols. Goonpo, Korea: Hansei University Logos, 2008, I: 311-344.

Lee, Y. 'Biblical Teachings on Prosperity Theology'. A Study Presented at World Evangelical Fellowship Conference, Seoul, Korea, 1995.

_____. 'Dr. Yonggi Cho's Influence on the Korean Church in Relation to His Pneumatology' [in Korean]. *Journal of Youngsan Theology* 7 (August 2004).

_____. 'Evangelism and Church Growth in Korea' [in Korean]. *Theological Thoughts* 100 (April 1998).

_____. 'Korean Churches and the Holy Spirit Movement' [in Korean]. *World of Faith* 343 (Oct. 1995), 134–39.

_____. 'Suggestions for the Holy Spirit Movement of Korean Churches' [in Korean]. *World of the Spirit* 12 (1992), 34–35.

_____. 'The Case for Prosperity Theology' [in Korean]. *Evangelical Review of Theology* 20 (Jan. 1996), 26–39.

_____. 'The Influence of the Pentecostal Movement on the Korean Church' [in Korean]. *Journal of Pentecostal Theology* (February 1998).

_____. 'The Life and Ministry of David Yonggi Cho and the Yoido Full Gospel Church'. *Asian Journal of Pentecostal Studies* 7:1 (2004), 3-20.

_____. 'The Understanding of Pneumatology in the Pentecostal Church' [in Korean]. Master's Thesis, Yonsei University, Seoul, 1983.

_____. 'Yoido Full Gospel Church: Its History and Structure'. A Report for 95th AWF and World Congress of the Sung-kyul (Holiness) Church, Seoul, 1995.

_____. *The Holy Spirit Movement and Korean Church* [in Korean]. Seoul: Seoul Books, 1982.

_____. 'The Influence of Dr. Cho's "God Is So Good" Faith in the Korean Church' [in Korean]. *Journal of Youngsan Theology* 7 (2006); also in Youngsan Theological Institute (ed.), *Dr. Yonggi Cho's Ministry and Theology.* Goonpo, Korea: Hansei University Logos, 2008, I, 57-80.

Lee, Y. *The History of Korean Church* [in Korean]. Seoul: Concordia, 1978.

Lim, David S. 'A Missiological Evaluation of David Yonggi Cho's Church Growth'. In Wonsuk Ma, et al. (eds.). *David Yonggi Cho: A Close Look at His Theology and Ministry*. Baguio, Philippines: APTS Press, 2004, 181-207.

Lim, T. (ed.) *Testimony of Miracles in Chosun Jesus Churches* [in Korean]. Seoul: Chosun Jesus Literature, 1921.

Ma, Julie C. 'Korean Pentecostal Spirituality: A Case Study of Jashil Choi'. *Asian Journal of Pentecostal Studied* 5:2 (2002), 235-254.

Ma, Wonsuk. 'Tasks and Challenges for Korean Pentecostal Churches in the Twenty-First Century'. *Australasian Pentecostal Studies* 5-6 (2001), 63-94.

_____. 'The Effect of Rev. Cho's Sermon Style for Church Growth on the Development of Theology'. In Sung-hoon Myung and Young-gi Hong (eds.). *Charis and Charisma: David Yonggi Cho and the Growth of Yoido Full Gospel Church*. Oxford: Regnum Books, 2003, 159-71.

_____. 'David Yonggi Cho's Theology of Blessing: A New Theological Base and Direction'. In Youngsan Theological Institute (ed.). *Dr. Yonggi Cho's Ministry and Theology*. 2 vols. Goonpo, Korea: Hansei University Logos, 2008, I: 179-200.

Mathew, Thomas K. 'Oral Roberts and David Yonggi Cho: A Comparative Evaluation of Their Theologies of Healing'. In Youngsan Theological Institute (ed.). *Dr. Yonggi Cho's Ministry and Theology*. 2 vols. Goonpo, Korea: Hansei University Logos, 2008, I: 263-294.

Menzies, William W. 'David Yonggi Cho's Theology of the Fullness of the Spirit'. In Youngsan Theological Institute (ed.). *Dr. Yonggi Cho's Ministry and Theology*. 2 vols. Goonpo, Korea: Hansei University Logos, 2008, II: 175-192.

Min, K. 'The Influence of Yong-do Lee's Theology on the Holy Spirit Movement'. A Paper Presented at the Fourth International Theological Seminar, Seoul, 1995.

_____. *Church History of Korea* [in Korean]. Seoul: Christian Literature Society of Korea, 1982.

_____. *History of Korean Christian Faith Movement under Japanese Occupation* [in Korean]. Seoul: Korean Christian Literature, 1991.

_____. *History of Korean Nationalistic Church Formation* [in Korean]. Seoul: Yonsei University, 1974.

_____. 'The Revival Movement of Ik-doo Kim and His Healing Ministry' *Oriental Studies* 54-56 (1987).

Moffett, S.H. *The Christians of Korea*. New York: Friendship, 1962.

Moon, C.H.S. *A Korean Minjung Theology: An Old Testament Perspective*. Maryknoll, NY: Orbis, 1985.

Myung, S. 'Spiritual Dimensions of Church Growth as Applied in Yoido Full Gospel Church'. Ph.D. dissertation, Fuller Theological Seminary, Pasadena, CA, 1990.

_____. *Church Growth and Sermons* [in Korean]. Seoul: Seoul Books, 1992.

_____ and Young-gi Hong (eds.). *Charis and Charisma: David Yonggi Cho and the Growth of Yoido Full Gospel Church.* Oxford: Regnum Books, 2003.

Nell L.K. *Dream Your Ways to Success: The Story of Dr. Yonggi Cho and Korea.* Plainfield, NJ: Logos International, 1980.

O'Grady, R. 'Reunification Hopes: Too Much Harm in Korea'. *One World* 140 (1988).

Ok, Che-Gyeong. *The Handbook of Korea.* New York: Pageant, 1958.

Oosterom, L. *Contemporary Missionary Thought in the Republic of Korea.* Utrecht-Leiden: Interuniversitair Instituut Voor Missiologie en Oecumenia, 1990.

Owens, D.D. *Revival Fires in Korea.* Kansas City, MO: Nazarene, 1977.

Palmer, S.J. *Korea and Christianity: The Problem of Identification with Tradition.* Seoul, Korea: Hollym, 1967.

Park, A.S. *The Wounded Heart of God: The Asian Concept of Han and the Christian Doctrine of Sin.* Nashville, TN: Abingdon, 1993.

Park, B. 'Christianity in the Land of Shamanism, Buddhism, and Confucianism'. *Asia Journal of Theology* 1 (1972), 33–39.

_____. 'The Encounter of Christianity with Traditional Culture and Ethics in Korea: An Essay in Christian Self-understanding'. Ph.D. theses, PA: Vanderbilt University, 1970.

_____Park, B. 'The Indigenization of Christianity in Korea' [in Korean]. *Christian Thoughts* (Jan. 1971).

Park, Myung-soo. 'Korean Pentecostal Spirituality as Manifested in the Testimonies of Believers of the Yoido Full Gospel Church'. *Asian Journal of Pentecostal Studies* 7:1 (2004), 35-56.

Park, Myung Soo. 'David Yonggi Cho and International Pentecostal/ Charismatic Movements'. In Youngsan Theological Institute (ed.). *Dr. Yonggi Cho's Ministry and Theology.* 2 vols. Goonpo, Korea: Hansei University Logos, 2008, II: 309-335.

Park, Y. *Biography of Ik-doo Kim: A Korean Evangelist* [in Korean]. Seoul: *Christian News*, 1968.

Park, Y. *Major Cults.* 2 Vols. [in Korean]. Seoul: Christian Literature Mission, 1976, 1984.

Park, Yong-gyu. *Biography of Rev. Ik-doo Kim* [in Korean]. Seoul: Word of Life Press, 1991.

Phillips, E.H., and Eui-Young, Y, (eds.). *Religions in Korea: Belief and Cultural Values.* Los Angeles: Center for Korean-American and Korean Studies, California State University, 1982.

Price, Stella. *Chosen for Chosun (Korea).* Essex, MA: Emmaus Road Ministries, c. 2007.

Rha, Y. 'An Analysis of the Terms Used for God in Korea in the Context of Indigenization'. Th.D. theses, Boston University, 1977.

Rhodes, H.A. *History of the Korea Mission Presbyterian Church U.S.A. 1884–1934.* Seoul: Chosen Mission Presbyterian Church USA, 1934.

Ro, B. 'The Korean Church: Growing or Declining?' *Evangelical Review of Theology* 19 (Oct. 1995), 336–53.

_____ and L.N. Marlin. *Korean Church Growth Explosion.* Seoul: Word of Life, 1983.

Ross, J. *History of Korea.* London: Houlston & Sons, 1879.

Rutt, R, and S.G. James. *History of the Korean People.* Seoul: Royal Asiatic Society Korean Branch, 1972.

Ryu, D. 'Korean Church and the Holy Spirit Movement' [in Korean]. In *A Study on the Pentecostal Movement in Korea.* Seoul: Korea Christian Academy, 1982.

_____. 'Rev. Yong-Do Lee and His Neighbors' [in Korean]. *Christian Thoughts* (July 1967.

_____. *The Christian Faith Encounters the Religions of Korea* [in Korean]. Seoul: Christian Literature Society of Korea, 1965.

_____. *The History and the Structure of Korean Shamanism* [in Korean]. Seoul: Yonsei University, 1975.

Schwöbel, Christoph. 'The Kingdom of God and the Trinity'. In Youngsan Theological Institute (ed.). *Dr. Yonggi Cho's Ministry and Theology.* 2 vols. Goonpo, Korea: Hansei University Logos, 2008, II: 127-146.

Shearer, R.E. *Wildfire: Church Growth in Korea.* Grand Rapids: Eerdmans, 1966.

Shim, Chang-sup. 'Assessing the Impact of Pentecostalism on the Korean Presbyterian Church in Light of Calvin's Theology'. *Chongshin Theological Journal* 3 (1998), 115-31.

Shin, Muncheol. 'Eco-theology of Young-san' [in Korean]. *The Holy Spirit and Theology* 22 (2006).

Sohn, B. 'Can We Call Minjung Theology a Theology and Korean Theology?' In *Minjung and Church.* Seoul: Inter-Varsity Christian Fellowship, 1983.

_____. 'Catholic Charismatic Renewal' [in Korean]. *Prospects of Theology* 67 (Winter 1984), 24–31.

_____. 'The Interpretation of the Holy Spirit by Korean Churches in Each Period'. *Theology* 31 (1980).

_____. *History of Theological Thought in Korea* [in Korean]. Seoul: Christian Literature Society, 1987.

_____. *The Three Stars of the Methodist Church under Japanese Occupation* [in Korean]. Seoul: Sung-gwang, 1982.

Studies in Korean Church History. *The History of Korean Christianity II* [in Korean]. Seoul: Christian Literature, 1970.

Sugirtharajah, R.S. (ed.) *Asian Faces of Jesus.* Maryknoll, New York.: Orbis, 1993.

Suh, D. (ed.). *Korean Studies: New Pacific Currents.* Honolulu: University of Hawaii, 1994.

_____. 'Korean Theological Developments in the 1970s'. In *Minjung Theology: People as the Subjects of History.* Maryknoll, NY: Orbis, 1983.

_____ et al. *A Study on the Pentecostal Movement in Korea*. Seoul: Korea Christian Academy, 1982.

Suh, D.G. *Theology, Ideology and Culture*. Hong Kong: World Christian Student Federation, 1983.

Suh, G. (ed.). *The Identity of the Korean People: A History of Legitimacy on the Korean Peninsula*. Seoul: National Unification Board, 1983.

Synan, Vinson. 'Roots of Yonggi Cho's Theology of Healing'. In Youngsan Theological Institute (ed.). *Dr. Yonggi Cho's Ministry and Theology*. 2 vols. Goonpo, Korea: Hansei University Logos, 2008, I: 263-310.

Tano, Rodrigo D. 'Dr. Yonggi Cho's Theology of Good God'. In Youngsan Theological Institute (ed.), *Dr. Yonggi Cho's Ministry and Theology*. Goonpo, Korea: Hansei University Logos, 2008, I, 17-30.

Tak, M. *New Syncretistic Religions in Korea*. Vol. 1. Rev. ed. [in Korean]. Seoul: International Religious Research Institute, 1992.

The Catholic Charismatic Renewal Committee. *Handbook of Charismatic Renewal in Korea*. Seoul: Catholic, 1986.

Thelle, N.R. *Buddhism and Christianity in Japan: From Conflict to Dialogue, 1854–1899*. Honolulu, HI: University of Hawaii, 1987.

Underwood, H.G. *The Call of Korea: Political-Social-Religious*. New York: Fleming H. Revell, 1908.

Underwood, H.H. *Tragedy and Faith in Korea*. New York: Friendship, 1951.

Walraven, B. *Songs of the Shaman: Ritual Chants of the Korean Mudang*. London: Kegan Paul International, 1994.

Weems, B. *Reform, Rebellion and the Heavenly Way*. Tucson, AZ: University of Arizona, 1964.

Weems, C.N. (ed.). *Hulbert's History of Korea*. Vol. 1-2. New York: Hillary House, 1962.

Woo, W. *Misfortune and Providence of Korean Church History* [in Korean]. Seoul: Mokyang, 1992.

World Missionary Conference. *World Missionary Conference, Report of Commission I*. Edinburgh, 1910.

Yamamoto, J.I. *Unification Church*. Grand Rapids, MI: Zondervan, 1995.

Yeo, W. *Thy Will Be Done: World Mission and Yonggi Cho* [in Korean]. Seoul: Gyujang, 1982.

YFGC. 'History: The Church at SeoDaeMun'. http://english.fgtv.com/yoido/History2.htm, 2007. Accessed on 2 Feb 2008.

_____. 'History: The Church at Yoido'. http://english.fgtv.com/yoido/History3.htm, 2007. Accessed on 2 Feb 2008.

_____. 'History: The Tent Church'. http://english.fgtv.com/yoido/history.htm, 2007. Accessed on 2 Feb 2008.

Yi, G. *Modern Transformation of Korea.* Seoul: Sejong, 1970.

Yoo, B. 'Response to Korean Shamanism by the Pentecostal Church'. *International Review of Mission 75* (1986), 70–74.

_____. *Korean Pentecostalism: Its History and Theology.* Frankfurt-am-Main: Peter Lang, 1987.

Yun, S. *Christianity and Korean Thought* [in Korean]. Seoul: Christian Literature Society of Korea, 1964.

General References

Abraham, K.C. and Bernadette, M. (eds.). *Spirituality of the Third World* (Maryknoll, NY: Orbis, 1994).

Asiatic Research Center. *Bibliography of Korean Studies.* Seoul: Korea University, 1965.

Barr, J. *Fundamentalism.* Philadelphia: Westminster, 1977.

Barrett, D.B. et al. (ed.). *The World Christian Encyclopedia: A Comparative Study of Churches and Religion in the Modern World.* 2 Vols. 2nd Ed. Oxford: Oxford University, 2001.

Bednarowski, M.F. *New Religions and the Theological Imagination in America.* Bloomington: Indiana University, 1989.

Burgess, S.M. and B.M. Gary (eds.). *Dictionary of Pentecostal and Charismatic Movements.* Grand Rapids, MI: Zondervan, 1988.

Burgess, S.M. and Eduard M. van der Maas (eds.). *New International Dictionary of Pentecostal and Charismatic Movements.* Rev. & Expand. Ed. Grand Rapids: Zondervan, 2003.

Burgess, S.M. (ed.). *Encyclopedia of Pentecostal and Charismatic Christianity.* New York: Routledge, 2006.

Cole, S.G. *The History of Fundamentalism.* Hamden, CT: Archon, 1963.

Cox, H. *The Seduction of the Spirit: The Use and Misuse of People's Religion.* New York: Simon and Schuster, 1973.

Daume, D. (ed.). *Britannica Book of the Year.* Chicago: Encyclopedia Britannica, 1992.

Douglas, J.D. (ed.). *New Twentieth Century Encyclopedia of Religious Knowledge.* Second Ed. Grand Rapids, MI: Baker, 1991.

Dupré, L, E.S. Don and M. John, (eds.). *Christian Spirituality: Post-Reformation and Modern.* New York: Crossroad, 1989.

Durkheim, E. *The Elementary Forms of the Religious Life.* New York: Free, 1965.

Eliade, M. (ed.). *The Encyclopedia of Religion.* Vols. 1–16. New York: MacMillan, 1987.

Elwell, W.A. (ed.). *Evangelical Dictionary of Theology.* Grand Rapids, MI: Baker, 1984.

Foster, A.L. (ed.). *The House Church Evolving.* Chicago: Exploration, 1976.

Freedman, D.N. *The Anchor Bible Dictionary.* Vols. 1–6. New York: Doubleday, 1992.

Frend, W.H.C. *The Early Church: from the Beginnings to 461.* 3rd ed. London: SCM, 1991.

Gang, M, and K. Il-Chun. *Christian Heretical Sects* [in Korean]. Seoul: Calvin, 1991.

Goetz, P.W. (ed.). *The New Encyclopedia Britannica.* Vols. 1–28. 15th ed. Chicago: Encyclopedia Britannica, 1991.

Greenslade, S.L. *Schism in the Early Church.* London: SCM, 1954.

Hadaway, C. Kirk et al. *Home Cell Groups and House Churches.* Nashville, TN: Broadman, 1987.

Haller, W. *The Rise of Puritanism.* New York: Harper & Brothers, 1957.

Han, Y. *One-Volume Christian Encyclopedia* [in Korean]. Seoul, Christian Literature, 1992.

Hanchen, E. *The Acts of the Apostles.* Philadelphia: Westminster, 1971.

Hesselgrave, D.J. (ed.). *Dynamic Religious Movements.* Grand Rapids, MI: Baker, 1978.

Higton, T. and K. Gilbert. *The Challenge of the House Churches.* Oxford: Latimer, 1988.

Hutchenson, R.G., Jr. *Mainline Churches and the Evangelicals: A Challenging Crisis?* Atlanta, GA: John Knox, 1981.

Kane, J.H. *The Christian World Mission: Today and Tomorrow.* Grand Rapids, MI: Baker, 1981.

Katz, S.T. *Mysticism and Philosophical Analysis.* New York: Oxford University, 1978.

Knitter, P.F. *No Other Name? A Critical Survey of Christian Attitudes Toward the World Religions.* Maryknoll, NY: Orbis, 1985.

Krieger, D.J. *The New Universalism.* Maryknoll, NY: Orbis, 1991.

Küng, H. *Global Responsibility: in Search of a New World Ethic.* New York: Crossroad, 1991.

Küng, H. and C. Julia. *Christianity and Chinese Religion.* New York: Doubleday, 1989.

Küng, H. et al. *Christianity and World Religions: Paths to Dialogue with Islam, Hinduism, and Buddhism.* Tr. Peter Heinegg. New York: Doubleday, 1985.

Kuyper, R.B. *Evangelical Theology.* Tr. Su-Joon Park. Seoul: Hope, 1980.

Lee, G. (ed.). *Christian Encyclopedia.* 16 Vols. [in Korean]. Seoul: Christian Literature, 1980–83.

Lewis, G.R. *Confronting the Cults.* Philadelphia, PA: Presbyterian and Reformed, 1966.

Littell, F.H. (ed.). *Religious Liberty in the Crossfire of Creeds.* Philadelphia: Ecumenical, 1978.

_____ (ed.). *The Growth of Interreligious Dialogue 1939–1989: Enlarging the Circle.* Lewiston, NY: Edwin Mellen, 1989.

_____. *Enlarging the Circle.* Lewiston, NY: Edwin Mellen, 1989.

_____. *From State Church to Pluralism: A Protestant Interpretation of Religion in American History*. Rev. ed. New York: Macmillan, 1971.

_____. *The Church and the Body Politic* (New York: Seabury, 1969).

_____. *The Free Church*. Boston, MA: Starr King, 1957.

_____. *The Macmillan Atlas History of Christianity*. New York: Macmillan, 1976.

_____. *The Origins of Sectarian Protestantism: A Study of Anabaptist View of the Church*. New York: Macmillan, 1964.

Mackay, J.A. *Ecumenics: The Science of the Church Universal*. Englewood Cliffs, NJ: Prentice-Hall, 1964.

Macquarrie, J. *20th Century Religious Thought*. London: SCM, 1963.

McGavran, D.A. *How Churches Grow*. New York: Friendship, 1959.

_____. *Understanding Church Growth*. Grand Rapids, MI: Eerdmans, 1970.

Meeter, J.E. (ed.). *Selected Shorter Writing (I) of Benjamin B. Warfield*. Nutley: Presbyterian & Reformed, 1970.

Mills, W.E. *Glossolalia: A Bibliography*. New York: Edwin Mellen, 1985.

_____. *The Holy Spirit: A Bibliography*. Peabody, MA: Hendrickson, 1988.

Panikkar, R. *The Intrareligious Dialogue*. New York: Paulist, 1978.

Peterson, E.J. *A Theology of Church Growth*. Grand Rapids: Zondervan, 1981.

Ryu, G. *Christian Spirituality* [in Korean]. Seoul: Yollim, 1994.

Schaff, D. *History of Christian Church* Vol. V: *The Middle Ages*. Grand Rapids, MI: Eerdmans, 1957.

Schaff, P.S. *History of the Christian Church*. Grand Rapids, MI: Eerdmans, 1953.

Schuller, R.H. *Your Church Has a Fantastic Future*. Ventura, CA: Regal, 1986.

Seeberg, R. *Text-Book of the History of Doctrine*. Grand Rapids: Baker, 1977.

Shulman, F.J. (ed.) *Doctoral Dissertations on Japan and Korea 1969–1974: A Classified Bibliographical Listings of International Research*. Ann Arbor, MI: University Microfilms International, 1976.

Shulman, F.J. (ed.) *Doctoral Dissertations on Japan and Korea 1969–1979: An Annotated Bibliography of Studies in Western Languages*. Seattle, WA: University of Washington, 1982.

Smith, D.L. *A Handbook of Contemporary Theology*. Wheaton, IL: Victor, 1992.

Smith, M. *Studies in Early Mysticism in the Near East and Middle East*. Amsterdam: Philo, 1973.

Song, C.S. *Theology from the Womb of Asia*. New York: Orbis, 1986.

Soon Shin University. *1996 Soon Shin University Brochure*. Goonpo, Korea: Soonshin University, 1995.

Swidler, L. *After the Absolute: The Dialogical Future of Religious Reflection*. Minneapolis: Fortress, 1990.

Swidler, L. *Christian Mission and Interreligious Dialogue.* New York: Mellen, 1991.

_____ (ed.) *Ecumenism, The Spirit and Worship.* Pittsburgh: Duquesne University, 1967.

_____ and Paul, M. (eds.) *Attitudes of Religions and Ideologies toward the Outsider: The Other.* Lewiston, NY: Edwin Mellon, 1990.

_____ et al. *Death or Dialogue?: From the Age of Monologue to the Age of Dialogue.* London: SCM, 1990.

The Catholic University of America. *The New Catholic Encyclopedia.* New York: McGraw-Hill, 1967.

Thurman, J.V. *New Wineskins: A Study of House Church Movement.* Frankfurt-am-Main: Peter Lang, 1982.

Tillich, P. *A History of Christian Thought.* New York: Simon and Schuster, 1967.

Torrey, R.A. et al. *The Fundamentals.* 4 vols. 1917. Repr. Grand Rapids: Baker, 1980.

Turner, H.W. *Bibliography of New Religious Movements in Primal Societies.* Vol. 4. *Europe and Asia.* Boston, MA: G.K. Hall, 1991.

Um, D. *Mystics and Their Thought.* Seoul: Eun-Sung, 1992.

Underhill, E. *Mysticism: The Preeminent Study in the Nature and Development of Spiritual Consciousness.* New York: Doubleday, 1990.

Underhill, E. *The Essentials of Mystics.* London: Methuen, 1920.

Wakefield, S.G. *The Westminster Dictionary of Christian Spirituality.* Philadelphia, PA: Westminster, 1983.

Williams, G.H. *The Radical Reformation.* Philadelphia, PA: Westminster, 1962.

Yonggi Cho, Untitled Sermon delivered on Jan 4, 2005 at Yoido Full Gospel Church, Seoul, Korea.

Documents

Global Christian Forum. 'Message from the Global Christian Forum to Brothers and Sisters in Christ throughout the World'. www.globalchristianforum.org, 2007.

'Mutual Understanding and Respect through Dialogue: the 4th WARC-Pentecostal Theological Dialogue' [in Korean]. *Full Gospel Weekly.* May 25, 1999.

'The Lausanne Covenant'. http://www.lausanne.org/lausanne-1974/lausanne-covenant.html.

Name Index

Subject Index

STUDIES IN GLOBAL CHRISTIANITY
(Previously GLOBAL THEOLOGICAL VOICES series)
Series Listing

Hubert van Beek (ed.)
Revisioning Christian Unity
The Global Christian Forum
2009 / 978-1-870345-74-3

This book contains the records of the Global Christian Forum gathering held in Limuru near Nairobi, Kenya, on 6 – 9 November 2007 as well as the papers presented at that historic event. Also included are a summary of the Global Christian Forum process from its inception until the 2007 gathering and the reports of the evaluation of the process that was carried out in 2008.

David Emmanuuel Singh (ed.)
Jesus and the Cross
Reflections of Christians from Islamic Contexts
2008 / 978-1-870345-65-1 / x + 226pp

The Cross reminds us that the sins of the world are not borne through the exercise of power but through Jesus Christ's submission to the will of the Father. The papers in this volume are organised in three parts: scriptural, contextual and theological. The central question being addressed is: how do Christians living in contexts, where Islam is a majority or minority religion, experience, express or think of the Cross? This is, therefore, an exercise in listening. As the contexts from where these engagements arise are varied, the papers in drawing scriptural, contextual and theological reflections offer a cross-section of Christian thinking about Jesus and the Cross.

Sung-wook Hong
Naming God in Korea
The Case of Protestant Christianity
2008 / 978-1-870345-66-8

Since Christianity was introduced to Korea more than a century ago, one of the most controversial issue has been the Korean term for the Christian 'God'. This issue is not merely about naming the Christian God in Korean language, but it relates to the question of theological contextualization—the relationship between the gospel and culture—and the question of Korean Christian identity. This book examines the theological contextualization of the concept of 'God' in the contemporary Korean context and applies the translatability of Christianity to that context. It also demonstrates the nature of the gospel in relation to cultures, i.e., the universality of the gospel expressed in all human cultures.

REGNUM STUDIES IN MISSION
Series Listing
In partnership with Paternoster (except titles marked with *)
Web: www.authenticmedia.co.uk/paternoster

Kwame Bediako
Theology and Identity
The Impact of Culture upon Christian Thought
in the Second Century and in Modern Africa
1992 / 1-870345-10-X / xviii + 508pp

The author examines the question of Christian identity in the context of the Graeco–Roman culture of the early Roman Empire. He then addresses the modern African predicament of quests for identity and integration.

Everett A Wilson
Strategy of the Spirit
J.Philip Hogan and the Growth of the Assemblies of God Worldwide, 1960 - 1990
1997/1870345231/214

Everett Wilson, a long-time Pentecostal missionary among the Hispanic people, wrote a well-researched contribution on the life and role of J. Philip Hogan, as the primary architect of the missionary work of the U.S. Assemblies of God (AG). The main strength of this work is the vast amount of material and information the author was able to collect, and the enjoyable descriptive way he presents the data as well as an evaluation that readers can easily comprehend.

Christopher Sugden
Seeking the Asian Face of Jesus
The Practice and Theology of Christian Social Witness
in Indonesia and India 1974–1996
1997 / 1-870345-26-6 / xx + 496pp

This study focuses on contemporary holistic mission with the poor in India and Indonesia combined with the call to transformation of all life in Christ with micro-credit enterprise schemes. 'The literature on contextual theology now has a new standard to rise to' – Lamin Sanneh (Yale University, USA).

Hwa Yung
Mangoes or Bananas?
The Quest for an Authentic Asian Christian Theology
1997 / 1-870345-25-8 / xii + 274pp

Asian Christian thought remains largely captive to Greek dualism and Enlightenment rationalism because of the overwhelming dominance of Western culture. Authentic contextual Christian theologies will emerge within Asian Christianity with a dual recovery of confidence in culture and the gospel.

Keith E. Eitel
Paradigm Wars
1999 / 1-870345-12-6 / x + 140pp
The Southern Baptist International Mission Board Faces the Third Millennium
The International Mission Board of the Southern Baptist Convention is the largest denominational mission agency in North America. This volume chronicles the historic and contemporary forces that led to the IMB's recent extensive reorganization, providing the most comprehensive case study to date of a historic mission agency restructuring to continue its mission purpose into the twenty-first century more effectively.

Samuel Jayakumar
Dalit Consciousness and Christian Conversion
Historical Resources for a Contemporary Debate
1999 / 81-7214-497-0 / xxiv + 434pp
(Published jointly with ISPCK)
The main focus of this historical study is social change and transformation among the Dalit Christian communities in India. Historiography tests the evidence in the light of the conclusions of the modern Dalit liberation theologians.

Vinay Samuel and Christopher Sugden
Mission as Transformation
A Theology of the Whole Gospel
Regnum Books (1999), 522pp, ISBN: 0870345133
This book brings together in one volume twenty five years of biblical reflection on mission practice with the poor from around the world. The approach of holistic mission, which integrates proclamation, evangelism, church planting and social transformation seamlessly as a whole, has been adopted since 1983 by most evangelical development agencies, most indigenous mission agencies and many Pentecostal churches. This volume helps anyone understand how evangelicals, struggling to unite evangelism and social action, found their way in the last twenty five years to the biblical view of mission in which God calls all human beings to love God and their neighbour; never creating a separation between the two.

Christopher Sugden
Gospel, Culture and Transformation
2000 / 1-870345-32-0 / viii + 152pp
A Reprint, with a New Introduction, of Part Two of Seeking the Asian Face of Jesus
Gospel, Culture and Transformation explores the practice of mission especially in relation to transforming cultures and communities. - 'Transformation is to enable God's vision of society to be actualised in all relationships: social, economic and spiritual, so that God's will may be reflected in human society and his love experienced by all communities, especially the poor.'

Bernhard Ott
Beyond Fragmentation: Integrating Mission and Theological Education
A Critical Assessment of some Recent Developments
in Evangelical Theological Education
2001 / 1-870345-14-2 / xxviii + 382pp

Beyond Fragmentation is an enquiry into the development of Mission Studies in evangelical theological education in Germany and German-speaking Switzerland between 1960 and 1995. This is carried out by a detailed examination of the paradigm shifts which have taken place in recent years in both the theology of mission and the understanding of theological education.

Gideon Githiga
The Church as the Bulwark against Authoritarianism
Development of Church and State Relations in Kenya, with Particular Reference to
the Years after Political Independence 1963-1992
2002 / 1-870345-38-X / xviii + 218pp

'All who care for love, peace and unity in Kenyan society will want to read this careful history by Bishop Githiga of how Kenyan Christians, drawing on the Bible, have sought to share the love of God, bring his peace and build up the unity of the nation, often in the face of great difficulties and opposition.' Canon Dr Chris Sugden, Oxford Centre for Mission Studies.

Myung Sung-Hoon, Hong Young-Gi (eds.)
Charis and Charisma
David Yonggi Cho and the Growth of Yoido Full Gospel Church
2003 / 1-870345-45-2 / xxii + 218pp

This book discusses the factors responsible for the growth of the world's largest church. It expounds the role of the Holy Spirit, the leadership, prayer, preaching, cell groups and creativity in promoting church growth. It focuses on God's grace (charis) and inspiring leadership (charisma) as the two essential factors and the book's purpose is to present a model for church growth worldwide.

Samuel Jayakumar
Mission Reader
Historical Models for Wholistic Mission in the Indian Context
2003 / 1-870345-42-8 / x + 250pp
(Published jointly with ISPCK)

This book is written from an evangelical point of view revalidating and reaffirming the Christian commitment to wholistic mission. The roots of the 'wholistic mission' combining 'evangelism and social concerns' are to be located in the history and tradition of Christian evangelism in the past; and the civilizing purpose of evangelism is compatible with modernity as an instrument in nation building.

Bob Robinson
Christians Meeting Hindus
An Analysis and Theological Critique of the Hindu-Christian Encounter in India
2004 / 1-870345-39-8 / xviii + 392pp

This book focuses on the Hindu-Christian encounter, especially the intentional meeting called dialogue, mainly during the last four decades of the twentieth century, and mainly in India itself.

Gene Early
Leadership Expectations
How Executive Expectations are Created and Used in a Non-Profit Setting
2005 / 1-870345-30-4 / xxiv + 276pp

The author creates an Expectation Enactment Analysis to study the role of the Chancellor of the University of the Nations-Kona, Hawaii, and is grounded in the field of managerial work, jobs, and behaviour, drawing on symbolic interactionism, role theory, role identity theory and enactment theory. The result is a conceptual framework for further developing an understanding of managerial roles.

Tharcisse Gatwa
The Churches and Ethnic Ideology in the Rwandan Crises 1900-1994
2005 / 1-870345-24-X / approx 300pp

Since the early years of the twentieth century Christianity has become a new factor in Rwandan society. This book investigates the role Christian churches played in the formulation and development of the racial ideology that culminated in the 1994 genocide.

Julie Ma
Mission Possible
Biblical Strategies for Reaching the Lost
2005 / 1-870345-37-1 / xvi + 142pp

This is a missiology book for the church which liberates missiology from the specialists for every believer. It also serves as a textbook that is simple and friendly, and yet solid in biblical interpretation. This book links the biblical teaching to the actual and contemporary missiological settings with examples, thus making the Bible come alive to the reader.

Allan Anderson, Edmond Tang (eds.)
Asian and Pentecostal
The Charismatic Face of Christianity in Asia
2005 / 1-870345-43-6 / approx. 600pp
(Published jointly with APTS Press)

This book provides a thematic discussion and pioneering case studies on the history and development of Pentecostal and Charismatic churches in the countries of South Asia, South East Asia and East Asia.

I. Mark Beaumont
Christology in Dialogue with Muslims
A Critical Analysis of Christian Presentations of Christ for Muslims
from the Ninth and Twentieth Centuries
2005 / 1-870345-46-0 / xxvi + 228pp

This book analyses Christian presentations of Christ for Muslims in the most creative periods of Christian-Muslim dialogue, the first half of the ninth century and the second half of the twentieth century. In these two periods, Christians made serious attempts to present their faith in Christ in terms that take into account Muslim perceptions of him, with a view to bridging the gap between Muslim and Christian convictions.

Thomas Czövek,
Three Seasons of Charismatic Leadership
A Literary-Critical and Theological Interpretation of the Narrative of
Saul, David and Solomon
2006 / 978-1-870345484 / 272pp

This book investigates the charismatic leadership of Saul, David and Solomon. It suggests that charismatic leaders emerge in crisis situations in order to resolve the crisis by the charisma granted by God. Regarding Saul, the book argues that he proved himself as a charismatic leader as long as he acted resolutely and independently from Samuel his mentor. He failed, however, because in Samuel's shadow he could not establish himself as a charismatic leader.

Jemima Atieno Oluoch
The Christian Political Theology of Dr. John Henry Okullu
2006 / 1-870345-51-7 / xx + 137pp

This book reconstructs the Christian political theology of Bishop John Henry Okullu, DD, through establishing what motivated him and the biblical basis for his socio-political activities. It also attempts to reconstruct the socio-political environment that nurtured Dr Okullu's prophetic ministry.

Richard Burgess
Nigeria's Christian Revolution
The Civil War Revival and Its Pentecostal Progeny (1967-2006)
2008 / 978-1-870345-63-7 / xxii + 347pp

This book describes the revival that occurred among the Igbo people of Eastern Nigeria and the new Pentecostal churches it generated, and documents the changes that have occurred as the movement has responded to global flows and local demands. As such, it explores the nature of revivalist and Pentecostal experience, but does so against the backdrop of local socio-political and economic developments, such as decolonisation and civil war, as well as broader processes, such as modernisation and globalisation.

David Emmanuel Singh & Bernard C Farr (eds.)
Christianity and Cultures
Shaping Christian Thinking in Context
2008 / 978-1-870345-69-9 / x + 260pp

This volume is a way of marking an important milestone, 25th anniversary, of the Oxford Centre for Mission Studies (OCMS). The papers here have been exclusively sourced from Transformation, a quarterly journal of OCMS, and seek to provide a tripartite view of Christianity's engagement with cultures by focusing on the question: how is Christian thinking being formed or reformed through its interaction with the varied contexts it encounters? The subject matters include different strands of theological-missiological thinking, socio-political engagements and forms of family relationships in interaction with the host cultures.

Tormod Engelsviken, Ernst Harbakk, Rolv Olsen, Thor Strandenæs (eds.)
Mission to the World
Communicating the Gospel in the 21st Century:
Essays in Honour of Knud Jørgensen
2008 / 978-1-870345-64-4 / 472pp

Knud Jørgensen is Director of Areopagos and Associate Professor of Missiology at MF Norwegian School of Theology. This book reflects the various main areas of Jørgensen's commitment to mission. At the same time it focuses on the main frontier of mission, the world, the content of mission, the Gospel, the fact that the Gospel has to be communicated, and the context of contemporary mission - the 21st century.

Al Tizon
Transformation after Lausanne
Radical Evangelical Mission in Global-Local Perspective
2008 / 978-1-870345-68-2 / xx + 281pp

After Lausanne '74, a worldwide network of radical evangelical mission theologians and practitioners use the notion of "Mission as Transformation" to integrate evangelism and social concern together, thus lifting theological voices from the Two Thirds World to places of prominence. This book documents the definitive gatherings, theological tensions, and social forces within and without evangelicalism that led up to Mission as Transformation. And it does so through a global-local grid that points the way toward greater holistic mission in the 21st century.

Bambang Budijanto
Values and Participation
Development in Rural Indonesian
2009 / 978-1-870345-70-5
Socio-religious values and socio-economic development are inter-dependant, inter-related and are constantly changing in the context of macro political structures, economic policy, religious organizations and globalization; and micro influences such as local affinities, identity, politics, leadership and beliefs. The three Lopait communities in Central Java, Indonesia provide an excellent model of a rich and complex negotiations and interactions among all the above factors. The book argues that the comprehensive approach in understanding the socio-religious values of each local community is essential to accurately describing their respective identity which will help institutions and agencies, both governmental and non-governmental, to relate to these communities with dignity and respect.

Young-hoon Lee*
The Holy Spirit Movement in Korea
Its Historical and Theological Development
2009 / 978-1-870345-67-5
This book traces the historical and theological development of the Holy Spirit Movement in Korea through six successive periods (from 1900 to the present time). These periods are characterized by repentance and revival (1900-20), persecution and suffering under Japanese occupation (1920-40), confusion and division (1940-60), explosive revival in which the Pentecostal movement played a major role in the rapid growth of Korean churches (1960-80), the movement reaching out to all denominations (1980-2000), and the new context demanding the Holy Spirit movement to open new horizons in its mission engagement (2000-). The volume also discusses the relationship between this movement and other religions such as shamanism, and looks forward to further engagement with issues of concern in the larger society.

David A. Kerr, Kenneth R. Ross (eds.)
Edinburgh 2010: Mission Then and Now
2009 / 978-1-870345-73-6
No one can hope to fully understand the modern Christian missionary movement without engaging substantially with the World Missionary Conference, held at Edinburgh in 1910. As the centenary of the Conference approaches, the time is ripe to examine its meaning in light of the past century and the questions facing Christian witness today. This book is the first to systematically examine the eight Commissions which reported to Edinburgh 1910 and gave the conference much of its substance and enduring value. It will deepen and extend the reflection being stimulated by the upcoming centenary and will kindle the missionary imagination for 2010 and beyond.

Ande Titre
Leadership and Authority
Bula Matari and Life - Community Ecclesiology in Congo
2009 / 978-1-870345-72-9

This book proposes that Christian theology in Africa can make a significant development if a critical understanding of the socio-political context in contemporary Africa is taken seriously. The Christian leadership in post-colonial Africa has cloned its understanding and use of authority on the Bula Matari model, issued from the brutality of colonialism and political absolutism in post-colonial Africa. This model has caused many problems in churches, including dysfunctions, conflicts, divisions and lack of prophetic ministry. The book proposes a Life-Community ecclesiology for liberating authority, where leadership is a function, not a status, and 'apostolic succession' belongs to all the people of God.

Alan R. Johnson
Leadership in a Slum
A Bangkok Case Study
2009 / 978-1-870345-71-2

This book looks at leadership in the social context of a slum in Bangkok from an angle different from traditional studies which measure well educated Thais on leadership scales derived in the West. Using both systematic data collection and participant observation, it develops a culturally preferred model as well as a set of models based in Thai concepts that reflect on-the-ground realities. This work challenges the dominance of the patron-client rubric for understanding all forms of Thai leadership and offers a view for understanding leadership rooted in local social systems, contrary to approaches that assume the universal applicability of leadership research findings across all cultural settings. It concludes by looking at the implications of the anthropological approach for those who are involved in leadership training in Thai settings and beyond.

OTHER REGNUM TITLES

Vinay Samuel, Chris Sugden (eds.)
The Church in Response to Human Need
1987 / 1870345045 / xii+268pp

Philip Sampson, Vinay Samuel, Chris Sugden (eds.)
Faith and Modernity
Essays in modernity and post-modernity
1994 / 1870345177 / 352pp

Klaus Fiedler
The Story of Faith Missions
1994 / 0745926878 / 428pp

Douglas Peterson
Not by Might nor by Power
A Pentecostal Theology of Social Concern in Latin America
1996 / 1870345207 / xvi+260pp

David Gitari
In Season and Out of Season
Sermons to a Nation
1996 / 1870345118 / 155pp

David. W. Virtue
A Vision of Hope
The Story of Samuel Habib
1996 / 1870345169 / xiv+137pp

Murray Dempster, Byron Klaus, Douglas Petersen (eds.)
The Globalization of Pentecostalism
A Religion Made to Travel
1999 / 1870345290 / xvii+406pp

Peter Johnson, Chris Sugden (eds.)
Markets, Fair Trade and the Kingdom of God
Essays to Celebrate Traidcraft's 21st Birthday
2001 / 1870345193 / xii+155pp

Deryke Belshaw, Robert Calderisi, Chris Sugden (eds.)
Faith in Development
Partnership Between the World Bank and the Churches of Africa
2001 / 978-0821348482 / 246pp

Robert Hillman, Coral Chamberlain, Linda Harding
Healing & Wholeness
Reflections on the Healing Ministry
2002 / 978-1- 870345-35- 4 / xvii+283pp

David Bussau, Russell Mask
Christian Microenterprise Development
An Introduction
2003 / 1870345282 / xiii+142pp

David Singh
Sainthood and Revelatory Discourse
An Examination of the Basis for the Authority of Bayan in Mahdawi Islam
2003 / 8172147285 / xxiv+485pp

For the up-to-date listing of the Regnum books, see:
http://www.ocms.ac.uk/docs/Regnum_Studies_In_Mission_Listing.pdf
http://www.ocms.ac.uk/docs/Studies_In_Global_Christianity_Listing.pdf

regnum

Regnum Books International

Regnum is an Imprint of The Oxford Centre for Mission Studies
P.O. Box 70, Oxford, OX2 6HB
Web: www.ocms.ac.uk/regnum

June 2009